Jim Dale
2d Oct 2012

Praise for Neon through the Pines:

Jim,

Thanks for the kind words. Putting people in touch with their past is an important and I think 'therapeutic' role for a community newspaper and you do an excellent job of it. It also gives a good perspective for those younger folks who think things "have always been this way".

Thanks for devoting the time to these columns that you do.

Leo (Leo Holman was editor of the West Georgia Beacon newspaper when I wrote my column).

Note from a reader of my column, Ellen Arnold Davis:

Thank you for your nice comments about my dad, Dr. Arnold. It was a joy to read your favorite reminiscences; many people in Hogansville didn't know him and I was so pleased you remember him fondly. I moved back to the area after many years away and enjoy reading your column in the Beacon. I'll make sure Chip, Richard, and Frank see it, too.

Leo and Marty have a great local newspaper. Again, thank you.

Ellen Arnold Davis

An excerpt from a letter of a reader of my column:

Dear Jim, I enjoy your columns in The Beacon and especially the one on Oct 5 about the doctors in Hogansville. I can relate to all of them and agree Dr. Arnold was special.

Leo is putting out a good paper – but is not getting rich. Forgive me for running on but would like to hear from you.

Virginia Hamby (Mrs. Cecil)

Another reader comment:

These are great! Well written and funny but touching, too. Thanks for bringing these in for me to read. Elaine.

A friend at work:

Hi Jim, I was clearing out some books, etc and came across your book again. It is way too good to toss and I thought you may have someone else to share all your stories with. Your writing is soooo good and the stories are never dull. I pray all your hard work will pay off and your talent is shared by many others. Jan

NEON THROUGH THE PINES

Southern Memories

By

Jim Dale

Copyright 2012 by Jim Dale

Neon Through The Pines
Published by Yawn's Publishing
210 East Main Street
Canton, GA 30114
www.yawnsbooks.com

All rights reserved. No part of this book may be reproduced or transmitted in any form, electronic or mechanical, including photocopying, recording, or data storage systems without the express written permission of the publisher, except for brief quotations in reviews and articles.

The information in this book has been taken from various sources, and is presented with no guarantee of its accuracy. All photographs used were submitted for this publication. We assume no liability for the accuracy of the information presented or any photos used without permission.

Library of Congress Control Number: 2012948126

ISBN: 978-1-936815-59-3

Printed in the United States

DEDICATION

For my daughter Emily and her daughters
Audrey, Madelyn and Delilah

PREFACE

Neon through the pines. It used to be moonlight through the pines. This book is primarily about my experiences as a Southerner, how the South has changed, and how some of us feel about the changes.

Someone somewhere said, "Everyone has a book in them." We'll see. What I have written here may not meet the specifications for a book much less literature but I'm not trying to win a Pulitzer Prize. Many people have written, talked, and clowned about the south and southerners over the years. To my mind none of them manages to touch the soul of a southerner, with the possible exceptions of Lewis Grizzard and Margaret Mitchell. I was born the same year as Lewis Grizzard and grew up not more than thirty miles from him, but we never had occasion to meet. However, I believe because of our similar experiences growing up so close to each other we shared a common southernism that has been distorted in one fashion or another in writings about the South.

What I hope makes this effort stand apart from others is the clear expression of the essence of that southernism demonstrated by the lifestyles of average people in a small town in western central Georgia during the era of the 50s and 60s, before being diluted by the influx of non-southerners. Our current society's negative mindset regarding southern heroes, ideals and heritage make it difficult to think about the South the way its people actually are. A need exists today for someone to demonstrate the many noble qualities of the people of this unique region. This is the objective of my book. A secondary objective is to show how the modern south affects one raised in a small Georgia town when life was a little slower and people had time for each other. Letters, calls and e-mails received over the years from readers of my columns validate a need for these kinds of stories to be told not just for my family but for theirs, too.

The format chosen for the book is a series of edited articles from columns I wrote for my hometown newspapers published under the titles "Let Me Tell You a Story" and "Lines from the Lake." A composition made up of stories from columns needs some kind of introduction to chapters and in some cases further explanations within those chapters to establish logical flow readers can follow. So I have decided to incorporate this feature into the book, with the hope it is as useful to you as it appears to be to me.

Originally, my wife suggested I write this as a sort of memoir, or maybe a novel. While I feel I have some natural ability to tell a story, I'm not certain I'd be up to writing something as comprehensive as a novel with a plot and sub-plots or a narrative of my life since it doesn't have a lot of direction I can assess. Short bursts of inspiration seemed the best way to go and these articles were primarily written that way. All but a few of the stories are not fabricated, but are a real part of my life told from the perspective of a child as he grew up in a small close knit community and who eventually faced adult life in the suburbs of an impersonal and unfamiliar Atlanta that was growing out of control. Although told with tongue-in-cheek embellishments to keep things interesting, the stories in this book are not just a collection of anecdotal musings. They are a series of life lessons taught by and learned from people who did not consider themselves out of the ordinary because of their high standards of respect, honesty, honor, friendship, and their love for and devotion to their fellow man. There is no knowing or willing intent to slander/liable anyone in these stories, so when the need occurs to change or simply shorten names to protect reputations and avoid embarrassment, I do so. Credit is given where credit is due to celebrities and products mentioned in the articles.

The first thing I did in preparation for this project was to read the history of my hometown, Hogansville, Georgia. A small white pamphlet is the only source known by me to exist of written history of the town and the pamphlet chronicles it from the early beginnings in 1830 through 1970. The town is named for its founder, William Hogan who was a very wealthy landowner. While I lived there from 1946 until 1968, Hogansville was a vibrant cotton mill town. My parents worked for the U.S. Rubber Company making duck cloth for the construction of Uniroyal tires. Actually, there were three mills in Hogansville: the old mill (Reid), where my parents worked; the new mill (Stark), where my mother eventually retired from; and the Asbestos Plant that claimed the lives of too many of my parent's friends before and after the EPA shut it down in the 70s. I and a few of my friends pulled tours in the mills during the summers while we were home from college and fortunately none of us worked in the Asbestos plant.

Hogansville, during my tenure, had a population of approximately 3,000 inhabitants. It only had one main street, on which the majority of the local businesses were located. There was a secondary street, Commerce, running parallel to Main Street that contained a few more businesses. It wasn't hard to find your way around town and you only had to park in one spot to get to everything you would need when shopping. We also had written in readable long hand on our city limit signs the phrase "City of Friendly People." There was one grammar school on Johnson Street, and a junior high school co-located with our high school on the same campus on East Main. Then, in the section of town called West End where the black population was located, they too had a grammar, junior and a senior high school. Yes, we were segregated when I went to school in Hogansville. It wasn't until 1966 that most schools in the country were required by Federal Law to integrate. My high school graduating class of 1964 comprised sixty-two students. I still have a copy of the *Hogansville Herald* with the class picture on the front page – if it hasn't crumpled into dust. Like any baby boomer I won't forget where I was when President Kennedy was assassinated. I was sitting in Mrs. Chapel's fifth period English class when the intercom over the blackboard suddenly popped and crackled into life with a call to attention for a message. We all thought Mr. Pridmore, our Principal, had turned the thing on accidentally as it was playing a news broadcast.

This tragic event heralded the intrusion of a not so idyllic world into our nearly perfect little southern town, but this wasn't where it stopped. I grew up, went off to college, did my stint in the military and returned to an alien homeland. Nothing prepared me for the changes I witnessed in Georgia upon my arrival home, changes that continue to this day eroding attitudes and dimming the atmosphere that provided inspiration for the romantic southern chivalry Margaret Mitchell vividly describes in her classic novel of the old south. So before southern culture is folded into the rest of the country and lost to future generations it seems about time someone adds another volume to the stories of small southern towns.

Writing can be a lonely task unless someone is there to make it tolerable and at times even pleasurable. A good number of authors credit their spouses for inspiration and support in the successful completion of a work. There is no reason why I should deviate from this tried and true pattern; however there are many more reasons than inspiration for naming my wife Yvonne as the prime driving force in the completion of this book. She edited the articles for grammar and structure, and also performed a sanity check sometimes known as quality control to try to assure the overall work fell into place properly. Some of the articles are purposely left written and punctuated as they appear in the newspaper. This means they do not always meet the rules and specifications of English grammar but in my view makes them all the more human. When work and other responsibilities interfered with my efforts, Yvonne took on the tasks of cataloging and organizing the work and putting it on floppy disk and hard drive so it wouldn't be lost. She never gave up on me nor let me lose sight of the objective. If you like what you see and read then you should thank her too.

Of course, there are two other people who are instrumental in making this book a reality. They are the two most significant people in my life, my parents Tom and Sara Dale. They are no longer with me but I believe they were the best parents anyone could ask for and I truly believe I asked for them before I came here to this earth. They raised me to respect people of all personalities and that is why theirs is the most valuable contribution toward making this story possible.

There are always too many people to acknowledge by name who contribute to the completion of a book, as is the case with this one. However there are a few key individuals who need mention for without them this book could not have seen the light of day. I must not fail to recognize Laurie J. Lewis, past Editor of the Hogansville Herald, and Leo Holman, Editor of the former West Georgia Beacon, and to thank all those folks who read my columns over the years. If not for the two editors named above taking a chance on an unknown writer, none of this would have ever been possible. My thanks also go to the Troup County Archives and high school classmates Jan Walls Chaffin, Linda Breed Smith, and Mike Ayers for providing picture memories of my hometown Hogansville, Georgia. I owe a debt of gratitude to my cousin by marriage Michael Frosolono and life long friend Charles E. Harlow III. Both of these gentlemen never failed to provide advice and encouragement to continue working on this book. I would like to offer my thanks to Mrs. Nadine Yawn and Mr. Farris Yawn owners of Yawn's Bookstore in Canton, Georgia, and publisher of this book. Their guidance and advice, and the quality of their publications are unequaled.

Finally, I must thank the City of Hogansville which provided a powerful inspiration to write and remember. The people of this town, their lives and times are among the fondest memories anyone can have about growing up. I wish you all could have been there to share them.

INTRODUCTION

NEON THROUGH THE PINES

The shadow of the pines against the early dawn represented to me all of what it is to be a Georgian, and moreover a southerner from a small town like Hogansville. It was still dark when I got to the intersection with the road that would eventually dump me onto I-75 South. I sat there looking across at the pines, and even though it was dark I could see their silhouette against the early beginnings of sunrise. My eyes were compelled to follow the needles down to the limb and eventually to the red, white and blue neon-lit roof of the Amoco Station. What! It wasn't sunrise that had provided the light for the silhouette it was neon tubes. Those awful florescent lights that stood a few feet above the tree line didn't help either. This wasn't the beauty of nature at all. It was "progress." And if this wasn't enough they had put up a Wendy's just across the street without telling me.

I had a few minutes to reflect on all this, as the traffic light where I sat is notorious for holding most of rush hour. What would Hoagie Carmichael and Ray Charles have said about all this? I think they preferred the lyrics "moonlight through the pines" to "neon through the pines." Moonlight has a better ring, I think too. Neon is better for rock concerts than at an intersection with stately pines.

The landscape changes so fast it seems I can't go out for gas or to get bread without having to buy a map to find my way back home. Just recently the dark and sleepy little lane I take to the interstate turned into Sunset Strip. There's so many businesses with neon I don't even need my headlights anymore. A new Shell gas station appeared overnight at the first intersection where I turn in the morning. I'm sure a traffic light will follow soon after the first five accidents caused by the gas station business. At least if I give out of gas just after pulling out of the driveway, I won't have far to walk to get more.

And why was I surprised by the neon lighting through the pines? I guess because I wanted it to be natural, maybe like in old movies when you pan from the trees to the moon. I'm too much of a romantic, or too small-town southern, to appreciate glittery city life. I believe too many neon lights are only one symptom of a deeper problem, overpopulation. It isn't the fact that we continue to build more, cut down more trees and crowd the streets with more cars, but why we do this. It's because of economic "progress" we are attracting wall-to-wall people here, and I guess this is why we're attracting MORE NEON LIGHTS.

You're probably already asking yourself what this has to do with Hogansville. People in Hogansville don't usually get lost because something changed from the time they left the house. The intersection of Askew Avenue and Johnson Street has had the same red light since 1958. I know because Noel and I bent that shade over the green part facing Johnson Street. No one has built a convenience store on the empty lot across from the Community Building and there isn't a gas station younger than thirty inside the city limits. Nevertheless, I've seen some of it in Hogansville; it is there. What? That nasty word called "progress." I used to think this was a nice word before things got out of hand. The good book teaches you moderation in all things is good; it's only when you tend to overdo something that it becomes vile.

Last Friday I needed to visit my mother and handle a few things at the "home" for her. I also needed a get-away from the overpopulated neon-lit metropolis where I unfortunately have to spend most of my time. I had not had an easy week at work either. In fact I had taken too seriously a comment from a superior that was not well thought out nor considerately made. There was a real need to touch base with home and find some self worth. I knew there would be pines at home with less neon, real moonlight would do. It was still early morning, and cool enough to appreciate sitting and reflecting for a while when I reached the exit for Hogansville and Lutherville. I looked forward to stopping and just looking at the tranquil scene of Emmaus Church that I knew would be there just off the exit. It would renew me and I could go on to face life in the fast lane, whether I wanted to or not.

I turned left to go back over the interstate, already anticipating the intersection just ahead that would take me to the church. I knew the little white wood framed structure would be waiting. I would get out of the car and sit on the fender, breathe the good unspoiled country air and soak up the needed transfusion of a simpler life. But I'm doomed to live in the twentieth, soon to become the twenty first, century. There it was another Shell gas station waiting to spew that damned neon all over the pines just after dark. Fortunately, it was daylight and I didn't have to see the full effect. The station did a really good job messing up my bearings and I almost didn't see the little road that ran behind it and led to the church. Thank God (appropriately), the little church was still there and still looked the same. Its neat little yard, well laid out cemetery and covered eating tables reminded me of why I am what I am. It was another time set in the present.

As I began to calm from the effects of the Shell gas station lurking just behind the tree line I was again awakened by progress. This time it was a massive garbage truck with a driver who just realized there was no more road past the church. He almost took the stubby tail of my Honda in tow when he decided to use the church yard as an emergency exit. When he finished ruining my recent wash job, he wheeled around in the church yard and left a trail of dust as he sped back up the road. Progress again, and this was Hogansville or close to it.

Progress can sometimes work to our advantage and this time it caused me to see something I had missed as a teen when once I came to this church with a friend, and again the time I first stopped for revitalization. It was an old cemetery across the road from the church. Some of the graves were the familiar stone and concrete boxes you see frequently on the coast. They had deteriorated from sheer age and lack of maintenance but the grass was cut and I knew I had to go inspect the place. The cemetery revealed graves of people who were born in 1812, 1817 and the 1830s. They were "Phillips." Many were women and children who didn't endure well the hardships of rugged pioneer life. There were three graves of veterans of the War Between the States who had served with the Confederate States Army. To a history minded boy this was the tonic needed to revitalize the spirit. What I had stopped for was accomplished. The neon, the nasty comment at work and progress in general were all put into their proper prospective in my mind, last place.

CHAPTER I

Recently, I was walking out of my daughter Emily's front door headed for home when she asked if the house where I was raised had an outdoor bathroom. A strange question, indeed, that needed to be answered before I departed. So, we went back into the house and sat down for what turned out to be a lengthy explanation. Most of our visit had consisted of a discussion of genealogy, a subject she's deeply interested in at the moment. She's had good luck tracing her mother's lineage but can't say the same for my father's side of the family. No record seems to exist on them before 1897 as the court house in Randolph County, Alabama burned. Seems there was a rash of wooden courthouse fires in the south around that time. Makes one wonder if there weren't a few scalawags who didn't want their past to follow them and took everyone else's records along with theirs in the fire. My mother's side faired a bit better and Emily's hard work resulted in my recent acceptance into the Society of the Sons of the American Revolution. Since my lineage isn't too clear on my Daddy's side, I suppose I am what he called many of our dogs during my youth, a "sooner." Sooner be one kind as another.

I explained about how mill village houses were laid out and why she may have had the notion I didn't have indoor plumbing. I asked how she happened to focus on the subject and she said her mother had once told her my family had an outdoor bathroom. My first home was a small rectangular white wood frame structure with four rooms counting the kitchen and a front and back porch. It is located among the blocks of similar houses built in the early part of the twentieth century by the U.S. Rubber Company for their employees. In a sense I suppose the bathroom was outdoors as one did have to go on the porch to get to the thing. Many of the families in my neighborhood eventually enclosed the porch to the bathroom. We never did. Eventually, my parents sold the mill village house and built the house Emily used to visit as a child. It had all the modern amenities including an indoor bathroom.

When I finished relating the story of my first home, Emily hunched her shoulders and said, "You and mom sure come from different backgrounds." "I guess we do," I said, remembering her mother was from a more urban and larger town very near Atlanta. I thought Emily knew as much about me as I do but it seems there are some blanks that need to be filled and. . .

PART ONE:

THE BEGINNING.

This small town boy entered life in LaGrange, Georgia at the City-County Hospital about five minutes till midnight, November third, nineteen hundred and forty-six according to my mother who was there for the event. It must have been a relief for the doctor and most of the patients in the hospital when I went home as I was born with a severe case of colic. Actually, this chapter starts a little earlier during World War II. It carries through my daddy coming home from four years of steady combat and pretty much still in one piece, but with a few ounces of German lead added to his slight frame.

Before launching into stories of wonderful people and places that made life so good, you should get to know the person who is authoring this book. In the second half of this chapter are selected articles involving a little character analysis or maybe for a more accurate description, assassination. They will introduce you to my personality and acquaint you with some of my idiosyncrasies that fortunately or unfortunately still exist today.

IT ALL BEGAN WHEN …..

I have a picture of mother and daddy sitting on a grassy field. I guess they were somewhere in their twenties. Mother's curls are funny, indeed, in comparison to today's styles, but I guess what is most intriguing to me is that they were once young, much younger than I am now.

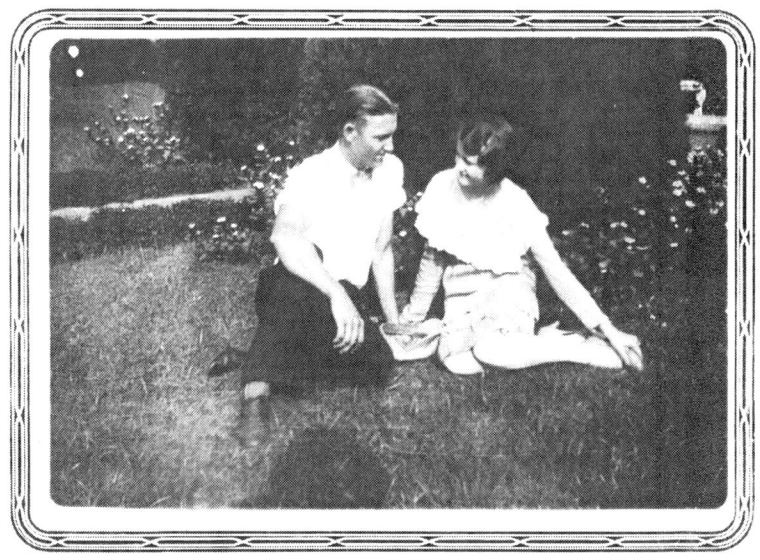

My mother and daddy in La Grange, Georgia, circa 1933, shortly after their marriage

Mother never had that many dates before daddy came along, and even with him she had to babysit her little brother "Bud" on their dates. This kid even had to sleep with her at night because he easily spooked. Finally, in 1933 my mother and daddy got married. Tom's running around with the guys immediately ceased and they settled down in Hogansville, GA, working for the U.S. Rubber Company. Daddy always had problems with his stomach, a legacy he handed down to yours truly and through me to my daughter. The significance of this will be apparent as you read further.

When the war started daddy and mother's cousin, Eely (pronounced e-Lee) Hines who was then Daddy's best friend, decided to enlist in the Navy. They went down and signed up. Eely was taken immediately and Daddy had to wait for medical tests to come back. When the test results came in, the Navy told Daddy they couldn't use him because of his stomach problems and sent him back home. This was a happy camper and when he got his draft card, making him eligible for the draft, he merely put it away. This lasted approximately one month until he got a notice to report for induction. He told mother he would see her in a few hours as he left the house for four years and a purple heart later. Obviously by then, the Army considered him healthy. Daddy was able to call mother to say he couldn't make it home for dinner and not to worry he was being well-taken care of. He was sent immediately to Camp Leonard Wood, MO, where he received basic training.

During that phase, he was having his heel stepped on by a fellow recruit when they marched. This was an intentional act that had to be stopped. Daddy yanked the guy out of ranks and placed a well-planned right hook on him. It didn't happen again. Seems this is something that plagues the Dales every generation. Not being a fighter in high school or college, this same thing began happening to me in the Air Force. I was reluctant at first to move. Then I remembered what my daddy did and I fell out of rank and grabbed this guy by the collar and we both went to ground. But before anyone could throw a punch, the flight leader was on the spot. The feud continued through basic but he never marched behind me anymore.

Back to the story at hand: Daddy got sent to Camp Hood in TX and trained on tank destroyers. When he and Truman Griffin were finally sent to Camp Patrick Henry, a port of embarkation, he decided he would let mother know where he was. Since the Army censored all mail, Daddy's letters looked like they had been assaulted by mice. He sent home a really tacky pillow with lots of loud colors and gold fringe. I remember seeing it once and recall it was written plainly, well flamboyantly, across the front in big letters "CAMP PATRICK HENRY VIRGINIA." This was boxed up with a picture of him and Truman and sent to mother. The Army doesn't censor pillows and we know that now.

Daddy was to eventually spend a year in North Africa suffering from malaria, which he got within days of landing. After being pronounced well, he was attached to an anti-aircraft gun and spent a glorious year in Rome watching a relatively empty sky. Only problem was they weren't allowed out of camp except for a visit to St. Peter's Basilica once. He always talked about going to see the Sistine Chapel again but, unfortunately, he and I were never able to make the trip to Italy after the shooting stopped. During his time in Rome, Daddy's biggest "little" problems were trying to keep up with the puppies he and two of his friends inherited and keeping the Italian kids from using their helmets for commodes. It was not a pretty sight when those GIs, who didn't check first, pulled on their helmets in an emergency situation.

Knowing his good fortune wouldn't last, Daddy was prepared when General Mark Clark addressed his battalion and said he knew they all wanted to go home soon so he was going to help them do that. It was reminiscent of the Total Quality Management speech given just the other day by our Chief of Staff more or less saying we were going to lose some people (positions) to do things smarter. Daddy's unit was converted to infantry and they did lose some people, he almost being one. It was on a hill in the Po Valley after they had just won it from the Germans. It wasn't smart for him and another guy and their sergeant to stand up to have a cigarette, but they did. Wonderful targets for German mortars, at least the Germans thought so and they launched one right on target. The Sergeant and other guy "bought it" on the spot and Daddy ended up with a couple of pounds of metal in his back and leg.

Just a month before the end of the war, they were loading a very unhappy GI into a field ambulance. At this point Daddy was not enthralled with Germans and he found himself lying next to none other than a German officer. This guy spoke no

English and Daddy knew he was motioning for a cigarette from the pack he had just taken from the medic. Mad as you know what and in some considerable pain, my Daddy pretended not to understand what the German wanted and failed to give him a cigarette. Later the officer died. Daddy always regretted until the day he too died that he never gave this man a cigarette. He told me many times this German, like him, didn't start the war and that the man probably didn't want to be there fighting anymore than he did. When you think about it, not too many men or women today really want to go into combat, but they sometimes do.

Mother was living with Mrs. Rosser, an older lady, whose son Glen was Daddy's friend and serving in the Pacific. Mother worked a lot of overtime and spent her few free hours listening to the radio and reading newspapers. She and Mrs. Rosser consoled each other every time they heard of a big battle taking shape. It was nerve wracking for both of these ladies waiting to hear from their loved ones.

Still angry about having to watch all his buddies, especially those from Hogansville, get out of service and come home, Daddy had to remain in the hospital for almost a year after the end of the war. His wounds were so close to the spine the Army wanted to make sure there were no problems, so they kept him under observation. Mother dressed up every day expecting that to be the one when he would come walking in. It seems when you finally decide to drop your guard, it happens. She got up one morning and didn't wash her hair or put on a fresh dress, and didn't put on any makeup. Yep, you don't even have to guess. He came waltzing in and found her in this condition. It didn't matter since he hadn't seen or been that close to a female in almost five years. What's a few out of place hairs? It was approximately one year since the cessation of hostilities and nine months after the return of the Hogansville crew from the war that I was born. He had to make up for lost time. That's probably why I was one of the youngest kids in my graduating class at Hogansville High School.

So, you see I am what you call a baby boomer. When Daddy and Mother decided I needed to be brought into the world, there was still another problem. The doctor told mother that to have a kid would probably kill her; that's why they didn't have any children before the war. But this time they were so glad he was home and in one piece they tried anyway. Incidentally, if you hadn't already guessed nobody died. So, that's what I'm doing here. What about you?

Corporal Thomas L. Dale in 1944 Italy, before he relinquished his rank to a fellow soldier who protested to HQ that he had more time in grade and believed he deserved it more. Daddy didn't care and bowed out, all he wanted was to get home in one piece, which he did more or less.

ME

  Southern is first, then Protestant, Methodist to be precise, and male by gender. I am Caucasian by race and likely of Scot/English ancestry. I have post graduate work and I like history. Those are the major characteristics most job applications or any kind of paperwork require. There is much more to me than those things tell. However, very few people are interested past that point.

  I don't tell them on applications that I am basically lazy, have no interest in yard work, and had rather be tortured by cannibals than do handyman tasks around the house. I'm not artistically creative, have trouble spelling, and am still trying to learn how to play guitar after thirty years. I procrastinate at the level of a master and forget at the Ph.D. level. I am somewhere between poor and fair at matching clothing and have a tendency to wear the same set of clothes each week even though there are some shirts and pants I've never worn because they are not near the front of the closet.

  I sometimes have to be reminded to take pills, brush and floss, take clothes to the cleaners and shine my shoes. I do manage to remember to take baths regularly and wash my hair. Shaving is no problem since I don't like fur on my face. Waking up falls in the area of forced participation and my wife refers to me as a possible manic depressive. I suppose you can call me that if you are my wife. Mentally, I lack a lot of the kinds of things that make me interested in being aggressive on the job, but not on the highway or in restaurants with uncaring hired help. If I could reverse that, I'd retire rich and be a much nicer person for it all. As it is, I don't do badly except I can't get rid of the ants that crawl on my desk at work when it's cleared off enough for me to see them.

  It seems we are all quirky in some ways; I mean this in a positive manner. I like cars, boats, airplanes, and collecting stuff on all of them. My wife tolerates my collecting scale models but the collecting of full-sized cars is beyond her scope of rationality. I've always liked fast, sleek, sporty, and unfortunately, expensive sports cars. Having owned a couple in my life, I can say I succeeded in a desire that has plagued me since adolescence. In addition, my wife is not thrilled with the eight million other things I have collected which threaten to overrun the house on a steady basis. It has gotten to the point where things are in the floor of the once neat and orderly area we fondly call the hobby room. She went to great lengths and monetary expense to bring this room from the brink of condemnation by the health department to a picturesque and lovely area that could have easily made *Southern Living* magazine. I have, in a few short years, returned it to its original status with an updated state of the art of collection mania.

That's me. In summary, I am not an inspired worker-hobbyist, handyman, or yardman, nor am I inspired period. I like to watch TV whether it is something I want to see or not and can sleep at the drop of a hat. However, I am loyal, true, usually follow instructions and also get along well with the cat. That's why my wife keeps me around, but then there are drawbacks like the quite large feeding bill and I do need a flea dip on occasion.

Another thing I like to do is reminisce and ramble, so let me tell you a story or two....

THE MOST AGGRAVATING MAN
IN THE WHOLE WORLD

That's me. Yep. It started when I was born. I wouldn't stop crying just after the doctor slapped my rear end. They found I had colic, and when that was cured I still didn't stop crying. It felt good, so why not? Mother often had to give me over to Ruby, our maid, so she could get some rest. Ruby quickly found some household chore that required her attention so she could hand me back. Eventually, even I got tired of this and started believing my parents might really give me up for adoption if I didn't stop crying. Besides, I needed them to stay sane as I was too young to work.

As a child I was always extremely restless. When we went to visit relatives I constantly found something to excuse myself for and go do. If I didn't break something, get hurt, or cause a general panic, I wasn't feeling good. Sometimes I just went to sleep, not my choice. I couldn't be still otherwise. I can't tell you the number of times mother said, "Be still, you're driving me crazy."

I guess going to my grandmother's was probably the best opportunity I had to exhibit my true aggravating nature. The house was always dark as it seems all of my parent's relatives had some aversion to light. I often wondered if I was descended from vampires. Grandmother, my Aunt Lydia (we called her Liddy) and Uncle Pappy were definitely strange enough to make you wonder. Grandmother just sat around and ate peaches, grapefruits, and drank Dr. Pepper. She didn't talk much but when she did it didn't make any sense. My aunt and uncle were classic TV characters. She was overbearing and he was kind of oblivious and happy. They were amusing, and I probably wouldn't have gotten into as much trouble as I did had not the whole atmosphere been so extremely boring to a kid. The furniture was from a different century and not the one before this one. I usually was placed in an overstuffed chair and told to stay. This just couldn't happen. When they became engrossed in conversation, I would sneak away to see what was going on outside the house. Usually it was nothing. The street was a picture book Victorian neighborhood, very formal and everything in place. There were no kids around anywhere and there were only so many rocks to throw or trees to climb, so I had to create my own excitement. This meant I would find a dog to play with or perhaps just stray too far away and cause them to get excited and think I had been kidnapped. Daddy never accepted this logic because he knew no one could stay around me long enough to do the act.

My Aunt Mary's was another place where I was watched like a hawk. She had lots of good ceramics and things sitting around in her formal living room. This was a gold mine I never tired of checking out, but I wasn't allowed to touch anything. Even thinking about it caused Aunt Mary to scowl, which by the way she did most of the time anyway. Uncle Willie was probably the sternest man I have ever known short of my first father-in-law. Uncle Willie didn't smile much either probably because Aunt Mary didn't. He was a very straight and tall man who always wore formal slacks, probably part of a suit, and a tank top undershirt of the period. He was sort of a Noel Coward and Humphrey Bogart combination of a guy. He played banjo a lot with the Easterhood's, but would never do it for us when we visited. I wanted to get my hands on that banjo really bad, but my daddy knew Uncle Willie would probably want to kill me with his straight razor if I hurt the thing. There was something about it being passed down in his family for generations. He always kept his Cadillac locked for obvious reasons. I did manage to get into the basement on one visit and found some old straight razors. Mother was always quick to take them away from me and return them. Uncle Willie never shaved with anything else. His medicine cabinet with fluorescent lights on the sides, razor strap, and sink were in the den instead of the bathroom. Since they only had one bathroom, I guess he relinquished it totally to Aunt Mary. She liked it so well she even died there.

The only thing that saved me from falling into the mill pond behind Aunt Mary's house was the concrete storm drain that separated it from the very abbreviated backyard. I fell into the storm drain a couple of times scaring everyone to death. A big hill, a house or two over from Aunt Mary's, was always good for a thrill. My cousin Jenny and I would get cardboard boxes and break them down flat. Then we would ride them down the steep grassy hill. Only problem was you either fell off and rolled or you rode them into the storm drain. My reflexes weren't any better then than they are now so I spent a lot of time in the storm drain which was fortunately a lot shallower at that end than behind Aunt Mary's house. I didn't really become controllable until my hormones changed and I met the girl two doors down in the other direction from the hill.

Now that I'm all grown up, my daughter says I aggravate her sometimes. But, I think that's only because I am a concerned parent. Just because I ask eight million questions about her boyfriends and worry about what she does every minute she's not with us, I ask you, "Is that aggravation?" Of course, when I cringe every time she's driving or sometimes try to do things for her that she can do better for herself I ask you again, "Do you consider that aggravation or perhaps a father's love?"

When I went to work for the Army, I worked with a close-knit group of guys. My boss, the other two analysts on my team, and I were really more than just a work team; we were friends. Homer, a large black guy with a heart of gold was my best friend and we always worked on projects together. Then there was Nick, also a big guy with a very big heart and a good friend. We spent eight years together and over that period I did all kinds of things that required Nick and Homer to save me both professionally and personally. I can still remember hearing Nick say, "Jim Dale, you are the most aggravating white man I have ever known." Homer also began to say this but they did appreciate my good work and willingness to pitch in no matter what the cost. Eventually, he began to say "that's mighty black of you" when I did something he really appreciated. Oh, I unintentionally renamed Homer. I called him Homer Lee Honeycutt, after a Kris Kristofferson song. It got so bad Carl, our boss, began calling him Homer Lee. And when Homer began to get phone calls from other Army people asking for Homer Lee they were all in agreement I was most definitely aggravating.

To this day I am still a practicing aggravator. I bother my wife when she is reading, cooking, sewing, watching TV, or you name it. I'm always wanting attention or otherwise interrupting her reading or watching of her favorite science fiction programs to make unnecessary comments. Do I feel bad about it? Well, just a little but not enough to give up the hard earned title as "The most aggravating man (not just white man) in the whole world."

"I LOVE TROUBLE" (AND IT LOVES ME)

I guess stealing a movie title is not the best way to start this article. I was never a thief, really. Well, a few government pens and occasionally a sticky pad over the years that were accidentally taken home but not in the sense I was doing something that would result in the Army suffering a major loss. I've always been pretty good about following rules of law in society and at home. Trying to stay inside guidelines at home has always been like walking a tightrope. My wife has a code of health and cleanliness I run afoul of on occasion. But probably the most stringent of codes were my mother's, when I was growing up. She insisted on strict honesty and I got into trouble more times trying to stay out of trouble, than I did when I just surrendered and confessed.

The one time I was tempted to do some real stealing was at Belk's in Hogansville. My friend Johnny and I bought a model airplane each when we went shopping with my mother. Johnny's kit had a tube of glue inside and mine didn't. He pointed out the oversight, noting the manufacturer just probably forgot to put one in mine. We had just peeped in some other kits and noticed they had glue, so it hit me maybe since my kit didn't have any it wouldn't hurt to just take one from another kit and put it in mine. We were very careful not to be seen doing this but I had such an attack of conscience when I got home I had to tell my mother. Of course, I could see the

Hogansville Police dragging me off to jail never to be seen again. I had a vivid imagination at eight years old.

Did you know putting a dime on railroad tracks can stop a diesel passenger train? It was another friend, Mike E., and I who learned this little known fact or at least it appeared to be a fact. This is a story for later on. Be patient, it's worth the wait. The problem with me is I have this conscience that is overwhelmingly honest and my mother knew it. I've had this problem (blessing?) throughout my life. I just can't do something dishonest because I'm my own worst enemy about keeping it a secret or just plain fighting the urge in the first place. It's not so much now a fear of what authorities might do to me as much as not being able to live with doing something that isn't right. I've been thinking about returning those pens and note pads to the Army that I couldn't remember to return before. Excuse me while I go gather them up and call my former commanding officer. Well, maybe not; some of the pens don't write now and I doubt the Army will want sticky notepads with our grocery lists written all over them. But I still love trouble, so I don't always tell my wife when I miss a vitamin pill or pilfer extra brownies on occasion.

AN ENDLESS SUMMER

I was riding down the beach in a three-year-old 1962 Corvette, sitting between the driver and my friend Noel. Of course Corvettes have only two seats, so I was propped precariously on the car's rear deck with my legs firmly secured inside the cockpit on either side of the seats as we cruised along observing the local scenery. The sun was bright that July morning on Daytona Beach and the wind from the sea was brisk. It was heaven and I was there, really there, and it was an endless summer day.

As you know from reading all my miscellaneous ramblings in this paper that it doesn't take much for me to drift off into one of my states of mind riding with Roy Rogers or holding the line with General Longstreet against insurmountable Yankee odds. I might even join forces with my old but loyal cat to expel an invader from her territory. So, I suppose you could say I am easy to drift off into an "Endless Summer" Beach Boy's daydream.

Reality, unlike imagination, doesn't give one the luxury of making it go on forever. So, the Corvette ride was a short one and eventually I had to get out of the car; it wasn't mine. My wife reminds me it's nice to spend time day dreaming, but we have to live in the present and not the past. She'll have a difficult time convincing a hard core history lover there is something out there other than the past. Not long ago I forced her to sit through three showings of "Palm Springs Weekend," so I could relive a little bit of innocence known as the early 60s. Now my wife is an extremely tolerant woman, but she does have a limit. She threatened to pack up and go live in a separate room if I made her watch that movie again as I was about to insist she do. So, I put away the VCR tape.

To tell you the truth my outlook hasn't changed much since the early 60's. I'm still living the life of Walter Mitty. I guess I didn't start thinking so much about it until recently when some of that era's icons started to depart. Considering Carl Wilson of the Beach Boys was the same age as me, and John Denver wasn't much older, I've awakened to the fact that this 60's teen has already passed the half century mark.

Just the other day at work I stopped in the restroom to comb my hair (Kooky style). I suddenly realized that it's grayer now than brown and a tad thinner, too. No, I won't resort to Hair Color for Men and I won't go out and get a hair transplant or buy a Corvette, either. My wife will be glad to know these things. Just the same I won't compromise my daydreaming as long as it doesn't cause me to wreck my car or run my wife off.

Daydreams are wonderful things to have as long as you know when and how to control them. So any time I want to ride down the beach in that Corvette and relive my youth, I'll just put on a 60s movie, grab my car books and collapse in the backsaver recliner. Eventually, I'll close my eyes and there I am in an "Endless Summer."

ALL YOUR TASTE IS IN YOUR MOUTH

It wasn't that long ago, when I was commenting on some of my favorite things, when a colleague at work said, "All your taste is in your mouth." This is the same person who said, "What do you cut a 'C' with?" Well, do you know? I'll tell you what she said, "A C saw." I wasn't sure we were joking around about the taste thing, so I carried the thought back to my desk.

I sat and contemplated the statement wondering if it might just be gender. Males are not noted for their taste, but then you have people like Noel Coward, Peter Lawford, David Niven and Cary Grant who seemed to be very tasteful gentlemen, but none of them are alive today. Is having taste hazardous to your health? Is it true women have more impeccable taste than men? It doesn't seem to bother their health because I could name you many of them living today including my wife, but I don't have the space to do it.

Since Noel, Peter, David and Cary didn't come from small towns, well at least in the U.S., maybe that was the key? I don't know though because I believe I learned some really good taste growing up in Hogansville, USA. Take for instance I learned to say "yes ma'am" and "no sir" to adults. That is after I had the rear of many fine pairs of pants thinned by a belt or a very hard hand a few times. Tastefulness might be taught on the spot if you were taken many places like church, town, and visiting. Truthfully, those were about the only places we could go for entertainment in small towns. In big cities you've got the opera, dinner, theaters and balls to hone your taste. There you had better have taste or you don't get invited back. Even if your tastes fell off a bit in a small town atmosphere you might get invited back for a second try, especially if it was family. I did try many times to intentionally do tasteless things to terminate my invitation for good when it was a certain family we were visiting. Getting their docile indoors dog riled up so he would chew up half the furniture and break the rest of it chasing a ball I threw should have demonstrated all my taste was definitely in my mouth, but they still told us to come back (through gritted teeth).

After I outgrew those kinds of antics I decided just being a teenager would demonstrate I was without a doubt, tasteless. I came close, but still it didn't work. Had I been drawn to the hippie lifestyle, I think it might have though. You know, in spite of the generation in which teens are raised, they all have a knack for tastelessness. For instance, when my daughter reached her teens she demonstrated there was nowhere to include the word taste in her choice of music. Deaf Leopard was not a way to describe her basically hearing impaired daddy, and neither were Bon Jovi or Guns and Roses. If you don't recognize these names you may actually have taste, don't fight it.

It took many hours of serious headache-rendering thinking cap sessions to come up with a solution to the inherent lack of taste I suffer from. I'd say where you are born has nothing to do with taste. I would also surmise gender also has nothing to do with taste. What I think has to do with the fact that all my taste is in my mouth are my tireless efforts to eat everything in sight.

Jim Dale

PART TWO:

A SPECIAL PLACE

I'll give you a little tour of downtown Hogansville where you will find a few of my favorite places and people. You'll share some special holiday memories that take you back to a magical time we can only dream of today, and I'll bet before you finish you'll wish you had been there.

A view of downtown Main Street Hogansville Georgia, in the early 1960s. The banner wasn't a military one. The word 'rubber' is just under the huge 'U S' circle on the banner. The U.S. Rubber Company was Hogansville's major employer and probably the reason the town existed at all in the twentieth century.

GOING TO HOGANSVILLE IN MY MIND

"Going to Carolina in My Mind," a song by James Taylor, is what I experienced lately. Except it wasn't Carolina, it was Georgia, and more specifically Hogansville, Georgia. It's near the end of the day and my creative juices and memories are flowing. I want to write this down now before the words leave me for good. It seems I'm being summoned on a mental trip to my hometown.

How do I know I need a mental trip home? Well, recently I felt this overwhelming desire to leave my normal interstate path when returning from a visit to my mother's apartment in LaGrange, and detour past my old homestead on U.S. Highway 29. Once I got to Hogansville's only stoplight, I felt compelled to drive up Main Street right through town instead of following Highway 29. I had no idea where I would go once I drove up the one and only business street. I pondered turning left at the Presbyterian Church and going down Johnson Street past the famous McKibben Funeral Home. It's the only one in Hogansville but ranks high funeral-home-wise in Troup County for its kind, caring, and quality service. It has been in the McKibben family for generations. Claude Junior and his brother John run it now.

I could have continued on Main Street, going past the High School to see what was left of the fifth and sixth grade building that just recently burned. I figured since it only happened a week before, there might still be a lot of other cars with rubber-neckers passing the scene. The last big high school fire was in 1954 and that one really brought out a crowd. People from Corinth, Harrisonville, Louise and Mountville came to see the sky lit up for miles. It was worse than Halloween around there. Halloween, when I was growing up, was when all the kids with pickup trucks lined the streets to throw water balloons at those of us who didn't have transportation. They would load the back of a pickup truck with water balloons and kids and take to the streets. If today's politicians had been around then, the entire adult population of Hogansville would have been in jail for neglect, child abuse, violation of safety laws, and probably for having fun.

Anyway, I saw many of the buildings downtown being gutted

and torn down or in some stage of being rebuilt. It couldn't be Jimmy Carter and Habitat for Humanity because it didn't appear that there were that many people left in Hogansville. This kindled my desire to find out what was going on. Since I didn't know anyone anymore, I couldn't stop and ask a total stranger why downtown Hogansville was being torn down. I figured, based on the fact the high school had become county maintained and most of the remaining residents are on Medicare, that the town would soon disappear. But I expect it to do it on its own and not with the help of a wrecking crew.

I drove slowly because I didn't know if Buddy was still police chief. Back when I lived there a black Honda (non-American car) without Troup county plates was dead meat at any speed. City Hall wasn't City Hall anymore, it was the police department and a LaGrange Police car just in front of me turned in at the driveway. Wait a minute; has the City Government dissolved? Was Buddy without a job, and has LaGrange assumed responsibility for law and order? I was really worried until I reached the Royal Theater and discovered the building where I had passed so many pleasurable Saturday afternoons watching movies. It had later sat empty many years as I grew up but had suddenly become "CITY HALL." At least there was still a city government even though it looked like a movie house. They should have taken down the marquees because I'm sure we don't want to know what's playing inside now. The Post Office had moved too, but just across the street in a newer and slightly larger building. And there was a new library so it seems maybe there is still life after all. But, why tear down uptown?

I decided not to fight the traffic jam to see the burned school, so I turned left on Johnson Street. It looked the same except the city was doing work on the street. As I recall they were always doing work on the street at the same place. Why not just replace whatever it is and be done with it? Surely, after thirty years, they ought to have fixed that problem? So the street work and all still looked the same. I saw McKibben's and it is still well kept; the white paint looked fresh and the lawn was immaculately cared for. I had to hand it to those boys, the black hearse gave the place class. They never fell for the silver or white ones or the more modern Pontiac and Oldsmobile hearses. They still have their Cadilacs with the wide whitewalls.

Something inside tugged at me as I approached the intersection at Marshall Avenue where my parent's and I lived until I was nine. I passed the house by in spite of the strong urge to stop and stare. The next street is Greenough Street and I turned to the left to circle the block and come back up to Marshall. When I turned onto Greenough Street I saw someone sitting on a porch swing. It was like seeing a ghost as she looked the same sitting in the same place as she always sat when I was a boy. The woman was Miss Jane, my friend and playmate Jerry's mother. I couldn't resist so I pulled up next to the house. After making sure she was who I thought she was, I told her who I am and she asked me to get out and come in. I did, and she got up I thought to give me a big hug. The look on her face was pure amazement, but I knew it had been a long time. I immediately realized when she ran past me I was not the object of her concern. My car was rolling down the street without me. Fortunately, the car had only gone a short distance. Given the condition of the street it couldn't build up too much speed hitting pot holes every few feet. I caught up with it in front of Paul Haye's house and wrestled it under control just as it reached Lena Pearl's. I tried to hide my embarrassment but Miss Jane said, "Jimmy, you haven't changed a bit."

We had a good conversation and I learned about Jerry and his brother Randy and how they are doing these days. I found the neighborhood was not doing too well, as was evident without a word. I also found out why downtown Hogansville is being wrecked. It seems a man from Atlanta with more money than he can figure out what to do with is redoing Main Street into little shops and curios to attract outside interest. He is going to make what my wife calls a "cutesy" little place for antiques and crafts and whatever. Good luck converting Whit's Western Auto into a crafty ribbon-laden macramé outlet. However, it would make a wonderful antique shop without changing the inventory very much. And, I can't imagine how or what the City Barber Shop will be converted to as P.L., Jackson, and Whip left too many memories stored in the back to completely remove. If the Royal Theater can be turned into City Hall then I'm sure the rest of the town can be converted into Cabbage Patch USA. I hope the cast of the "Bob Newhart" show (the one with the Connecticut Inn) isn't doing anything because they'd make perfect citizens for downtown.

It was late when I left Miss Jane's. I don't know if I will ever see her again but we spent priceless time and renewed a friendship that has endured changing times. I never made it up Marshal, but it's just as well as I don't think I would have found the number six house like I remembered or expected it to be. As I crossed the railroad to rejoin Highway 29, I looked into the rear view mirror and didn't see anything that reminded me of home. Perhaps, I needed this to finally break the link that drew me each time I see the Hogansville exit on the Interstate. My former girlfriend Pat, whom I haven't seen in years, recently prepped mother for surgery. When we talked she said something to the effect, "The Hogansville I knew isn't there anymore and I have no reason to visit the one there now." Pat's words are true, but Hogansville as it was is still there in our minds. It's still there when I see Pat and she sees me. It is there when Miss Jane and I talk. And, it was there just last week when I found another refugee from the past, but that's another story.

A TOWN YOU'D KNOW BY HEART, PART ONE

Those of you who live in Hogansville today probably don't know almost everyone in town like we did. So I thought I'd share some memories of what Hogansville, the town and its people were like when I grew up there in the 50's and 60's. Amazingly, a lot of the physical town is pretty much the same but not quite. Let me explain.

The downtown buildings are still there but the City Hall of the fifties and sixties is on the opposite side of the town. The Royal Theater building hasn't changed since our parents put us kids out at the ticket window around noon on Saturdays when the marquees advertised "The Creature from the Black Lagoon in 3-D" and "The Body Snatchers" for the matinee, and later during the week "Butterfield 8" with Elizabeth Taylor. Okay, so I wasn't allowed to see "Butterfield 8." There was always a big race to get tickets first so we could claim the seats closest to the front. I can't figure out why we did this since we had to look up at the screen and it made everything look out of whack. My eyes would hurt for the rest of the day. Once we had seats staked out and someone to protect them we'd go back up to the counter for popcorn, candy and a coke which we'd do away with before the previews ended. Hum? Today my wife wonders why I eat almost all our popcorn before the feature begins. Well, anyway on Saturdays they showed a double feature and we didn't get out until about 4 p.m.

When mother picked me up, we'd do a little shopping before going home. Allen's Five and Ten was just down Main Street from the theater. In fact across the side street, which has a name I can't remember, from the theater were Belk Gallant and Jabley's Men's Stores, and then Allen's. Mother would always talk to Motty, the store manager. Motty was a short cute blonde girl (of course that didn't mean much to a ten year old) who always had a story to tell. I'd check out the toy department in the back while they talked. Then we'd go to Henson's Furniture Store next door to pay on our new furniture. Mister Henson was a tall lean man with crew cut hair and horn rimmed glasses. After paying on the furniture, mother and I would leave downtown driving down Johnson Street past McKibben's, Jap Keith's store and the Community Building. The buildings are still there except McKibben's is the only one still in the same business. Of course Mr. Claude McKibben, Sr., was one of our stellar citizens and community leaders when I was a kid. I remember his red hair and he always drove a black station wagon. When my parents met him on the street, he'd always have a kind word and go out of his way to speak to me.

Mother headed to Green Street next and her friend Lottie Clark's house which still stands just across the street from the Reid Mill site. The Reid Mill is gone now. There is a vacant overgrown field where it once stood. The "Old Mill Village" was a beautiful place then with well maintained houses and yards. Diagonal from the Clark's and across the street was U.S. Rubber Company mill management office. The building was a single story brick, trimmed in dark green. The little park in front of the office was composed of neatly manicured trees, grass, and shrubs with converging sidewalks from each end of the street that led to the office steps.

Well, I'm getting carried away so next time I'll continue this little tour and tell you more about the Hogansville you may not recognize today.

A TOWN YOU'D KNOW BY HEART, PART TWO

"If you don't stop eating you're gonna be fat as Herschel S.," my mother scoffed as I went back a third time for seconds. Now Herschel in all fairness was a bit, well maybe more than a bit, overweight. But, he was one of the strongest, friendliest, and most decent men I remember my parents knowing. He worked the first shift with my daddy at the Reid Mill which was and is still referred to as the Old Mill, the one that stood on Green Street where now there is just an overgrown vacant lot. The New Mill or Stark Mill is still standing on Hwy 29 just as you leave Hogansville headed north.

My parents worked in the mills and so did most of the folks

who lived in Hogansville in the 50's and 60's. There were also support businesses like downtown merchants, car dealerships, food markets, utilities, and the local police. And yes, there were Pritchett's Cab Company, Bad Eye Cardin's Texaco, Don Howington's Shell gas stations, Pee Wee Hubbard's, and Thompson's auto repair shops. All these professions were populated with some of the most interesting, an understatement if I've ever made one, people I've ever known. A name that keeps coming back to me from my parent's acquaintances is Duck Morgan. I don't remember much about him except I liked his name then and still do. Then there was Joe Pink. The name Joe Pink, for me, recalls a 50's kid show host who wore a hideous plaid suit and straw hat and who had two teeth missing in the front. I don't recall Joe Pink really looking or dressing that way. There was another fellow I didn't get to see a lot, Nim Childres, who drove a tan 1961 Chevy Biscayne taxi. He surely must be related to the Childres who own a race team in NASCAR. I'm sure the reason I don't remember his face is because he never slowed down enough for me to see it clearly, but I don't recall him ever having an accident.

Then there were the ladies in waiting, including Mary Alice and her best buddy Deana, who every afternoon, when mother and I would drive to the mill for the shift change, were always there sitting or leaning on the executives' cars having a last cigarette before the whistle blew to change shifts. Lena Pearl always waited until close to the shift change to show up and Avaleen usually sat on the porch with Lottie just across from the gate. I never figured out why mother and Lena Pearl never wore shorts since all the others did, at least in the summer. The mill wasn't air conditioned, you know.

I'd see a lot of these same folks at church on Sunday too. Mary Alice's husband Clinton, when he wasn't rotating with Harry B. as singing leader, rotated with my daddy as Sunday School Superintendent. We had a good community mix at our little church which still stands on Granite Street. It's called St.

James United Methodist now, but was just plain St. James Methodist then; that's before the Methodist had their Civil War. We always had a good crowd on hand for Sundays and the choir was always the most interesting (understatement again) to me. Mrs. Iris B. played organ, and a very good one at that, and Miss Floy W. played an equally good piano. Together they were unbeatable. Mildred and Lottie were the premiere vocalists and always managed a special number for each Sunday's service. Their voices had a unique effect on me and the whole congregation. I won't elaborate. Of course, I was pretty infatuated with Angela so you'll have to pardon me if I don't remember much about the church service. There's still more, as a boss I had for longer than I want to think about often said, "Stay tuned."

HOG HEAVEN

"Mama, why is that man talking like a woman?" "What man are you talking about Jimmy?" replied my mother looking at me like I was not her child. We were in Belk Gallant or Gallant Belk; I can't remember which it was. Now-a-days, it's Belks. So I guess either Mr. Gallant got out of the business or died? It was the department store on the corner of Main and the short alley way, which had a name that now I can't recall. It went between Belk's and the Royal Theater connecting Commerce to Main streets. Jackson, the only name I remember him by, was a slight man who would remind you of the actor Wally Cox if you can go back to "Mr. Peepers," the sitcom of the fifties. His voice was rather high but he, like most of the men in Hogansville, had come up through the mill. He worked his way out of the lint and cotton to this job wearing a white shirt and suit with the mandatory yellow tape measure around his neck. He lived on the Blue Creek Road near the Sportsman's Club, I think. He had a wife and two daughters. My parents both knew him so he was a good friend. Of course, at three or four I didn't know anyone too well. I found out later on as I grew up that Jackson was one of the cornerstones of Hogansville and so were a lot more folks that most Hogansvillians of today probably won't remember or ever knew existed.

Jabley's Men's store was right next door to Belk's and it was owned by two brothers. They were Lebanese and knew my Aunt Josephine, who was also Lebanese, along with our neighbor's wife Lena who I think was the Jableys' sister, and a relative of the Mansour's of LaGrange. Integrity was their middle name, but it was pretty much everyone else's too at that time in Hogansville. The Jabley's ran a total of your purchases and at the end of the month all you had to do was come by and pay. It worked better than a credit card and there was no interest. I got all my jeans and shirts for school at Jabley's and my shoes, too. But my suits and other stuff came from Jackson at Belk's, or if my parents were in a generous mood, from Mansour's.

On down the street was Allen's Five and Ten. I know we've talked about this before but it's my favorite store so I'll mention it again. I was personally responsible for keeping that store in business from the time I was three until I graduated from high school. My mother was never one to buy me a toy when we went to town but my daddy was a pushover. So when I spotted something at Allen's on a trip with mother, I'd make certain to point it out to daddy when we went to town to pay bills after he got off from work. But like all less than honest schemes, it got figured out and they agreed I wouldn't do this anymore. I had to start using my allowance for such needs in the future.

As we made the rounds we'd also go to Ray Cheatham's Economy Auto to pay the phone and electric bills and then to Whit Barrett's Western Auto to pay our bill. There, daddy would talk to the head cashier Kaiser and Whit's brother-in-law Garnett, who spent a lot of time at the store doing things I never figured out. Once we'd make the rounds on that side of the street we'd go by Henson's Furniture store and pay for whatever piece of furniture mother had bought that week.

Lastly, but never my favorite thing to do as a four year old, was the City Barber Shop. Haircuts as far as I was concerned were for men and not boys. I guess if I had had my way I'd have cheated the Beatles and Stones out of their trademark long hair by a few years. Either P.L. or Jackson (a different Jackson than the Belk guy) was determined to cut my hair regardless of my occasional loud protest. I had to sit on a board placed across the arms of the barber chair so they could reach me. Like my dog, when we gave him a bath, I had no choice but to tolerate the aggravation until they finished. Once the cutting stopped and the sweet smelling stuff was combed into my hair with an application of cooling powder on my neck, I thought I was in heaven: Hog as in Hogansville, heaven that is.

CHAPTER II

A SOUTHERN BOY'S LIFE IN THE 50's AND 60's

PART ONE:

SURVIVING ON THE MILL VILLAGE

This chapter begins with what I remember from when I was living twelve miles up the road from the hospital where I was born in the little town of Hogansville, Georgia, in a four room house on the Mill Village. My family resided there for the first nine years of my life. There were always kids who lived nearby on the Mill Village and we played daily. We all went through school together and some of them I still know today. No, this isn't a tell-all book, so don't worry buddies, although it does tell it like it was. We were generally good kids, but on occasion would do a few things I don't believe some of our parents ever knew about or parts of our bodies would still bear the scars of them finding out. There was the hunky man, coal houses, Roy Rogers and Davy Crockett, air rifles, rusty nails, and Mrs. Whaley's infamous granite countertop driveway that all figured prominently in our adventures.

TO MY MOTHER

My wife asked me why I was following her around in the kitchen. Actually, I was trying to figure out a way to help her. She then asked if I did this to my mother when I was little. Before I could answer the first question, I was thinking about the second one. The first question never got answered, for when I told her I did in fact follow my mother around in the kitchen when I was small, she then asked if I held on to her dress. How does my wife know these things? The woman is psychic!

I was probably way too young when it happened to remember

very much about hooking onto my mother's print dress and getting towed around the kitchen. The only thing I can think of that would give me some indication of how she felt was when my dog Herman bit the seat of my pants and wouldn't let go. I dragged him around from one end of the yard to the other with that grip steadily clamped down on the denim. It was aggravating to say the least, and the dog was heavy for such a small compact package as me. Mother, no doubt, had the same thoughts about me even though I helped her by walking and not being dragged like Herman.

The mill village house where I lived, until I was nine years old. It took me a while to get the hang of balancing a bike, re: the training wheels. I think my daddy had just about given up on me ever getting it figure out. But, I did.

I usually did my following around when it was raining or too cold to go outside. Our house on Marshall Avenue was quite small and there were only a couple of rooms I was allowed to play in. I could only go in the kitchen when someone else was there. Our living room was not for people either. We kept furniture in there but mother didn't allow anyone to go in. But when Preacher Webb came to visit, she and daddy would take him in the living room. I'm not sure I understood. There were a few times when no one was looking that I'd slip in there, and to this day I don't see anything so special about it. When we moved up on North Highway, the same furniture went into our new living room, but then I was allowed to go in anytime I wanted. It wasn't nearly as much fun as it was when it was off limits.

I always went with mother to the Colonial Store, I guess because she didn't trust me at home by myself; I might go into the living room. I didn't mind going to the grocery store because I liked to see my neighbor Tommy Whaley working the cash register. He was pretty friendly and I liked his dog Spot. I didn't care for all those pigeons he raised under his mother's house. They were pretty nasty birds and made too much noise. At least that's what mother always said. I was pretty good about adding comments to the conversation with our neighbors when she ran into them at the grocery store. It got me popped a time or two. There is one good thing about mother carrying me along: it tended to get the bull sessions over with quickly. She could count on saving about thirty minutes every time she took me shopping.

Even though she didn't always welcome my making comments at the grocery store, mother was my constant protector. There were times when I actually did some things that were wrong. I broke a lot of stuff, by accident of course. Then there were report cards too. We won't go there. Did I tell you I eventually was accepted to and graduated from college? So you know those early report cards weren't that bad; either way my daddy was from the old school that says you always pay the price for not so good grades. That payment always somehow involved pain. Either it was the palm of his hand which he finally figured out probably hurt him as much as it did me, or his belt which didn't hurt him at all. I hated that belt, and the wait for him to come home and spank me with it was like being on death row with no more appeals. Mother would tell me if I behaved and didn't commit whatever ungodly atrocity I had done again, then she would tell daddy I didn't mean to do it. That wouldn't prevent the inevitable spanking but it would reduce the number of licks. I am forever indebted to my mother for that because my rear has never been padded well, not even today.

The final act, for which I remember my mother protecting me, occurred when I was in high school. This time it really was an accident. I managed to lose a hubcap off my daddy's '61 Chevy. It was one of the expensive ones Impalas had, and I gave mother all the details. She offered to help me find another hubcap before daddy got home from work. We spent the better half of the day in and out of junkyards and sifting through all kinds of things. Mother was good at looking through stuff as she had plenty of practice at J.C. Penny in LaGrange. When I was about five or six, I'd hang onto her dress and get pulled through numerous racks of clothes. We finally found the matching hubcap and I used my allowance to make the purchase. We picked daddy up from work and he never knew he had been short one hubcap for most of the day. I was too big for a spanking by then but his "hard talks" were just as painful.

So, you see, I owe a lot to my mother. So mother, if I haven't told you lately, or tugged on your print dress in a while, I want to take this opportunity to say I love you.

DON'T CALL 911, JUST SCREAM FOR DR. MOM

When I was a little boy, I can say without reservation, I was accident prone but not as much as my mother thought. Life wasn't always easy while living on the mill village, because you weren't more than 20 feet from the street when you were sitting on your own porch. There was always glass somewhere for you to cut your wrist on or slice your foot with as my mother always assumed I'd do immediately upon locating it. Then there was the ever present opportunity to run out in front of Boots Lankford's old Pontiac he bought from my daddy. My mother felt I had no sense of impending danger when I ran to the street to hear the old car's transmission whine as it turned on to Marshall Avenue. But oddly enough, I didn't do any of those things her imagination told her I would.

What I did do was run a lot in Mrs. Whaley's yard, the mine field of the neighborhood. Unfortunately Mr. Whaley, about twenty years before he died, had unknowingly set a booby trap for me. It was his drive paved with rock he had worked diligently to finish so that in the future I would scrape half the skin off my left arm because I didn't pay attention to the uneven surface. When a seven year old is chasing the Durango Kid and runs over uneven surface while riding Trigger at Mach One, you couldn't expect the stallion not to bolt and throw him off. Could you? My mother couldn't either when she heard the wrenching screams of the wounded sheriff. She'd grab up a bottle of mercurochrome and head out the door. I knew my shirt didn't have that much red in it when I put it on that morning. Blood is my most unfavorite liquid and upon seeing it I went into afterburner hysterics. I put the entire neighborhood on notice of my predicament. It brought out Mrs. Whaley, and naturally Mrs. Payne, Mrs. Rainwater and Mrs. Henry Smith. There was no sign of the Durango Kid, the cause of the whole thing. But there were enough nurses to fill a hospital ward.

Mother was on the scene in minutes. The paramedics of today have nothing on her. Without field training, she applied the mercurochrome on the spot. I was fine until it began to take affect. The blood, the scraped skin, none of it was as terrifying as the pain I experienced after she put that stuff on me. She tried to calm me by saying it would only hurt a little while. After about five minutes of this I decided the pain was too much and I passed out. Mother thought I had died and rushed my limp little body to Dr. Harvey's office. Doctor Harvey never got excited about anything, at his age it was a pretty good idea. His cure for most stuff was to wrap it up in bandages. This cure came about the same time the pain was easing, not from the mercurochrome but the toothache medicine my mother had applied to 90 percent of my arm. How do I know it was toothache medicine? Well, when we got home mother noticed the label when she grabbed up the bottle to throw it away so I would come in the house.

It wasn't quite a year later when I went to play with Larry Smallwood, a friend who lived on Askew Avenue on the opposite side of the athletic field behind our house. The field doubled for Normandy or any South Pacific beachhead. Larry and I had air guns. To clarify this term for non-southerners, an air gun is a BB rifle your parents took the feeder mechanism out of, and it will only shoot air out and not BBs. That was mild aggravation to us, so we decided to play war with them anyway. We knew, even then, we needed assault rifles and not just regular M-1s. So we pulled the breech down to pretend they were clips for Tommy guns. Only thing was I forgot I couldn't pull the trigger or the breech would automatically return to its original position. I still can't tell you how I did it but I pulled the trigger and the breech flew into position cutting my left thumb severely. Well, it was time for the old blood again. It was plentiful and flowed freely as I again alerted the neighborhood of what I was convinced was my imminent death from blood loss. Mother arrived soon, having recognized my well known shriek. Instead of me, it was she that almost passed out from seeing the blood. Mrs. Smallwood was left to take care of both of us. They eventually wrapped up my wound tightly and taped it.

Mother was somewhat of a contradiction and she still displays this even now at eighty-four. You would think she would've insisted on taking me directly to the doctor as in past instances. You would have thought wrong. When I didn't see blood anymore I stopped crying. She decided if I stopped crying I was all right even though Mrs. Smallwood, who had seen the cut, knew it needed stitches. Mother disagreed and said she could take care of me at home. I now have a nice little lump on my left thumb, but that's not bad. It has always been immensely helpful in telling my right from my left hand. In times of doubt I just feel my thumbs.

If you can't run or play with guns then what can you do? The world is a big place and I was not short on ideas. Airplanes have never been far away from my heart. I remember sitting on the edge of the long porch that extended the length of the front of our house. It was covered by a roof that slanted down to four white posts. One of these posts was on each end of the porch, and mother had planters running from the house to the posts on each porch end. Barge Garner and I would sit in the white metal lawn chairs on the porch using a planter as rudder petals for our B-17 bomber. This was really fun when it was raining hard cause we could pretend to be in a storm on a bombing run. This is to prepare you for the rest of my airplane exploits.

The swing that sat in the side yard between our and Mr. Henry Smith's house was the fighter plane I had always envisioned in my mind I'd fly one day. The higher I swung the faster the plane would go. We all know that even good fighter pilots have to bail out sometimes. When the swing got even with the pole holding it, I lost my nerve. Instead of going out the front and landing on my feet and hands, I took the old ejection seat method and went out backwards. I landed on my back and momentarily was knocked unconscious. When I came to I couldn't breathe, which meant I couldn't give my standard neighborhood alarm of injury and imminent death. I guess the sucking sound from trying to catch my breath or either the thud of my sudden connection with the ground sent my ever vigilant mother out the front door to my rescue. I was thoroughly convinced this time she was too late. I couldn't move or make a sound. A quick diagnosis by Dr. Mom was a certain broken back possibly resulting in paralysis. As always she believed it was all her fault and her only child would be a paraplegic for the rest of his life. Without considering that a broken back could be worsened if she moved me, she snatched me up and off we went to Dr. Harvey.

Doctor Harvey was in fine form that day. He decided to

innovate and instead of bandaging me he used strapping tape. Within minutes of an x-ray which proved there were no broken bones, I was strapped from my shoulders to my navel in white tape. I resembled the Mummy minus the head wrappings. Of course, it didn't buy me time out from school as I had hoped, but it got me a certain amount of sympathy from the teachers. There were two problems with the tape, it got dirty and it began to itch. Mother did not let me remove any tape to scratch. She proceeded to make me take sponge baths, over tape and all, saying I shouldn't get into the bathtub because it would get the tape wet. I'm sure Gracie Allen is somehow related to my mother's side of the family. Eventually the tape came off and my ego recovered from the swing bailout, but my back never did.

I remained accident free for a few more years, but there were times when it didn't seem I would maintain that record. At age fourteen I had expanded my capabilities to doing seriously dangerous things, like jumping off mountains. Well, the mountain was a huge pile of gravel stacked by the highway department between my neighbor's house and the one next to his. The house next door to my neighbor was inhabited by the Gay family. Bobby was about my age and was the most rambunctious one of the three Gay kids. He and I couldn't resist that pile of gravel. We first started having races up to the peak. Then we were joined by his brother and sister, Sidney Michael and Goo Goo, to play King of the Mountain. Other kids joined in and this kept up until the parents intervened. Then it was back to Bobby and me seeing who could jump further off the gravel pile. The object was to land clear of the base of the pile. It was fun, and I wish to report I was never hurt during this particular pastime.

I managed to survive to adulthood without giving my mother another opportunity to save my body. Kids are a lot tougher than they look. Why, if my mother had been able to doctor today's kids, well maybe there wouldn't be so many clinics popping up in every neighborhood to take care of minor medical problems.

SWIMMING INDOORS

When I hear someone talking about indoor swimming pools, I think of big time money. It wasn't the case in Hogansville in the 50's, at least not in my family. Nevertheless, I learned to swim in an indoor pool. If they haven't yet torn down the Community Building on Johnson Street, then you might stop by and take a look at my indoor pool. It's in the basement.

I was six when my mother decided I'd need to learn to swim. We went to Panama City every year on vacation whether we wanted to or not. Just habit I guess. My parents weren't much on exploring, so when they found a place they liked we just kept going back. I believe I inherited that trait or at least my wife thinks so. Mine wasn't the only mother who decided to enroll me in a swimming class to prepare me for those vacations. Tony's mother and a few others also enrolled their kids. You have to understand, from the beginning, I never liked to get wet. Mother had a hard enough time getting me to take a bath on a regular basis. My wife still does on occasion, but I suppose I got used to it just like I did going to the pool for lessons every afternoon in the summertime. One of the reasons I fear getting wet, is water tends to fill all my breathing apparatus and makes it extremely difficult to get oxygen to my lungs. Our first lesson was learning to "duck," you know, take your head underwater. As I recall, swimming lessons were much like military basic training where you did as you were told or someone standing over you would make you pay.

Calvin Hipp was a young guy and great swimmer who earned money to go back to college by teaching kids to swim. In spite of the fact Calvin did an excellent job teaching us, the pool was always permeated with too much chlorine, enough sometimes to affect our breathing in or out of the water. Now most indoor pools, at least the ones we think about today, are pretty opulent. But the Community Building pool left a lot to be desired. The basement had no windows, the lighting was poor and the echo didn't help my understanding of orders even before my hearing went bad. Overall, it was pretty dank in that basement and everything was done in black and white checked tile, including the showers. It was all we had and we loved it even when our lips turned blue.

Once we kids had the hang of swimming in the unheated Artic-like pool water, Calvin gave us some free time to practice. By then most of the mothers had decided to leave us in his capable hands, except mine. It was a little embarrassing when she was the only one sitting around patiently waiting with my towel in hand. Mother was a good swimmer and had been on the swim team at LaGrange High and wanted to be there in case Calvin needed help pulling me or some of the others off the bottom of the pool. It's surprising I never gave her an opportunity to show off her skill. That doesn't count the time I slipped and grazed my head on the side making a rather unusual entrance into the water. My movements weren't and still aren't graceful when I swim, so neither mother nor Calvin noticed anything unusual about my arms flailing around wildly when I entered the water. Of course, over the ten years my wife and I have owned a pool, she's never worried about my swimming form either. Come to think of it, I thought I would drown a couple of times over those years but as you can see I'm still here and I managed to stay on the surface if you can call it that. Thanks Calvin!

COAL HOUSES AND HOT HOUSES

After washing two cars in a row and suffering a minor heat stroke, I collapsed on the sofa to join my wife watching Bob Villa's home improvement show. I'm not much on doing home improvement but I enjoy watching someone else do it. Bob was building a solarium on the front of a house in Cape Cod. I watched the progress and the more I saw the more it reminded me of Mr. Henry Smith's version, built from his coal house.

In case you don't know what a coal house is, I'll try to explain. Until I was nine years old I lived on the Mill Village, precisely Marshal Avenue. For those of you who never experienced the mill village, it's a group of little houses all built to the same specifications by the U.S. Rubber Company for its employees to live in so they could be close to the factory. Of course, you could count on the residents changing the houses to fit their particular tastes, and each neighborhood took on its own personality. But there was one standard thing no one seemed to ever change. It was a little building that sat behind the house and had a door on each end. This was the coal house. Its purpose was to serve as a storage bin and a place to put, what else, coal. The houses on the Mill Village weren't centrally heated and had fireplaces for burning coal. I know because I made a personal inspection of our coal burning fireplace, hands first when I was three years old. Doctor Harvey wrapped them up and hoped for the best. Turns out he was a pretty good country doctor, evidence, my typing this story today. Of course he didn't do much for my spelling.

There was a narrow strip of yard between each coal house and main house. When your imagination is only about six or seven years old, it doesn't take much to envision the narrow streets of a western town lying before you. I would always ride my mother's broom, alias Trigger, to the coal house and tie him up to go in and have some sarsaparilla. Mother didn't care much for me foraging around inside the coal house, so she told me there were wharf rats the size of my dog running around in there. I was certain with all the stuff they had packed away in there that some rodents might be about, but I never saw one personally. Of course, it also never occurred to me we were a good two to three hundred miles from any kind of wharf. This didn't stop my furtive imagination from conjuring up all kinds of monster mice living inside the small building.

Our neighbors, the Henry Smiths, didn't have any kids so they spent most of their money improving their property. Miss

Bessy loved plants and Mr. Henry loved his yard. Most of us kids loved to play cowboys and that didn't mix well with the Smith's yard. We were all forewarned that if we treaded on Mr. Henry's fenced-off Bermuda grass and hung around his yard we would lose our ears to his work knife, and probably never recover anything dropped while trespassing. He turned his coal house into a "hot house" for Miss Bessy's plant collection. I recall it looking just like one Bob Villa built on his TV program. It was about four feet into the ground and walled with concrete, and the rest was a frame with glass panels curving all the way over the roof. It was just too enticing for a six year old not to want to explore. Every once in a while Miss Bessy would invite mother to come over and see her plants. Naturally, I came along and got to go in the hot house to find out first hand how it got its name.

One summer afternoon, Mr. Henry and Miss Bessy went out visiting in their Mercury Turnpike Cruiser, so I wandered over for a closer look at that hot house. Usually Miss Bessy locked the door when she wasn't using it, but on this occasion she left it open. I guess the beauty of the exotic plants and the fact that I wasn't supposed to be there lured me inside. Whatever it was, I managed to somehow accidentally lock myself in. You know glass is a pretty good insulator of noise and capturer of heat too. So after what seemed like an hour, but was probably only a few minutes, mother happened to come out into the backyard. She saw my little face mashed flat against a glass pane gasping for breath and my little hands beating the crap out of the two adjoining ones. Fortunately for Miss Bessy I didn't break anything, and not so fortunately for me my mother tried her dead level best to break something of mine. Numb rear or not I could at least breathe again and my little sweat soaked body never had a hankering to go back into Miss Bessy's hot house, not to mention our wharf-rat-ridden coal house. Trigger would be allowed to roam free from that time on. Where's a broom going to go anyway?

COWBOY HATS AND PISTOLS
I HAVE KNOWN AND LOVED

It was last night outside on the patio with a warm breeze blowing and a balmy eighty degrees to relax me when I decided to do it. When I have the time to relax the same thought crosses my mind. And since there were no major issues on the table requiring my attention, I decided to relive those days of yesteryear with a hidey hi yo Silver and away.

I went into the house and straight to "my room." My wife knows I've never quite accepted adulthood so she lets me call it "my room." I perused the various mementos telling the world who I am. There it was, sitting on top of the wall unit right next to my Yankee Cavalry Hat and the Teddy Roosevelt Rough Rider's slouch, the "Longstreet" hat. The cream colored slouch is my favorite. By the way, a slouch is a "cowboy hat" with wide brims that cover your eyes, only you can't wear it when driving a modern car because it hits the headrest and pushes down and covers up your face. I have a Texan friend at work that drives an old '68 Plymouth Fury his parents bequeathed him. It's a great gold colored vehicle looking somewhat like a Desert Storm tank without a turret. This car provides him with a low headrest permitting the wearing of his Ken Maynard genuine Texas cowboy hat. I wonder what he'd take for that car.

Cowboy hats, such as in the case of the "Longstreet" hat (named for Georgia's most famous Confederate General James Longstreet), need the accompaniment of other accessories like a pistol. It was pretty hard in the old west and in the Hogansville of the 50's for a cowboy to be without his trusty pistols. Right below the hat on a lower shelf of the wall unit is my original replica Colt model 44 caliber New Army Pistol (Confederate version). It doesn't shoot real bullets but it does look and work just like the original ball and cap pistol used in the Civil War. That is just as well because a gun that fires a cap fits my mood perfectly.

On the way back out to the patio I picked up a little something to quench my thirst and proceeded to enjoy the weather and my days of yesteryear. I had the patio all to myself because my wife was on the phone with one of her relatives and the fence blocked the view of all the neighbors. As I sat there in my chair, feet propped on the table with the umbrella open above my head, I noticed the pistol felt good in my hand as I digressed into a semi-dream state. I cocked and fired it several times and always hitting my imaginary target. I could see the brim of the hat just above my eyes and the color reminded me of days of old.

I was always Roy Rogers when we played cowboys. He was quite a hero to live up to. To even begin to put myself in this character I needed a white hat. Actually, I needed a cream colored hat. Even though we didn't have color TV when I was a child, I knew Roy's hat was cream and not white. Don't ask why because I can't tell you today. The first cowboy hat I can remember owning was cream colored and had a little brown cord that weaved its way through holes at the outer edges of the brim and a brown hat band. It had a little tie rope to keep it from blowing off my head while riding Trigger at a brisk pace. The hat could also hang behind my back and choke me, as it usually did. This was cool and I did it a lot especially when at a full gallop.

I spent much of my cow punching days with the kids on my block like Linda Payne, Butch Hight, and a few others. They always wore black hats because they liked Bob Steel, The Durango Kid, and Poncho and Cisco who all wore some sort of dark colored hat. We had many gun battles usually ending in a draw since nobody wanted to admit to being killed even if they were shot at point blank range. I knew I always had the fastest draw because mine were the "official" guns Roy Rogers wore on his show. I saw to it that Santa knew exactly which ones they were and the store where they could be found. I took mother and daddy on separate occasions to specifically point them out. They had a close relationship with the "Jolly Old Man."

I suppose of the arsenal I eventually amassed, my favorite gun set was the official Roy Roger's with the stainless steel barrels and the copper colored handles. Those guns, just like Roy's, had little black wood grains running through the copper and a revolving cylinder that held real play bullets. I'm not sure at all if Roy's guns held play bullets? I can still remember how thrilled I was when I got up that Christmas morning to find those guns and holsters, boots, spurs, and a brand new cream colored cowboy hat sitting under the tree. And this cowboy hat didn't have the kid-looking brown cord around the outer edge and the rope to choke you. It was taller and had tucks in just the right places and looked a lot more like Roy's. This outfit let me give fair warning to the rest of the kids on the block that the "King of the Cowboys" was still living at six Marshall Avenue.

The next year when I was recovering from a serious bout with Chicken Pox, mother bought me a special gift from Allen's Five & Ten to cheer me up. Since I couldn't get out with the other kids, she felt I needed a little inspiration to recover quickly before she turned into a domestic servant and nurse for life. Usually she was careful with her money but this time her guard was down and I got exactly what I asked for, a Hop-a-Long Cassidy six shooter. It was big, and the cylinder flipped out just like the real one. The grip was white and it had a brown longhorn cow head on it. Only problem was it didn't fit any of my holsters. It wouldn't stay in my pants either. More than once I had to retrace my steps to find it, but because it was big it was always easy to find. After a while of carrying the thing around in my hand, I got too tired to chase bandits. And since most of my summer days were comprised of cowboy chases with my friend Butch, the Durango Kid, I eventually retired the big gun to my closet. That "black hole" never returned any of the toys relegated there and the Hoppy gun was one of them.

   I suppose the last of my cowboy days are remembered in the pictures taken of me at Young's Mill Bridge where the waterfall could be used as a background. I had a straw cowboy hat on that day, but the trusty Roy Roger's six shooters were there in each picture. There are poses of me with the guns drawn shooting crooks and just being a cute kid (to my mother anyway). The boots and spurs were there too, as well as my checkered Roy Roger's shirt. I wouldn't take gold for those pictures even though they are black and whites. I only wish my cream colored cowboy hat had been taken along that day and I hadn't made the mistake of putting my official Roy Roger's six shooters in that closet when I finally outgrew them.

   So, having a floppy styled cowboy hat around is in my nature. And getting the real replica Civil War pistol made me realize I need a belt and a holster too. I don't guess it would be appropriate now-a-days for a guy my age to ride a broom for a horse. If I'm gonna ride maybe I'll need a real horse. But of course, if I get a real horse I'll need a blanket and saddle and probably a pasture and barn, and feed too. Does this sound like someone who reverts back to his childhood a little too easily? Forget the horse; I'll just keep my hat and pistol, and the real replica Civil War saber given me at Christmas by my stepson and stepdaughter. It's amazing what a little balmy weather and free time can do for a middle-aged kid.

'Stick em up!" It's none other than Roy Rogers. Okay, it's me, Jimmy Dale, around six or seven years old when cowboys were our heroes and a set of Roy Roger's pistols was the envy of every kid on the block.

PICTURE THIS

The first TV we had when I was growing up was an Arvin. You don't see too many Arvins these days unless you are in an antique mall, or more likely, a flea market. It was an amazingly good TV for its time. Television technology was new then so you really didn't expect the TV to work too long. Ours did. It got us through ten years of Dave Garroway and the Today Program, Uncle Milty, Howdy Doody, and Davy Crockett. I remember well sitting in front of that screen wearing my coonskin cap and eating dinner from my Davy Crockett cup, saucer and plate while watching Davy hunt bear. We didn't have VCRs then so either you watched it when it came on or you missed it. And there were no thirty-minute commercial breaks allowing you to eat a leisurely meal and get back before the program started again. Disney always came on about the time mother got supper done. I'd usually have to miss something I wanted to see because my parents didn't like to eat cold food. But on special occasions like Davy's show time, they'd compromise and let me eat in the front room where our TV resided.

As time passed and TV technology improved, we owned more sets that hadn't improved. The repair rate on our Admiral was not the best. I became a good friend of the TV repairman, John Arrington, who could have made his daily wage off us alone. I saw John so frequently that his two sons and I still recognize each other today. It seems John never had to take the TV to his shop in those days. He always had a tube or some kind of part he carried around in that little case. I guess things were simpler then and if they weren't maybe repairmen were better. I don't know which. I do know the 50's and early 60's were good times to live and a small town made them better. If anything went wrong with our appliances we could call men like John or Whit Barrett and they'd be right over. And if things went wrong with our bodies, Dr. Arnold or Dr. Harvey would be at our door. We knew we could trust them and they never let us down.

 Too bad things aren't like the 50's and 60's today, but those days are gone and so are the local professionals. I can't tell you the man's name that came recently to see about our projection TV when it committed suicide in front of our very eyes. He didn't bring a little case of tubes like John Arrington; he just looked blankly at us and said the TV had to be taken in but he didn't have his truck that day. He didn't bother to come out again until I called the manufacturer, ready to threaten a lawsuit. I didn't have to do either, as the manufacturer said to my amazement, "No problem; for you GI, we fix for free. Call this man to come out." Wow! They were going to fix it for free? That was in July of this year. I called the TV repairman regularly and got a recording giving us eighteen choices and none of them seemed to fit just asking the status on the progress of our set. I usually ended up holding twenty or twenty-five minutes to get a preteen receptionist chewing gum and not being able to speak very plainly because of the wad she had in her mouth. Actually, I guess the child labor laws prevent preteens from working, but maybe not those who just sound that way. She never seemed to know exactly who or what was working or going on with our set. I'd end up holding for another thirty minutes while she went to check. Sometimes she'd forget and hang up and I'd have to call back and repeat the process. Most of the time though she would come on and say, "Oh, well I just talked to them and they say in two weeks." I could almost repeat it word for word with her.

 Two weeks went by four times before the set came home. By then we had to go out and buy a new theater sound system because our 1982 model receiver and speakers had died and couldn't be repaired. They simply don't make parts for things that old. Putting the new sound system together took expertise far beyond my capabilities, so my wife did it. I pulled out my purchased version of "Gettysburg" to test the new system and to see if Lee's cannonade sounded as good as in the movie house version. It did. But it must have shaken something loose in the TV because the entire picture had little red highlights all around the blurred people and places on the screen. So I called the TV people to come back out. They sent a guy who said he didn't have to take the TV in. Oh, boy! But I spoke (yelled) too soon; he said he had to take the computer part of it in.

It's been two weeks now since he took our computer part away, and we have a large black box sitting in one corner of the room decorating the area just in front of our wall unit, which, by the way, we can't get to. Maybe I'll phone the TV repair service, or maybe I'll just save the call and get a big wad of chewing gum and tell myself that it'll be two more weeks before I get it back. Excuse me, I'll just go and give them a call.

THE HUNKIE MAN AND THE ROLLING STORE

My wife handed me a popsicle, as she passed my chair, while I was watching a Formula One race. She doesn't like the bumble bee sound made by the high performance engines, so when I'm watching races she retreats to the bedroom for a little peace and quiet to read her mysteries and science fiction.

The taste of the icy frozen grape juice, and yes it was one of those "healthy" popsicles, brought back a memory of childhood. Of course, the race didn't hurt either. My mind drifted back to second grade (not too far from where it is now) when I stayed in constant trouble with Mrs. Faith Smith for my screeching of tires during the reading of the Bobsey Twins. I should be working for Toyota because my "mind is always racing" as it was then. When I got home from school in the afternoons, I would cool my brakes and don my Roy Rogers's hat and guns just in time for the "Hunkie Man."

The "Hunkie Man" pushed a square white cart with a pointed nose. The cart was of a tricycle design with big-spoked bike wheels on the side and a little wheelbarrow type wheel at the pointed nose for steering. The box contained the ice cream and the pointed nose carried an additional load of "dry ice," you know the kind that if your tongue gets stuck to it you can't get it loose. It was Butch, Don, Noel and I who would race home from play at the sound of that whistle blowing a block away. We had to get our nickels or dimes for ice cream and be back before the "Hunkie Man" disappeared around the next corner.

My problem is I never liked ice cream; I just got caught up in the excitement. Now before you decide there is something wrong with me I did usually eat part of my "hunkie" before Don or Butch asked me if they could have the rest. My all time favorites were fudgesicles or orange popsicles, but occasionally I would buy a "hunkie" if the other two were sold out. For those of you not born before 1956 a "hunkie" is a vanilla ice cream bar on a stick and covered with a thin shell of chocolate. I'd usually take one bite, as I couldn't and still can't abide vanilla ice cream, and I would then peel off and eat the chocolate shell. But, never fear, one of the guys would always take the remaining hunk of vanilla I didn't want to eat. Sometimes I'd just buy the thing and give it away without ever tearing the paper off. Funny thing though, I'd fight to the death over mashed potatoes, fried okra, corn bread and meatloaf.

When my folks went visiting relatives at Abbot's Ford near LaGrange, I would have to make sure to catch the country version of the "Hunkie Man." Abbot's Ford was just that, a ford spanned by a covered bridge over the Chattahoochee River leading to some of the best farm land in Troup County. My daddy's sister and her husband had one of those farms and eight kids to help run it. My cousins Butch and Peck and I were always ready on Saturday morning to wait by the dirt road in front of their house for the Rolling Store. We'd do this even if it meant missing a Hop-a-long Cassidy or Rex Allen serial. It was a real decision whether or not to watch our favorite cowboys, but the Rolling Store always won out. When we saw that converted school bus coming down the road, the fun started.

The door would open and reveal a collection of things you would never believe could be gotten into anything short of the General Store at Lee's Crossing. In fact there was little difference except the aisles were a bit more restrictive. There were pots and pans, canned goods, dry goods, animal feed, Coca Cola, candy, bubble gum, ice cream, gardening tools, utensils, and clothes of all sorts. I usually bought a Mounds bar and a couple of pieces of bubble gum with baseball cards enclosed. I remember I got my Nellie Fox card that way.

I'll never forget how the owner had stuff arranged. He used every bit of space to maximize efficiency. I need him to help me pack for my upcoming business trip. It would take a genius to find a way to pack that bus so full of things and then make them so easy to get to. In fact, the Rolling Store was a stroke of genius itself and I'll bet it paid handsomely too. That bus wasn't easy to miss with its outlandish paint scheme that resembled a cross between a 70s psychedelic tie dyed T-shirt and a Salvador Dali painting. On the sides in big black letters outlined in white was written "Sims Rolling Store". It'd fit well in some of Jimmy Buffett's stories about the Caribbean like the bus Desdemona was converting to a rocket ship.

By the time I came to my senses in the present where I was watching the Formula One Race, I saw the checkered flag fall on the race. I can't tell you how the guy won but it doesn't matter anyway since he wasn't the one I wanted to win. What did matter is the grape juice popsicle had melted on my white shorts. Needless to say I didn't eat that iced treat either. Some things never change.

DALE AND ME

No, you read it right. The Dale I'm talking about in my title isn't me. To understand you'll have to really concentrate on this little set of lines. You see, back when I was living on Marshall Avenue in Hogansville I had a next door neighbor who was a girl, I think. She was a good deal bigger than me and a lot tougher. She didn't take guff of any of the boys in the neighborhood, not to mention other girls. Unfortunately today she isn't with us to read this and then come break my face, so I can tell you this little story.

One of our favorite things to do at the tender age of seven or eight when we got home from Johnson Street School, which was just up the hill at the end of the street, was to watch our favorite TV programs after supper. Since there were only three channels then and the programming day ended before it got dark, the selection was greatly limited by today's standards. But we were never short of cowboy shows. We enjoyed the fifteen minute and sometimes half-hour adventures of our favorite cowpokes like Gene Autry, Roy Rogers, Bob Steele, Jimmy Wakely, Tex Ritter and Hop-a-Long Cassidy. Then after supper we'd all get together in the street, or better yet between our houses and the infamous coal houses and pretend to be in Dodge City.

Butch was always the Durango Kid. Noel would be Hoppy or maybe Gene, and I'd always be Roy Rogers who was my favorite hero, and he still is. But then Linda would show up. She wore a gun belt few if any of us could carry while we pretended to be riding Trigger or one of his colleagues. That gun was twice as big as any of ours. My matching copper handled official Roy Rogers's gun set I got for Christmas in 1952 was dwarfed by Linda's. Anyway, Linda, we hoped, would like to be Dale Evans or maybe Annie Oakley but that was never the case. She kind of liked me and she always wanted me to be on her side. Since she preferred to be Roy too, there wasn't much else I could be because I didn't want to be Pat Brady. Pat never got to shoot anyone and he never got to ride a horse, even Buttermilk. Besides, there wasn't anything around to be Nelly Bell but one of those glide pedal cars I never got the knack of peddling, and they didn't work very well in grassy areas.

In order to stay in the game, I had no choice but to be Dale. No not me, but Dale Evans. I never quite learned to speak with a tenor voice nor did I ever don a skirt but I did go in the house and get an old flannel plaid shirt and using the arms I tied it around my head. One day my daddy came outside and said, "Boy what are doing with that shirt on your head?" I told him, "I'm Dale Evans and this is my hair." I'm sure the man worried about me until the day he died. But honestly, I didn't see a problem being Dale, me or her. Of course, a little later in life I realized my reasoning could be misconstrued so I never told anyone I pretended to be Dale Evans. And since Butch's whereabouts are unknown and Noel and Linda aren't with us anymore I guess my secret is safe?

JOHNSON STREET SCHOOL

The closing of our beloved high school overshadows an event that happened too many years ago for any of us to quickly recall. It was another school closing and one that should be just as momentous as the one we face now. Those kids in today's Hogansville won't remember it because they weren't even born when this place disappeared forever. But if you were around in the 50's, then you will no doubt know I'm talking about none other than the "Johnson Street (maximum security) Grammar School."

I was never too far away from this school since it sat at the intersection of Johnson Street and Marshall Avenue, the street where I lived. As a matter of fact, it sat astride today's Granger Field. I won't go into too much detail describing the facility, but it did have some interesting characteristics you need to be aware of. The building was a three story brick rectangle with a huge set of doors, front and back. The broad stairs outside to the playground were flanked by flat concrete pillars that provided perfect platforms for us kids to sit on until the bell rang. And since it was maximum security, those were the only two exits. The most prominent feature of the building was the silver painted huge steel pipes on either side that ran from the top floor to the bottom at a 45 or 30 degree angle. At the bottom the pipes turned up level with the ground and went another few feet.

It's those pipes I need to talk to you about today. You see, they were our fire escapes. The way it worked was you entered the pipes from classrooms on each floor and slid down to safety. Only problem was it was dark inside and when you started sliding you didn't have any brakes. The more kids in front of you, the slicker the pipe became. Can you imagine the scariest ride at Six Flags? If so, then you have the fire escape pictured perfectly. If that wasn't bad enough, when you got to the bottom there might not be someone there to catch you so you'd plop to the ground before you could do anything about it. We got into this thing from impressive entrances with lots of reinforced polished wood and a big steel bar that prevented us from taking joy rides at will. Joy rides? As you progressed in grades (the school went from first to fourth), the higher in the building was your classroom which meant the further you had to slide down the pipe.

My problem is I'm scared of heights. Notice I didn't use the past tense. I had vertigo badly enough when I looked out my third grade classroom window, but I was a basket case when we had to do those fire drills. I decided right then and there when a real fire began I would burn to death and be done with it. What's the difference if I got in that steel pipe three stories up? I'd have a heart attack before I got to the bottom anyway. If a kid today was forced to slide three stories down a dark tube against his will, the teacher would be drawn and quartered and then put on trial for child abuse. But nothing I did deterred Mrs. Harris. I loved her and still do, but the woman always made me get into that contraption and go. My screams were never heard because all the girls screamed too. Thank God for the girls, because the guys would never have let me live that down. I think I just told them now. It doesn't matter because we never see each other that much anyway and besides my wife will beat them all up if they make fun of me today.

It was all I could do to go down the regular slide at school as I practiced for the infamous "pipes." I took the short slide most of those practice sessions. I also got real dizzy on the boy's merry-go-round. Why the "boys" merry-go-round? Well, I know that isn't allowed today, the Citadel and VMI temporarily excluded, but then there was "kid established" unofficial separate playground equipment. This particular merry-go-round went Mach One and had a ditch similar to a Civil War trench encircling it. The ditch was created by five or six guys pushing with all they had to achieve maximum velocity. The idea was to stay on as long as possible without being slung off and be the last guy aboard when the bell rang to end recess. This was something I never achieved. Anyway, it was fun trying and it helped to be a little dizzy when we started the math lesson. Because of the high speeds and rather rough behavior on the boy's merry-go-round, the girls preferred to use the other one located on the front side of the school. It didn't look like it was assaulted by commandos. I would have preferred it too, but then I would have been called a sissy. The monkey bars were also a male domain for the most part because the girls weren't allowed to wear shorts or long pants. A few didn't care and I'm not going to name them here. I don't need that kind of trouble.

Back to the steel pipe slide fire escapes. It didn't matter how wild the school ground equipment was, nothing could compare to the villainous steel pipes. I suppose now that I look back, those pipes helped me more than I realize. It's because of them I'm able to make a living as an Analyst. Yep, I spent a good part of my elementary years analyzing the pattern of the fire drills and trying to figure out when the next one was due so I could conveniently get sick that day. I had much rather have had a penicillin shot than slide down one of those dreaded pipes. Even though the analysis was never quite on target, the exercise was good practice for my job today as a Management

Analyst. Management Analysis is a whole lot like those steel pipes, you know. But that's a story I'll tell you later if you're interested.

The fact I'm slightly warped today isn't attributable to the steel pipes. As you can see, even though I wasn't able to avoid the steel pipes, I'm still here. I'm a better person for having slid down those pipes. If you'll permit, I want to philosophize a bit. I think today's kids need to slide down more steel pipes and spend less time being pampered to death. So many kids are never permitted to experience life because either we or the government protect them from the consequences of living in the real world. If our current society allowed kids to learn the lessons the way we did, then we'd have a lot more self-sufficient kids around today. As my daddy said, "I can't tell you everything about how to live. You'll have to learn some of it the hard way like everybody else." I think it's clear what he meant; if I didn't experience the slings and arrows of life for myself, I might not survive when he wasn't around anymore to run interference for me. If we are forced once in a while to do something distasteful but necessary, like learning to save our life by sliding down a steel pipe, we'll be able to take care of ourselves when the time comes.

Johnson Street School gave way to a more modern and better equipped one on a single level, Crocker Elementary School. We lived through that change fine and you'll make it through Hogansville High's transition to "Callaway" equally as well. The future is bright for the kids of Hogansville. I know these new schools will do no better job of preparing them academically than did our older ones. But there is one thing they may never do any better than the Johnson Street School, and that is preparing kids for life.

ST. JAMES

Today I'm in one of those moods where I just need to sit and think. It seems as we get older these "spells" happen with more frequency. So before I drift off into a sound sleep as I usually do, I must tell you about the one thing in my life that has influenced every decision I have made. My parents saw to it I was raised in the church. That church was the Methodist one in Hogansville, and more specifically, the one called St. James. Appropriate since I'm a James too. Not because of the church but because of my mother's family name.

The last time I passed through Hogansville, I came down Granite Street by accident. Meaning to turn at Johnson Street, I had accidentally gone past it and my only recourse to get to the Mill Village was to turn at a place that put me on target to pass St. James. I did, and it was still there. It even had added an annex which seemed to indicate that things weren't too bad after all, considering a large portion of the membership would probably be now approaching an average age of seventy-five or eighty. Many of the regulars, after some six decades of being there, are still around. The most remembered for me are P.L., Raymond, Roger, Karen, Floy (who I believe is now in a nursing home) and Eris (Eris has been Raymond's wife for over forty years; but mother never could spell her name right so why should I?)

St. James was originally built to satisfy two different groups of Protestants in Hogansville. In the south you took either one denomination or the other and these two sides accounted for about ninety percent of the population of the town. You probably already know I'm talking about Baptist and Methodist. We also had a Presbyterian church in town. As a matter of fact, it was uptown at the corner of Johnson and Main Streets. I never saw anybody go in or out, but the grass was always cut and the place was kept up good. Highland Baptist and St. James were on the Mill Village and represented the blue collar folks. The First Churches, Baptist and Methodist, and the Presbyterian were the white collar professionals. They always had brass horns and more expensive sounding instruments in their musical services. It was bordering on blasphemy if you brought a brass instrument into St. James. They even got excited when Lamar brought his electric guitar for gospel night. It was pretty much Eris and Floy accompanying each other on the organ and piano that we considered righteous music. If you really wanted to get into the high cotton you had Mildred and Lottie doing a duet to the piano and organ ensemble. To my child ears things got pretty loud even though we didn't have any horns.

I won't go into how poor the blue collar Methodist in Hogansville were during the depression but when the old Methodist church burned before WWII, the congregation offered to throw in with the Baptist and build a new church. The plan was to alternate Sundays using the facility. This sounded like a good idea to the Baptists who weren't much better off financially than the Methodist, so they built St. James. The Baptists insisted on having a baptismal pool in the church. Daddy told me early in my life that I was destined to be a Methodist because they didn't like water and neither did I, evidenced in the fights to get me into the bathtub. The Baptist make you get in the pool and then they duck you all the way under. The Methodists sprinkle your head as a token of baptism. My daddy knew what he spoke of.

This arrangement between the Baptists and Methodists worked fine until each congregation began to grow. Anytime you get more people you get more problems. The split boiled over into war, and because the Baptists always had more money they offered to sell us their share and build their own church. This suited the Methodists and after they bought St. James the first thing they did was plank over the pool and put a choir section there. This always bothered me 'cause they made the MYF (Methodist Youth Fellowship) sing in the choir at Wednesday Prayer Meeting. Every time I moved over that pool the planks squeaked. I was convinced I was going to end up like the guys on Truth or Consequences (how appropriate) and be dunked right in the middle of "Onward Christian Soldiers." Worst of all there wasn't a lot of room to swim. I could just see me sacrificed during the sermon and no one would notice. I usually didn't move when I had to sit over the pool during church.

My parents could never figure out why I was so well-behaved in the choir and was such a holy (pardon the pun) terror when I sat in a pew. I never told them, and I never fell in the pool. It was always a treat when the Men's Club opened the trap door to the pool just to check it. I always accompanied my daddy to these meetings; he had no choice as my mother worked the second shift. I got to see Methodists didn't keep water in the pool. That was only minor consolation since water would help break a fall. Air never stops anything. The fear switched from drowning to suffering a broken neck.

The Men's Club, which many in today's society would admonish you for having, especially if it's a church affiliated organization, was the center piece of St. James' extracurricular activities. It was a social as well as a business club. The guys ran everything in the 50's and they also ate everything too. When I hear Men's Club it brings back memories of John's Fish Camp on the Chattahoochee, Sprayberry's Barbecue, and many other restaurants they sampled and used to conduct the very short business sessions. Raymond especially enjoyed my mascot duties. He always had dibs on my salad and roll. But there was always a contest between him and P.L. and an occasional other to see who could get the portion of the main course I didn't eat. Being a rather small and picky energetic kid I didn't eat much, and there was always a vegetable, a piece of fish, chicken, or occasional steak available for bid. The business meeting always started while some of the guys were earnestly involved in finishing dessert. Oh yeah, Raymond never forgot to ask for my dessert.

A typical Sunday began with the men standing out front of the church smoking that last cigarette before Sunday School and us kids being wild Indians. The women were inside sitting on the pews discussing their atrocious hats and huge hat pins that held them on. When the organ beckoned them, the smokers would extinguish their cigarettes and file in. There was never a dull moment with these guys as they never seemed to agree on any approach as to running the affairs of the church. But together they were the power brokers and could spell the fate of any minister. The Methodist church rotates its minister assignments like the Army does soldiers. You can keep one if you give him favorable reports. Bill Webb was one such preacher that got favorable reports. His family and mine were close friends, living on the same street not more than a block from the church. He was a charismatic person and was hard not to like. He carried this over in his sermons.

I was an honest little guy who always spoke his mind. I usually acted badly in church when I got sleepy or tired of sitting in one place and never let my complaints go unheard. The droning on of the sermon would do this to a little five year old. Then there was one day when exiting an unusually long sermon I told Preacher Webb he preached too long and my daddy had said he wasn't supposed to go past twelve o'clock. Everyone pretended this didn't happen except me. But when asked what I wanted to be when I grew up, I always said, ". . . a Methodist preacher." Fortunately for the Methodist church this never came to pass. And, unfortunately there came a day when even Preacher Webb had to move along.

Life went on and we had many good ministers whose names I can't quickly recall; not that they were any less accomplished than Preacher Webb. My teen years were the best I spent at St. James. We had a group of kids that were together for many years due to our parent's affiliations with St. James. Our closeness transcended religious boundaries and resulted in friendships for life. I went through some very nonreligious perils with Larry and Lamar. Our exploits were widely known in LaGrange as well as Hogansville, and we left a number of brokenhearted girls in our wake. Of course, a number of girls left our hearts in pieces too. One of those was a little red-haired girl named Angela. I worked hard to get next to her on the pew where we kids always sat together. But then that's another story for another time.

 I will not forget our Christmas plays. Sylvia, our MYF leader, was then in her 20's and directed most of them. We had more fun doing our dress rehearsals than should be allowed in a church play. Those opportunities gave me access to both Angela and Pat, my two on-again off-again girlfriends. Plus the overall camaraderie was worth every minute of learning the long lines. Usually I was a shepherd who wore a bathrobe and a towel tied around my head. I looked less like a biblical character than a kid who had just exited the shower. One year I played a dad opposite Diane's mom. We both had to put talc in our hair to represent older parents to Larry and Pam. Today as I write I know the talc in my hair now won't wash out.

 Before I wax too nostalgic about former girl friends and get whacked up side the head by my wife, I need to tell you about the MYF. The Methodist Youth Fellowship was our connection to life in Hogansville as most of us were still in the preteen stage. It hosted some of the most "groovy" church parties in town at the big old Victorian house of Sylvia and Whitley. Before your imaginations get too wild, these parties only provided us lovers an occasional chance to hold hands and sometimes dance close, and not in today's definition of close. We went to other churches in other towns and made connections with kids that would enhance our lives a few years down the road. We also got to go to really neat places like the Chicken Treat and the local LaGrange Brazier where all the kids circled around in cars that ranged from hot rods to station wagons. We sponsored car washes that gave us the opportunity to learn to drive stick shifts like Bill Jackson's '50 Ford, and to cruise in Miss Thelma's futuristic '60 Chrysler Newport. I'll bet those people wondered why their transmissions and gas tanks weren't the same as when they brought the car in for a wash job. And not to be forgotten was Whitley's hayrides with newspaper for hay inside his truck's camper top, going 65 MPH down a major highway. What more good clean fun can you ask for?

When I started college and expanded my life outside Hogansville, St. James became less involved in my scheme of things. I still attended occasionally but was distanced from the life of the church by physical and spiritual miles. Finally when I graduated, the tie seemed to be broken forever as I never came back home to live. I suppose that's why divine fate or possibly luck brought me back to St. James that day I made the wrong turn. I never quite left, even though I thought I had. And just like Hogansville, it will always be in my mind. Even more, St. James is a bigger part of me than I realize. My character, values, conscience, and what I am today came from its careful molding and teaching. And I am eternally grateful to the spirit of that church even if its building can stand a little renovation.

CUTTIN' UP IN CHURCH

I suppose it all came to an end when the Preacher stopped cold in his sermon and stared at me and my co-conspirators who were momentarily frozen by fear that our short lives would not get any longer after the service was over. It was painfully obvious the whole row of us gained as much attention from the congregation as the minister.

How did I start this life of total disregard for silence in the sanctuary? From the recollections of my parents, it started just about the time I was able to form a complete thought. They talked to me a lot at home and wanted me to respond. So when the Preacher started talking to me from the pulpit, at least I thought he was talking to me, I naturally answered him back. It wasn't real clear to me why this didn't please my parents. Talking to this guy in church got me taken outside frequently for a good whack or two. What did these two bigger people want from me? I wished they would decide whether they were going to reward me or kill me for learning to talk. This getting a whack when I thought I was doing the right thing was becoming a real problem.

Deciding talking could be hazardous to my health, I resorted to another weapon in the arsenal of disturbing the peace in church. Wiggling and kicking are proven potent defilers of organized worship services. When I graduated out of soft baby shoes and into oxfords, I found kicking the pew in front of me alleviated boredom and created a reverberation the entire congregation couldn't ignore. It also created competition for that guy standing up there behind that pulpit who wouldn't let me or anyone else talk. I often wondered why no one else challenged him for the floor. So when he stopped to catch his breath, I would broach the subject with him only to get a hand over my mouth or another trip outside. Then I was talking about wiggling wasn't I? I was an excellent wiggler, and wallower too; from one parent to the other and back. Usually, I accompanied it with a few groans and an occasional rip as I tore something off my special Sunday suit. They finally decided to fight this by giving me a pencil and paper. It stopped the wiggling for awhile, but how much can a five-year old write or draw before his short attention span breaks? Oh, and how often does he stick himself with the pencil and cry out in pain? Eventually, it became apparent to me that there were other kids in our church suffering the same malady as me. We often got each other's attention and combined forces to create some very original forms of disruption.

By the time I started first grade I had found there were other places too where you had to be quiet. I knew the age of innocence had long since passed when my parents declared "no quarter." In military talk this means take no prisoners. I received an ultimatum, behave in church or die. It worked until my parents and the others made a serious tactical error by allowing us kids to sit together. At first we didn't talk. We used the old school trick of passing notes and smiling at each other a lot. We were told the grand experiment of letting us sit together would stop immediately the minute we became unruly. But you know kids, and soon the smiles became giggles and the notes spawned more potential opportunities to follow up with actions. It didn't take long before the old ladies at the front were glancing back and giving us and our parents a stern look. I believe this is where I came in, remember stopping the service? After having accomplished this feat, there was nothing more for me to achieve or die for, so I kept my mouth shut through most of my teenage years and listened. I actually learned a lot in church and I'm better for my experiences there. I know one of my co-conspirators is too because today he's a preacher, and a very good one I might add.

VISITING RELATIVES

Daddy's '88 Oldsmobile would be shined to a fare-the-well and the white wall tires would blind you if you looked at them too long. Doc's wash jobs at Bad Eye Cardin's Texaco were top notch, and if you don't believe it ask anybody whose daddy's car he washed. A clean black shiny '50 Olds '88 parked in our driveway at six Marshall Avenue meant only one thing, we were going to leave right after church and go visiting. Now, I could always guess who we'd go see because it was a limited list consisting of my Aunt Mary and Uncle Willie Lassiter, my Aunt Lydia and Uncle "Pappy" Smith and Grandmother Dale, or my Aunt Margaret and Uncle Reese Bowen. Of these choices I'd much prefer to go see my Aunt Margaret because she had two sons (out of her seven) who were about my age. They also lived on a farm and had some mighty good pastureland that would pass for the old west. I was about eight or nine then and had transcended my Roy Rogers stage for my John Wayne and Rin Tin Tin cavalry stage. We boys would always find a perfect spot to build a fort and defend against the renegade Indians who looked an awful lot like Holstein dairy cows.

If I guessed wrong, or if per chance my Uncle Pete and Aunt Anita were the targets of opportunity, then I'd still be a happy camper. Today, my Uncle Pete, who is eighty-seven, is the sole survivor of my parent's generation. I still love going to visit him in LaGrange. Back then he and my Aunt Anita, Nita as my family called her, were about the coolest folks I knew. Mother and daddy were a little taken aback by their laid back lifestyle. Nita wasn't exactly a perfect house keeper, and she and Pete loved reading paperbacks and had hundreds on shelves in metal bookcases in their living rooms that would look right at home in a warehouse. Nita was a collector of all sorts of things like dolls, spoons, art, and all kinds of stuff for an inquisitive kid to get into. She was a second generation Italian who didn't take much off spunky kids like me so when I picked up a fragile piece without her permission, well let's say I didn't do it again soon.

Their son Freddie was a few years older than me and an avid airplane model builder/collector. He also flew real ones later in his life. It was a huge treat, I still recall as I write this, for Pete to take me into Freddie's room and supervise my checking out all those airplanes. Of course he'd never do that when Freddie was around. Some of those models were almost big enough for me to climb into. When I got old enough, Pete gave me a gas powered model airplane of my very own. It was still in the closet of what used to be my room, when I lost my daddy back in 1983. Daddy kept a lot of stuff from my childhood and had I the good sense to have kept it after I lost him, it would be worth a lot of money today.

Last week my wife and I went up to Demorest, a little town in North Georgia where one of her brothers lives. I began to recall my childhood visits, as it was easy since he lives on an oak- and pecan-lined street in an old Victorian house. He, another brother and I sat on that porch with our feet propped on the railing talking about life, fishing and our daddies. The experience was soul renewing and the unusually warm weather permitted us to stretch out this quality time. These fellows are from the Cajun side of my wife's family, the fun ones. I guess you can say my Aunt Anita and Uncle Pete, although being from different places, are the Cajun types of my family. Now that visiting my family is behind me, this Cajun one is well worth getting the black Honda washed up to go visiting. Never mind it doesn't have whitewalls and a rocket V8.

AUNT SALLY AND UNCLE DAVE

Just the other day I was sitting in my favorite position, next to the cat in the little bit of space left to me at the end of the sofa. This is okay until the cat decides she doesn't like to be crowded. Anyway, the TV was boring and I decided to take down one of my "War for Southern Independence" books and see if I could get interested in reading again.

As I read I found there was a Captain W.D. Carlson of the Troup Artillery helping Wade Hampton and Cobb's Legion hold South Mountain, Maryland. Of course, everyone knows the South Mountain Gap was important to General Lee as he moved his army toward Sharpsburg, Antietam to you folks from up north. Well, reading about Captain Carlson got me to thinking about my own forefathers from Georgia who fought in the conflict. They all were on my mother's side since my daddy's folks aren't traceable, well not yet; my genealogist daughter hasn't given up. Mother's family has been in Georgia for several generations even back as far as the war. Well almost, as mother now tells me some of them were from South Carolina.

When I was little we used to go visit my mother's Aunt Sally. For brevity we all just called her Aunt Sally. It was rather difficult for an eight-year old to call her Great Aunt Sally. She was Uncle Dave Hunter's mother. Actually he was our cousin, not an uncle. But everyone always called him Uncle Dave so I didn't think I should be the one to break the tradition and tell them that he was only a cousin. Uncle Dave was an interesting character. He had been a high ranking officer in the LaGrange Fire Department, even the Chief I think. He had this fancy white fire helmet. It obviously wasn't like the red ones on the Texaco pumps at Bad Eye Cardin's Service Station that were made of the same kind of tin that your canned biscuits come in. Bad Eye's helmets were wrapped with red cellophane paper and had cardboard Texaco fire chief badges on the front. I went through about a dozen of them a season.

Uncle Dave's fire hat was real though and I wanted it very badly. Since he never spoke to anyone when we went to visit Aunt Sally, it was difficult for him to give anything away. He just sat in a corner and smoked his pipe and nodded a lot. I think it was because he was falling asleep, or he could have been agreeing with what mother and Aunt Sally were saying. Using Aunt Sally as an intermediary one day, Uncle Dave offered me his Chief's hat. I told Aunt Sally to tell Uncle Dave I said, "Yes I want the cap." Before he handed over the cap he proceeded to take the big gold badge off the front. When this happened my little face fell to the floor. I didn't want just a plain white hat without the decoration. Why, that badge was the best part of the hat. Otherwise it was similar to the ones the Sinclair guys wore at Pritchett's Service Station. I decided not to talk through Aunt Sally and told Uncle Dave directly I didn't want his old hat and he could keep it. Mother told daddy how I had been rude to Uncle Dave so when we got home I got a spanking. I made several under the breath comments about Uncle Dave for causing me to get a spanking. I really felt bad about it when about a month later he went to that big fire house in the sky. I still regret I never got to hear his voice talking directly to me.

Aunt Sally had to have been nearly a hundred when we used to go visit her because Uncle Dave had been retired from the fire department since the end of WWII. She and Uncle Dave lived in a big drafty Victorian house next to the elementary school on

Hill Street in LaGrange. The school had long since been closed and Aunt Sally got a lot of pleasure talking about all the vandals she saw as she kept a vigil on the school each day. She was too old to walk anywhere. Uncle Dave would always wait on her and I'll bet he had to talk when he did this. The house was big, dark and drafty, and everything in it was either too large or overstuffed including Uncle Dave. He ate a lot. Aunt Sally was sort of skinny and wore her hair in a bun. As I recall she never needed glasses and could read fine print on a bottle of Carter's Little Liver Pills. Even as a kid with perfect vision I got tired of not being able to see anything when we visited Aunt Sally's house because they never turned on any lights. If it had not been for the big windows with the glass that distorted everything outside, we would not have been able to see who we were talking to.

I always enjoyed hearing Aunt Sally talk about family history. Her maiden name was James. She remembered lots of folks in our family and one or two who fought in the War Between the States. She always said Aunt Ada Belle was the one to talk to about family history. You'd think I would remember to do this but then we'll talk about that later on. She did do enough talking to inspire me to think about it later and I not only found some of my and Aunt Sally's ancestors, but one on my mother's other side that led to my recent installment in the Sons of the American Revolution. It pays to listen to your elders even if you can't see them and if they sometimes don't talk directly to you.

SPRING BREAK (HOLIDAYS)

My wife suggested I write something about Spring Break since I like to talk about it a lot. I could tell you about spring break in college but if the right folks read this it might invite the Daytona Beach authorities to reopen the investigation of a reported seaborne invasion of their coast by West Georgia College commandos. So we won't be going there.

In my pre-collegian days our family would plan their vacation around the week I had off from school, the week we all called spring holidays. It never failed that we always went to Panama City Beach, Florida. I know you are thinking about the carnival atmosphere there and saying, "Hey, these Dales were real swingers," but Panama City in the mid-1950s was anything but carnival. When we got into town, the population figures were changed on all the sign posts. That's how desperate they were to get folks to come down. I think improving accommodations would have been helpful. We always stayed in a mint green cinderblock motel with louvered smoked windows that cranked out like blinds. It had a kitchen, so we didn't eat out much. Mother didn't want to spend the money and daddy didn't want to argue, so we pretty much ate the same kind of food on vacation we had at home. The only exception being we got to eat it on the round concrete tables and benches that sat just outside our door in the gravel parking lot. Daddy liked that because he got to look at his '88 Oldsmobile while he ate. Mother and I always got a kick out of seeing the pink flamingos painted on the side of the building.

The motel was a very good deal because it was only a block and a half from the beach. You couldn't see the ocean but the lone palm tree next to our door let you know the water wasn't far away. Walking over to the beach was a logistics nightmare. We had to carry everything including towels, suntan lotion, food, and all the snorkels and fins I never used and even my little brown leather sandals. They rubbed blisters on my heels so half the time I walked barefoot to the beach on the hundred and eighty degree streets. It was fun once we arrived and found a clear spot amid all the seaweed and other unidentified things that washed up with the tide.

There were no lifeguards to interfere with my fun, so one vacation I found a boat washed up on the beach and decided to investigate while my folks were greasing each other down with sunscreen. It had a cabin that seemed to need some exploration so I climbed in for a look. When they discovered me missing, my parents spent a pretty harrowing thirty minutes looking for me. Just about the time they decided I was a victim of Neptune, my daddy heard a little voice emanating from the washed up wreck. He ran to the boat and found me successfully managing to steer the craft to safety. Of course, the thing was permanently beached and never in any danger of again going to sea. Once I was safe, mother immediately got a headache and we had to go back to the motel for the rest of the day. This little incident cost me a major loss of valuable beach time since we never stayed more than three days per vacation.

We always took lots of pictures on our vacation. There are some good ones with me sitting in the Oldsmobile '88 with the door open; me on the hood of the 88; mother leaning against the '88; a picture of the '88 with the door open and no one in it; and finally my daddy leaning against the side of the '88 with the door open, a picture I still have sitting on a wall unit in the "office." Somehow my daddy made sure every picture we took ended up with that black car in it. My wife says I have the same habit. Nonsense, she just happens to be more photogenic around my cars. Sometimes we got a picture of mother wearing her pedal pushers and posing, you guessed it, next to the '88. She refused to wear shorts and only wore the pedal pushers on vacation when she was sure she wouldn't be seen by anyone she knew.

I guess I could go on some more about the exciting vacations in Panama City but I believe I've about covered everything except my motorcycle cap. Yep, I always got a "Brando" motorcycle cap every vacation. I've gotta look for one of those things when we go on our cruise this September. I know the cruise can never replace the excitement of Panama City in 1958, but the hat will bring back the spirit. Oh, and a few snapshots of my wife next to the black Honda with its door open.

Jim Dale

DE-STRESSING WITH HOWL-O-WEEN

I just got back from a class on "STRESS MANAGEMENT." Good thing too, because the people I work for used those two days to come up with a test they thought would give me a guaranteed cerebral hemorrhage and it almost did. While I was gone they reorganized, changed my seat and increased my responsibilities. This made me very unsettled about my surroundings, but I remembered what the teacher in the stress class said when she summed up her lesson. She said that being in surroundings you relate to in a positive way helps reduce stress and you might live longer. I wasn't relating very positively to work when I found my situation suddenly changing. In fact, I realized work was only a symptom of my real problem which is life in the big city. This was a good time to remember the past, a time of less stress.

We certainly didn't have that problem on the Mill Village. I remember in the fall when all the women in the neighborhood like mother, Mrs. Pike, Mrs. Rainwater, Mrs. Payne, and Mrs. Bessie Smith would rake up the gold, red, and brown leaves that fell from the old oaks lining Marshall Avenue. It was a ritual of fall and a time when they would take a break to catch each other up on the latest news. We kids did the best we could to undo all the raking by free falling backwards into the large piles of leaves. Mrs. Pike would report on Nita Fay's new husband and Tom's Air Force assignment in England, and the other women would listen intently. Then after that they each took their turn. When the social was over they would light fires under the stacks of leaves. The aroma of slow burning leaves would permeate the whole street and it was heaven. Nowadays all these homemakers would be under investigation by Al Gore's gurus for increasing global warming.

In the evening we would sit on the porch, and the Paynes, Smiths and Pikes would also be on their porches. Before you knew it there would be a conversation that would eventually result in everyone on one porch. We kids would be together in the yard playing cowboys or telling ghost stories, and having fun deciding what kind of ghoul to be on Halloween. I loved those socials, especially when one of the adults would decide to tell us a really scary ghost story. Some of them missed their calling and should have been writers. We tried hard to prevent anyone from noting our little eyes were involuntarily closing, but when one of us kids yawned, the social was over as quickly as it had begun. I don't remember the tricks we used to prevent them knowing we were asleep on our feet but I do remember if we could have made those gatherings last forever we would have done it.

Halloween was always my favorite time of year. I loved the fall colors and our classroom was decorated with pilgrims, Indians, and of course witches, black cats, corn stalks, pumpkins, bats and ghosts. It was all magical, especially the Halloween Carnival held at the high school gym. Not the new gym but the old wooden one at the bottom of the hill across the road from the junior high building. When you went inside, the place was decorated with spooks and the ceiling was draped with black and orange streamers. There were all kinds of game booths set up to win prizes. My most exciting thing to do was picking up ducks. The plastic red, green, blue and yellow ducks floated around this little canal on the counter. All you had to do was pay your quarter and pick up three ducks. If they had a label on the bottom with a prize printed on it, then you won the prize. I usually got a tacky ceramic figure of a dog or some other animal I insisted on displaying in our living room. To keep from stunting my growth and moreover my ego, my parents would comply for a little while anyway. The carnival was not complete unless you went into the Haunted House. This was not my favorite thing to do, but I did it anyway. It was always scary, with ghosts jumping out in your face and hanged witches (not very convincing stuffed clothing). Occasionally you would see a little fake blood. Suffice it to say that the "Haunted House" changed your life, at least for the night.

The best part of the carnival was seeing all your friends who you immediately recognized regardless of their disguises. The costumes ranged from well thought out home efforts to the standard school clothes with a plastic mask. I was usually somewhere in between. Since my mother worked the second shift, my daddy was always the one who got dragged to these things. He wasn't keen on taking me trick or treating, that is after I got up big enough to ask for a treat myself. He started letting me go with neighbors.

Sarah, our neighbor next door on North Highway, wasn't much older than most of us kids when she took us out on Halloween. She was always dressed in some kind of costume herself and enjoyed the fun as much as we did. There was always me, her daughter Lib and her son Lex. Lex was much younger than me and Lib, so we pretty much could go our own way while Sarah was busy with Lex. You were never in danger in any neighborhood. You knew almost everyone you visited anyway. Some of them you might not recognize because they went to a lot of trouble to scare you, as bad as you did them. I can remember in particular a lady dressed as a witch answering the door and the room behind her being black with eerie lighting and strange looking stuff all around. She laughed that witchy laugh and peered right into my little mask. When I saw those pointed teeth and the wart on her nose (part of her costume) I didn't stop to ask for a treat.

The streets were covered with kids and we talked and followed each other to every house in the neighborhood. I always hated to go to the house next door to ours on Marshall Avenue. Even if it wasn't Halloween, I was afraid of the man who lived there. He always threatened to cut our ears off if we got on his grass. But on Halloween his wife Miss Bessie made him behave and he always had the best treats to give away. Despite being a little apprehensive about Mr. Henry, my real worry was the passing cars and trucks filled with the big kids. They would splatter us with water balloons. You really had to be careful or you might be wet for most of the evening. And it was just cold enough then that you didn't want to finish your Trick-or-Treating in wet clothes. The last thing you needed was a cold that lasted all winter.

To me all this community spirit was better than Christmas or any other holiday. It could never have happened in a large city. Maybe in certain neighborhoods in larger cities there were such things, but I'm talking about a whole town here. So, I guess my stress management teacher was right I do need to be in a place I can relate to positively.

THANKSGIVING

Winter holidays in small towns bring to mind close families and a Currier and Ives setting. At least it does for me, even though I'm from the Deep South where one can forget snow and sleighs. Looking out my window where I'm writing this at work (during break) I don't see any snow but I do see something not encountered everyday. It's a buggy, or better yet a fancy buckboard, the equivalent of a nineteenth century sports utility vehicle. It is flat black with yellow matte wheels and red underpinnings. It's sitting on a trailer that seems to be tailor made for it. Finally, the trailer is hitched to a modern pickup. Why all this description? Well, mainly to satisfy my desire for detail but also to put you in the mood for this little tale of a rural American family and how they shared Thanksgiving with a small town boy.

The buckboard brings to mind farms, and farms bring to mind the Bowens. Who are the Bowens? Well, they are my cousins on my daddy's side. Margaret, the matriarch, is my daddy's sister. She has eight children, seven boys and one girl. They live in a place called Abbotts Ford. This is where the Abbotts forded the Chattahoochee River. I know I'm being a smart aleck. Reese, the patriarch, had a purpose for a large family. He worked full-time in the Callaway cotton mills in LaGrange and needed help keeping the farm going. As tasks were added on the farm, another son was born to eventually handle them. I often wondered how he ordered a boy every time one was needed. He never revealed that secret, but Reese was always a resourceful man. If there was a better or smarter way of doing something, it didn't usually get past him.

Margaret is, as mother says, a good old soul. She can't read a word but she counts money and does so very well. After she paid all the bills, the family never went wanting. She always had enough to buy the kids decent clothing and kept them in shoes. She wore what southern women call print dresses and usually no shoes except on the weekends when they all went to town. She has a laugh and cackle I still hear today when I visit her at the senior's apartments where she lives. She always greets me with, "Lordy, Lordy, Lordy if it ain't Jimmy. How are you, hon?" Of course now you have to compete with the TV that plays constantly at a fevered pitch during conversations. Worst of all, she is more interested in the TV than in conversing with you, especially if a Braves game is in progress. That's not bad for a ninety-one year old who entertains no intentions of checking out of life.

She always has a smile for everyone, and there are few times I can remember her any other way. But, believe me there were plenty of times in her life and the life of her family when it would have been easy for her to just give up and cry. In fact, life has never been easy for Margaret but she wouldn't have liked it if it were. She milked cows, slopped hogs, fed chickens, churned butter, washed clothes on the porch, hauled firewood, tended sick kids, and generally kept things going around the farm. Through all this she considered herself blessed, and above all she was happy. Being blessed has a lot to do with what you are willing to do for yourself; and self sufficiency is something Margaret and Reese instilled in all their young ones early in life. Reese was a taskmaster, and the boys knew it.

They all ate well, as evidenced by their daddy who was always a reminder to me that it was entirely possible there could be a real Santa Claus. In spite of his rotund body, he was as hard as a rock with muscle. All the Bowens were big folks anyway, and the additional bulk always made them look like giants to me. Reese and Margaret named some of their kids after their favorite people, such as Babe (George Herman for Babe Ruth), Gene (for Eugene Talmadge), Butch (Dewey for Truman's presidential challenger), and Peck (for Gregory Peck, the actor). Butch and Peck were too young to do a lot around the farm during the times I remember, so they helped with household chores and light work. The other guys would come home from school, study awhile, eat supper and begin their jobs on the farm. Working till after dark, they harvested corn, beans, and watermelons. They also plowed, irrigated, and repaired the barn and fences. They did inglorious tasks like slaughtering and dressing a few farm animals for sustenance in the winters.

Since the boys had almost no social life and were usually too tired to get into any trouble, eating was their favorite thing to do. There was no TV to watch, and besides if there had been, time would not have permitted. Margaret and Betty (her only daughter) got up before dawn to prepare dozens of eggs. Each boy ate five or six along with a fried slab of fresh bacon and a ton of sausage along with coffee and hotcakes by the dozens. The syrup flowed freely and freshly churned butter was always in abundance. Nobody ever went hungry in that house, with fresh food of all kinds available just outside the window.

I suppose this brings me back to my theme, as eating at Abbotts Ford was the highlight of my Thanksgiving weekend. Generally, visiting relatives on both sides of my family was not one of my favorite things to do when I was a small kid. Usually, it was boring grown-up stuff and talk while I sat quietly (Ha!) in an overstuffed chair for what seemed like years.

It wasn't that way when my daddy announced we were going to Abbotts Ford. I immediately ran to get my guns and cowboy hat. I put on my checked shirt, red bandanna and boots faster than Roy Rogers could leap on Trigger. It was time to go fight a few Indians and work on the fort. If it was warm enough I would also get to swim in the creek. Mother cautioned me on the way down not to dive into water I couldn't see through. She gave examples of the dead, deformed and mentally retarded children she knew that got that way because they dived into murky water and broke their necks on hidden stumps or shallow bottoms. It seemed mother knew a lot of very strange people but I always heeded her words and was never seriously hurt. I occasionally got my toes nibbled by a stray fish and once in a while I tangled with a limb that my imagination told me was an anaconda. I mostly found creek water tasted better than the chlorine pool water which I was accustomed to swimming in, but it was also much colder.

The trip down would be filled with songs and reminiscences of the other times we had been to the "country," as mother called it. I was usually too busy to participate because I was planning how we were going to fix the fort in the back pasture. When we passed the haunted house at Abbottville, mother never failed to tell me about the time Mary George heard the piano playing and chains rattling while A. B. was off running a revival. Mary George was our former neighbor whose fate it was to move into the haunted house. Eventually, the ghosts ran them off, or maybe it was because A.B. got transferred to Texas. The fork off Hwy 29 meant we were within range of the river. That too was exciting, because of the covered bridge. It was called "Glass's Bridge" named for a local black man who engineered and designed it. It was a typical wooden structure with lattice-work sides and a slanted roof. You could see the river between cracks in the floor boards, but the planking for the tires that ran the length of the bridge was firm and strong. To my knowledge no one was ever lost in the river due to a bridge collapse. It hurt deeply when I last crossed it seeing the condemned sign with a notification that a new concrete bridge would soon replace it.

When we finally arrived, my day was spent with Butch and

Peck riding out to the north forty to oversee the cattle and work on the fort. The bigger boys would have already disappeared into town making good use of their free time on a day not set aside for work. Reese, my daddy, Reese's brother Clyde, and usually a neighbor, would be sitting on the porch playing dominoes. The house was a typical farm style with a porch that wrapped around from the back to the front. The domino table would be sitting near the edge of the porch close to a post for foot propping and sun for lighting. The men would prop their feet on the post and lean back in their straight-backed straw woven chairs, carrying on a conversation while waiting for a move. Looking back I think those men on the porch just liked to sit and talk. The game was just an excuse to keep the women from finding something useful for them to do in the kitchen.

Mother, Margaret, Betty and Clyde's wife, Icy, prepared the food. The kitchen was a combination of this one and the last century. There was the open hearth fireplace with the standard iron pot. But there was also a modern gas stove fed by a propane tank just outside the window. The refrigerator was modern as was the freezer on the porch. There was also a wood burning stove used right along with the modern one. All the cooking hardware went back to another era. Somehow the old cookware made the food taste better. The dining room was filled by a long table with high-backed cane chairs. The table cloth was plastic with large blue and white checks. The floors were polished hardwood, and the room had a gentle formality not found in the rest of the house.

The table was set and laid out with fresh butter along with dish after dish of fresh green beans, mashed and sweet potatoes, giblet gravy, dressing and other things that my little memory banks ran out of room to store. But above all, when that turkey was brought out I saved a megabyte of memory for remembrance. It was one raised by the Bowens and I believe it rivaled a B-52 in size. Reese always carved the turkey, and everyone accepted that tradition. I would have a giant glass of iced tea and the farm boys had fresh milk. We all sat down and waited for the traditional thanks asking God's blessing for the food and fellowship we were about to enjoy that day. It was all I could do to make it though the prayer which fortunately never lasted long. The Bowens were always to the point when food was involved.

The meal and conversations were purposely extended for a couple of hours. When the desserts were finally brought out, there was a choice of sweet potato pie, egg custard, or pecan pie. Mother never failed to bring an orange cake and a chocolate pie that I had usually already graded with a taste test. Then we would move into the living room in front of the big stone fireplace. While the grown folks sipped their coffee, ate pie and talked, we kids would often get mesmerized by the fire and take a nap. If it rained it became very easy to sleep. The rain hitting the tin roof and a fire to keep our little full bellies warm was a perfect situation for Morpheus to sneak in a visit.

The years eventually swept away the Bowen farm life as the family began to grow up and apart. Almost to the last one, all the boys left as soon as practical, joining the service; three made it their career. Butch is now a Presbyterian minister holding a PhD in Theology and living in Texas. Peck works for the State Department of Transportation and spends a lot of time seeing after his mother's needs. The others too have experienced much success and one owns a textile plant and travels the world as a consultant. Reese passed on a few years back and Margaret is now in the retirement home I mentioned earlier.

The farm was purchased by the government, as well as the general store Reese and Margaret ran after his retirement from the mill. These landmarks now reside at the bottom of West Point Lake along with the new Glass's Bridge. But all my wonderful memories of Thanksgivings shared with them are still intact and dry. The Bowen's way of life is symbolic of what this nation is built on and why it still remains the greatest one on earth. I shake the dust off those memories every Thanksgiving and give thanks for having been provided them.

REINDEER DON'T BARK, JIM!

They do in my song. Do you know the tune "Grandma Got Run Over by a Reindeer?" After each verse just insert "ruff, ruff" and you got it. My wife, smart one-half Cajun she is, told me I had gotten the tune confused with the dogs that bark "Jingle Bells." It wasn't a mistake as I knew exactly what I was barking and it wasn't "Jingle Bells," just like I know Santa really exists.

All this reminds me of a particular Christmas past, not in the Scrooge sense. I was about four or five-years old when I saw him, Santa I mean. Yep, I really did see him. We were living on the Mill Village where the U.S. Rubber Company built all the houses to look pretty much the same. It got confusing sometimes even for us kids who lived there; and being a kid most of the cars looked the same to me too. Well, except Mr. Whaley's '37 Chevrolet that he kept to remind himself of the good old days of the Depression. Since all the houses looked similar and Santa wasn't a permanent resident of our town, it amazed me to think he could know who lived where.

I often wondered how Santa could know when somebody moved, or when a new kid was born, or when one left the world. I also wondered why he only talked to parents about what to give us kids. I realize I didn't always write him, or at least I never did before I learned to write. But even those letters written after I learned never got a stamp on them. I didn't get too caught up in trivial details then; all I knew was he somehow got it together every Christmas. My immediate problem was how to stay awake long enough to get a good glimpse of this sucker. I thought it would never happen because I knew he would not show up when I was awake. I wondered if this guy worked for the government or had friends in the CIA who bugged our houses to find out when kids went to sleep.

My bed was in the front room that faced the street and I had a perfect view of anything that moved outside. The street light just down at the intersection helped my cause immensely. I had just about given up seeing the old man, and it being Christmas Eve I had decided to turn in early so I could enjoy all the toys the next morning. The lights went out and my parents went off to bed. It wasn't long before I realized I had grossly miscalculated my departure time and was wide awake at ten o'clock at night. So being the kid I was, and inquisitive to boot, I sat up in the bed and started to look out the window. Sure enough, I pulled one on the old boy and his CIA buddies. He wasn't looking and I caught him red-handed. I saw him walking up the sidewalk toward the house. Suddenly I panicked because I had forgotten he would pass me by if I were awake when he got to my house. I tried with every ounce of energy to put myself to sleep. As he got closer, I closed my eyes tighter and pretended to snore – something I don't have to pretend these days. Occasionally, I would ever so slightly crack one eye to see if it was working.

Well, it didn't and he walked right past the house. I saw the red suit, the white beard, and the huge sack of toys pass right by the door. I knew Mr. Pike was already asleep. Lucille had made him come in early that night for Tom and Nita Faye's Christmas. He always played Santa at Belks so this couldn't be him. All of us kids knew it was him at Belks, but we went along to humor our parents. But this guy was not Mr. Pike and he was real, and he had passed me by. My crying brought mother into the room. I pointed out the window and through my sobs managed to tell her the situation. Just as she was wiping away my tears, she saw the jolly old elf walk into Mike Birdsong's house. She assured me he would come back as soon as I was asleep. That didn't wash as I knew the old codger wasn't going to leave me anything this time, and it wasn't even my fault I couldn't go to sleep. Finally, exhaustion set in and I had no choice about falling asleep.

Amazingly, I was able to open my eyes the next morning. Though they were matted with sleep and swollen from my previous night's disappointment, I saw toys in front of me. There on the floor was everything I had asked for in the unstamped letter I didn't write. Well, I thought, maybe he isn't such a bad guy after all. He did come back after I had gone to sleep. But how did he know when I went to sleep? It was another of those perplexing and complicated questions that never seemed to get answered to my satisfaction.

From that time on I was a true believer in the existence of Santa Claus. Even in my older years when guys told me it was really my parents, I said, "Nope, I saw him and he is real." I was an only child and my parents didn't want to lose their baby any sooner than they had too, so they didn't do much to dispel my belief in Santa. After a while it got too embarrassing, even for them. Because when older, I was still professing to believe in Santa Claus, so they finally told me my Santa was Mike Birdsong's uncle. Do you really think Mike Birdsong's uncle would walk clear up Marshall Avenue near midnight with a sack on his back and all that git-up on simply to put stuff out after the kid had gone to sleep? I don't believe it, either. I knew it wasn't Mike's uncle but I went along with my parents, who really think Mr. Pike is Santa Claus. Come to think of it, they probably never would have believed reindeer bark either.

HOMETOWN CHRISTMAS

Most of our memories are reserved for happy events at a special time in our lives. I can't think of a happier event or a more special time in my life than Christmas. On Christmas Eve in the fifties and early sixties my mind would overflow with anticipation of sugar plum fairies and Santa bringing toys, and I'd have a hard time getting to sleep. I still get a warm and fuzzy feeling just thinking of those cold mornings I'd get up and sit in front of the fire in the living room to unwrap presents with my parents. I'd be allowed to keep my pajamas on longer and eat my breakfast in the floor so I didn't have to leave my stuff.

My parents also never forgot the true meaning of Christmas as they always made time to remind me of whose birthday we were celebrating. If that didn't do it, then the Christmas cards on the mantle with the manger scenes and wise men following the star gave me a pretty strong hint. When we decorated our tree, we made a special occasion of placing mother's angel on top after we finished all the other decorations. The tree wasn't complete until the angel was in place. Of course it was a bit difficult after I had slung icicles all over the place, even in the next room on the kitchen floor. I wasn't the neatest icicle tree trimmer in Hogansville, but they endured it because it was our family ritual of decorating the tree together. My daddy was pretty shy, but he managed to bring himself to sing "Silent Night" with mother and me. I'll never forget him showing that side of himself each Christmas. You know, he wasn't such a bad singer either.

One of my fondest memories of Christmas was when daddy would take me to get our Christmas tree. We usually did this task in the evening while mother was at work. She worked the second shift at the cotton mill. The cold night air was always warmed by our mutual bonding, and all the lights of the Christmas tree lot and nearby town mesmerized my little mind and started the imagination soaring to who knows where. I can still remember stars seeming more abundant and nights clearer than ever before, during Christmas season. I always experience this same phenomenon every Christmastime. I recall the same vision all those years later when driving to work in the pre-dawn during the holiday season.

There was always the class Christmas party at Johnson Street School on the day before we adjourned for the two week Christmas vacation. The teachers would cancel classes and give a party where we kids would exchange gifts with those whose names we drew. Then on the Sunday before Christmas, we'd have the church Christmas tree where everyone who exchanged names in Sunday School would get their presents. Afterwards, the choir would sing carols and the Christmas play would replace the normal evening services. The tradition included special music by Mrs. Mildred J. and Mrs. Lottie C. which could have been an early contributor to my hearing loss. Nevertheless, they were good, . . .and loud. I'd risk hearing problems any day to get to listen again to those two ladies sing their rendition of "Come All Ye Faithful" and "It Came Upon a Midnight Clear."

When the Christmas play cast was selected, I'd inevitably be selected to play Joseph against Diane Duncan's or Pat Dodson's Mary. But to tell you the truth I never got used to wearing a bathrobe, summer sandals and my mother's thickest towel on my head in front of someone other than my folks. Come to think of it I never dressed that way in front of them either.

When I think back to those special days of childhood, I wonder if my granddaughters will have similar memories of their Christmases? It's not such a sure thing these days with our society distancing itself from Christianity. But for now, we can still wish each other a Merry Christmas.

PART TWO:

GETTING OUT OF TOWN:

LIFE ON NORTH HIGHWAY

When my parents had enough money to pay cash to build their dream home, yes, I did say cash, they built the small tan asbestos-sided and white-shingled ranch house about a mile north of town on Highway 29, which was the main thoroughfare heading south from Atlanta. The new location had lots of interesting woods to explore and neighbors to get to know, as well as adventures the Mill Village couldn't offer, and a two football-field-sized yard of grass to mow.

What is adolescence in a new venue if you can't get into trouble now and then to cost your parents a few gray hairs, and of course money? Some of us could even do it with a good deal of imagination. Then there were moments that made my parents feel I was worth all the trouble, and organizations they were happy to see their son volunteer for and which they didn't mind spending their money to support. Not all lessons were taught by parents, some of them were from adults like one particular fun loving uncle.

My daddy loved cars and he passed that love on to me. So when he offered to teach me to drive, I couldn't wait. Driving was just part of the excitement in the fifties and I definitely made it a bit more exciting. If you weren't alive during that time, you have no idea how thrilling it could be for both adults and children when car model years changed, usually in late September or early October. The best way to succinctly describe it is Christmas, the Fair and birthday all at once. Also it was easy to know who you were waving to from the porch if you knew what kind of car they drove, and my daddy and mother, too, were aces at that game.

THE NEW NEIGHBOR

When we first moved up on North Highway as it was called in the fifties, about a mile past the Yellow Jacket Creek Bridge on Highway 29, I thought my family had permanently exiled me. I liked history even then and at the tender age of nine I was comparing mine to Napoleon Bonaparte's exile to St. Helena out in the middle of the Atlantic Ocean. I knew I hadn't caused as much havoc as Napoleon and didn't understand why they felt it necessary to leave what I considered to be a perfectly good house in the "village." There were a lot of advantages to keeping the house in the village. It was smaller and less trouble to take care of and it didn't have a yard the size of two football fields. I guess the real reason I disliked moving was I lost my neighborhood friends like Noel, Don and the Huckabee brothers who I played with from daylight till dark every day. I didn't want to admit it but there was a girl I'd miss too, my next door neighbor Linda; but I had to move and that was that.

I can't deny the new house was a big improvement over our Mill Village house; first and best of all I didn't have to get as cold when I went to the bathroom. The new house had a bathroom right off the hallway and it had a tub too, so my daddy and I didn't have to walk to the community building to get a shower. I decided I could live with it but I'd miss looking for Santa coming down the sidewalk because we didn't have a sidewalk at the new house. At that time Santa was another concern as I didn't remember writing him a letter to say I was moving. Guess he'd figure it out since he knew a lot of other things I hadn't bothered to tell him. When I got settled in the house, I found there were lots more positives than negatives about living in the "country," and one of them was I had new neighbors.

A young couple occupied the house below us and they had a little girl and a new baby boy. I wasn't too fond of younger kids so I was reluctant to go meet the neighbors right away. The man was never at home because he had a bread route and he also cut meat at his father-in-law's butcher shop. The lady was home a lot because she didn't work, and she seemed to be very friendly. Her little girl screamed a lot and it hurt my ears. She was also very energetic but I didn't mind it, as she was a good playmate. So on the summer afternoons when mother was getting her nap before going to work on the second shift at the Old Mill, I would walk down to the neighbor's house. My neighbor's daughter Lib was fun to play with, except she always wanted to play house. So to placate her, I'd pretend the shaded mimosa tree that stood between the two houses was a part house/gas station while she would pretend it was a house to keep clean. While I was busy fueling up our bikes, she would be sweeping a lot of dust around in the back with a switch broom her mother had made for her.

Sarah, Lib's mother, was a terrific playmate herself. When we had to come inside, usually when it was raining, she would entertain us. I guess when you are about twenty- five years old you feel like chasing kids up and down stairs pretending you are the big bad witch. Her way of accomplishing this was to chase us up and down the stairs of the house pretending to be a "hag." When she'd catch us, she would goose us until we'd lose our breath. Worst of all, Sarah was faster than either one of us and usually caught us about the time we made it to the top of the stairs. Sarah was, and still is, a very attractive woman. To turn herself into a hag, she would muss up her hair, then proceed to scream and yell and scare the dickens out of us. She would never seem to run out of energy or ways to entertain us. Then if we didn't give her too much trouble, she'd take us to Jap Keith's store and buy us candy and cokes. She also sat and just talked with us about things of our choosing. Like my wife, Sarah always drove a manual shift car. Once they bought a brand new Ford Galaxy 500. It was a top of the line, a white and bechromed four-door hard top with a red interior and almost every imaginable option except one. The car had a three speed manual shifter on the column. I remember many good times in that car with all four windows down driving to town and singing in the manner of Bobby McGee "every song that driver knew".

I liked my neighbor's house because it was one of the first ones I'd ever been in that had an upstairs. The entire back end of the upstairs was a screened in porch. I still remember those rainy days I played up there. I also remember the wasps that were there, that chased me inside the house and stung me as I started running down the stairs. I once ended up doing a stunt man roll, head first, down to the landing that turned right and then down another few steps to the first floor. When Sarah checked me for broken bones, she only found about four whelps, compliments of the not-so-friendly wasps.

It wasn't just the fun times that made us close to our new neighbors. In 1956, they bought their first brand new car. This was the time when garages were separate buildings from the house, and a good thing too. About two o'clock in the morning we were all awakened by a bright light. It was our neighbor's garage on fire. According to the insurance company, the car had shorted out and set itself on fire. We were there to provide them transportation until they got another car. It was that kind of thing that consolidated the friendship we developed with these neighbors and made them part of our extended family.

When I went off to college, I lost contact for a while with these good neighbors as I did with many of my friends in Hogansville. In the latter years our families didn't get a chance to renew our Lucy/Ricky and Fred/Ethel relationships because our neighbors moved to Texas. But when they decided to return to Georgia, we once again were in touch. Of course their daughter Lib and my daddy were not with us then, but Sarah was and still is devoutly devoted to my mother. Now that mother has transferred to a nursing home closer to me, I may not get a chance to see my neighbors much anymore. But they have grandchildren to keep them busy; and when occasionally I get to LaGrange, I always hope to have time to go by and see them. They were an integral part of my childhood and I'll never forget the closeness we had with them. You don't find that often with today's cosmopolitan and busy professional lifestyles. I miss not having neighbors like them.

THE GHOST DOG

Don't be deceived by the title because this is not a recounting of "The Hound of the Baskervilles." This kinda stuff can't be made up. So begins the eerie tail (I mean to spell it that way) of "The Hound of Hogansville." Poochee the First was the predecessor of a long line of dogs I named Poochee. Not being real original thinkers, the Dale family owned a succession of dogs that ran all the way to Poochee IV. Poochee the First – I will simply refer to as Poochee – was a "sooner." This meant, as my daddy said, "Sooner be one kind as another," implying his heritage was not pure. The dog did have a lot of German Shepard in his ancestry.

Our next door neighbor's son Lex had a dog named Cleo, after Jackie Cooper's dog in "The People's Choice." If you are over forty you know what TV show I'm talking about. If you're not I've wasted a sentence. Lex heard us talk so much about Poochee being a German Shepard that he decided Cleo should also be German but something more original than a Shepard. He settled on Spitz. Lex usually was at our house more than he was home, so when we had company he always had to tell them about the dogs, Poochee and Cleo. Daddy, aware of Lex's enunciation of Cleo's given heritage, tried to divert his attention to something else as the description sounded very much like a very bad cuss word. He never quite succeeded and Lex would announce that Cleo was a . . . German Spitz! I'll leave the rest to your furtive imaginations.

One day a friend was over to play and we decided to go outside. Poochee was running around the house and looked as if he had been drinking from the car washing soap bucket daddy left when he suddenly decided to go have Doc paint his tires. Shiny tires really made the wash job. Doc really had a way with that tire paint and those white walls would put your eyes out when he was done. We didn't pay much attention to Poochee's frothing at the mouth as he ran along with us, that is until he decided he might make a quick lunch of us. This wasn't his normal behavior and we picked up on it fast. He chased us inside and then began to have some kind of really serious fit on the steps to the door. That's when mother decided he was dangerous. Being a big dog, still a puppy at six months, I felt he was just being frisky and would soon get over it, but the weird acting didn't stop. The dog had us trapped inside the house and we had no car to get away.

Poochee then began trying to get inside and did some heavy damage to the screen door, so mother closed the wooden one and called the police. She also called Lilla, our neighbor's maid, to warn her about the dog. She told Lilla not to let Lex out and to barricade themselves inside because Poochee was on a rampage and might be mad. When the police arrived, it was T. He was the local chief and a take-charge kind of guy. T told mother Poochee was an unmistakable case of distemper, or as mother preferred to call it "stempers." In his opinion, T felt the only thing he could do was put the dog down to which I was greatly opposed and said so. Nevertheless, T was in charge and he went to the '59 Chevy Biscayne police interceptor to take out his thirty naught six and put a shell in.

He never carried a loaded weapon in the car because it was too much risk as Hogansville only had one police car and it already had enough air vents. Poochee became very calm after T arrived and almost returned to normal which inspired my friend Ricky and me to again plead for the dog's life. But T had already decided to put Poochee out of his misery. In a split second it was over. Poochee didn't drop like T expected and instead made for the safety of the tall grass behind the neighbor's house. T told us some dogs reacted that way but within a minute he would drop. Our afternoon search didn't locate Poochee. It was pretty sad around the Dale household that evening. Daddy agreed with T, saying it was inevitable, Poochee could not have survived with distemper. Not much was said and we all went to bed.

Next morning the somber mood was still permeating the family but it was a bright sunny day. Lilla was out back of the neighbor's house hanging out wash. I was in the kitchen and could see her swaying to a self-accompanied rendition of "Rock of Ages," and mother was cooking. Suddenly, we heard the most awful screaming and yelping. Lilla took off like a NASA rocket leaving a dust trail up the shared driveway that would have choked a caterpillar tractor. It sounded like someone was killing her. Mother couldn't hear good even then and seemed not to be at all alarmed. I ran to call the police because I thought the way Lilla was screaming she was being pursued by a mad killer straight off the FBI's ten most wanted list. Although you would think with Lilla weighing about 200 pounds, it would seem to be the other way around? Mother finally looked up and said, "Here comes Lilla up here, Jimmy."

Lilla's arms were up, with her mouth open, and some of the most horrifying screeches were coming out that you could ever even imagine. When she reached the carport, she about pulled the screen door off its hinges. Incidentally, carports are semi-garages usually build onto ranch style houses that don't have sides and rain usually blows in on the car. Using the screen door to assist she ascended the three concrete steps in a single bound. She never broke stride. "Miss Sara, Miss Sara, I done seen a ghost." Before mother could ask Lilla any facts, she began again. "I done seen that dog Mr. T shot yesterday. I knows he's a ghost 'cause he stood right there and jist looked at me while I was a hanging out clothes. He didn't say a word, just looked, and he had a hole the size of your fist right 'tween his eyes. But he didn't take on or nothing, just looked. I thinks I could see through him." Mother finally calmed Lilla down and sent me out to investigate. I didn't see anything and wondered if the experiences of the day before hadn't bothered Lilla more than it did me.

Lilla wouldn't stop about the ghost so we called the police again. T was a bit bothered, telling mother he had already shot the dog once, "and that ought to have been enough 'cause he shoulda gone off and died." "That's not so T, that dog's not dead and you better come up here and shoot it again or I'll tell your wife," was mother's reply. T wasn't afraid of many people in Hogansville but his wife counted among the few he truly feared, at least to hear T tell it. Well, T came back and it took him the better part of the morning to track the dog, which by this time had weakened and lay in the tall grass near the railroad track. Again T took aim and this time he succeeded. But no one would ever convince Lilla she had not seen a ghost. She was still telling that story when I left Hogansville for college and Poochee IV, aka Herman, was roaming the same territory. Soon after the second shooting of Poochee, our neighbors bought a dryer for their washer. That was a wise investment on their part because Lilla never again treaded that backyard. The Ghost Dog you know.

DELIVERED DIRECT TO YOUR HOUSE

Two things bring to mind a convenience that no longer is a part of our lives in this modern self-serve society. You would think as we progress into the twenty-first century that we would have more things come to us rather than us go to them. HA! But, maybe we are about to reverse all that. I recently heard an advertisement by Cub Foods that they're delivering groceries. I didn't check it out because by now I'm so used to going to get my own I didn't want to ruin a good thing. Besides, who wants to spoil a perfectly good habit that takes you away from your home life, especially when there's a thousand jobs to stay there and finish?

The second thing that brought to mind the loss of convenience came as a total surprise. I attended my wife's high school reunion recently and while we were eating I was talking with one of her more than well-to-do classmates. He asked me where I was from and when I told him Hogansville he laughed and said, "I'll bet you know Jasper." I said, "What does that name have to do with Hogansville?" My response stopped his laughing and he looked at me like I was playing with less than a full deck. Then he said slowly, "No, I mean Jasper Keith." Hearing that despite my sometimes on, and most times off, hearing aids I said, "Well, I don't actually know anyone from Hogansville named Jasper but there were some Keith's there when I was growing up. We called them Jap and Jim." "That's him," he retorted in voice that would have attracted attention anywhere else other than a high school reunion, Jap Keith and I were counselors together at Boy Scout Camp for many years."

After the reunion and hearing that Cub Foods will begin delivery services I wondered why things ever changed. I remembered when Boots Parham and Jap Keith delivered your groceries right to your door as a matter of routine. I guess Cub Foods will have to invest in folks to ride shotgun when they begin deliveries. Anything of value these days is at risk. Maybe good things like door-to-door deliveries became too dangerous as time went on? Maybe we ourselves drove them away?

Back in the fifties the only holdups of the grocery deliveries were natural disasters like when Yellow Jacket Creek flooded or an occasional unnatural disaster such as when some idiot missed the curve in front of our house and took out another one of daddy's pine trees. Of course, you could never tell when an old west bandit may be awaiting that cache of groceries once the trusty delivery vehicle rolled into the yard; especially during the hot summer months while school was out. I would be constantly on the lookout for Roger Parham's delivery of groceries to mother every Wednesday. I sat there behind that big Pecan tree with my trusty horse, spell that Western Flyer bike, bandanna tied over my nose and ready to chase that green '53 Dodge wagon all the way around the house. Roger hated that worse than being chased by my dog Herman who was a lot faster and ran closer to the wheels. It was just plain aggravation for a sixteen year old who used that driveway to test the limits of that old wagon's suspension. He couldn't do that very well while looking out for the Western Flyer and Herman, the little blonde-mane dog. Roger did all the deliveries for his daddy Boots when school was out, and most of them when school was in too. He worked hard and worked that old '53 hard, too.

It wouldn't do for Boots to be one up on Jap, so Mr. Keith also started up a delivery service. I used to see the familiar powder blue '61 Falcon Ranchero with the sign on the door saying "Keith Brothers Grocery" speeding up and down the highway. Competition was hot but friendly. We traded with Boots mainly because he went to our church, and for whatever reason mother preferred Ralph's butcher shop to Jim's. I never saw much difference in them and I didn't care to know. All I did know was each store had its own personality. Jap sold some stuff you couldn't get at Parham's and vice versa. I particularly liked Jap's salt fish, I guess because daddy did. They both had something that was interesting to me though, the candy shelves. I never went into either one without buying a Hershey Bar, a Milky Way or a Three Musketeers . . . Well, you get the message I hope because I'm getting hungry.

I never will understand how mother could order things that had to be seen before you could accept them. I mean things like vegetables, and some cuts of meat. I think why she could do that without worry was both companies cared enough about their customers to spend time selecting what was good and not just throwing something in the box. They also took time to listen and know their customers as people and not just as customers. They took stuff back if it wasn't all right and this usually didn't require mounds of paperwork or an affidavit to do it. If it was their fault, they immediately turned the delivery boy around and sent him back with the right stuff.

There was credit before there was a credit card. Did you know that? All you had to say when you called in an order is, "Put that on my bill", or when Roger showed up every Wednesday with a delivery you simply wrote him a check or paid him in cash. He was always pretty good about giving you a receipt. Of course, you got the same prompt and efficient service from Keith's too. It was great being a customer in the fifties, much better than the impersonal grocery buying we have today. I hate it when the little grocery clerks say the same thing week after week as you walk out of the stores that don't deliver. They ask, "How you doing today sir?" without even looking at you. That distracts from important issues like plotting your next move on how to escape from the jungle of cars in the parking lot which are all trying to go to the same place at the same time. Back in the 50s, not only did you get your groceries delivered by Roger, you also got the benefit of finding out how everyone was doing on the route and if anything big happened in town that day. Roger was friendly because he wanted to be and not because Boots directed him to be. And the good thing about Roger was he was original. He didn't say the same thing week after week. I believe there is still hope we can get back a little of this kind of thing because I've formed some very good friendships with some of the clerks at my local Publix. It's always nice to get a smile and find out how the grocery guy's house is coming along, since it was blown away in the recent tornado.

This yesteryear kind of consideration didn't just apply to our neighborhood grocers. If you bought something big at Crawford's Hardware, they took the thing to your car and helped you get it situated in the trunk. Try that at Home Depot or Lowe's without feeling guilty, after having to hunt someone to do it. Belk's and Jabley's took things back after you had taken them home and put them on and washed them, provided you didn't wear them to school for a week. Of all people, doctors did the unthinkable; they came to your house to treat you. As a matter of fact we consumers had it made in the fifties. We had everyone come to us instead of us having to go to them. I remember Doctor Arnold coming into my room at home to treat me for colds, stomach aches, and you name it. And he came at all hours of the day and night and in all sorts of weather. Doctors today make you wait sometimes hours past your appointment time at their office, and then they act like they hardly have time to spend looking at your problem. About the only time I went to see the doctor when I was young was for emergencies like nails in the foot, massive cuts from BB guns, falls from swing sets, or serious scrapes from being thrown from pretend horses.

When I am standing next to the gas pump these days and trying to make sure I don't overfill the thing and slosh gas down the side of my car, I remember Doc McVey who worked for Bad Eye Cardin at the Texaco. By the time you got the engine turned off Doc was at the window asking, "Filler up Tommy Dale?" That's what he called me as my daddy was Tom. He checked the oil, washed the windshield and rubbed any grease off he might have gotten on your finish, whether you wanted him to or not. You may as well just let him do it, as it was quicker in the long run. And you knew if you needed any water in the radiator it would be put in there. How did we let this "Delivered Direct" attitude escape us so that today we've became the service people instead of customers?

MAMA'S COOKING

Southern cooks are without question the best on earth. I'm sure I'll get arguments from some non-southerners but then you gotta expect that. My mother never wrote down how she fixed things because the next time she made the dish it might be different. Actually, there weren't too many times she deviated in her preparation. Unfortunately, since she only kept the recipes in her head I never paid enough attention to what she was doing to remember any of them or write them down. I didn't have time to write and besides boys didn't cook then, and there were too many Indians and Germans about to overrun the place while she was cooking dinner. Somebody had to hold them back until it was time to eat. But I guess one thing all mothers put into their recipes that can't be duplicated is love, and you can't write that down anyway.

When school was in session, I was lucky enough to get one of my mother's delicious meals a day. I never ate breakfast unless you count an occasional biscuit sopped in a little Alaga Syrup while running out the door for school. My noon meal was whatever Mrs. Keith decided to prepare for us kids at the school lunchroom. But the summer was different, and I got a chance to eat my mother's cooking at least two times a day. As we all know the fifties and sixties were all about clogging up our arteries with all that good grease southern cooks like to use, and mother was no exception. I was never too busy to stop what I was doing even if it was cutting the grass when she yelled out dinner was ready. Never mind my daddy had three heart attacks and a pretty nasty ulcer. I was a growing boy then and my wife tells me that might still be the case even though I'm fifty-eight years old. Like a lot of people I didn't slow down on the filling food and managed for a while to be overweight as a youngun. I have managed to get down to a decent size in my old age and it wasn't easy since my wife is as good a cook as my mother.

From what times I did manage to pay attention to mother's cooking, I remember some of what she did, especially when she was preparing my favorite meal of chicken and dumplings. Mother objected to strong drink so there was no alcohol in the house and she never used it when cooking. But, that didn't stop her using a huge wine bottle for a rolling pin. She never explained how she got that bottle. She would mix up her flour and salt in a large blue pottery bowl which my daughter now has in her kitchen. I'd see her add milk and water to the mixture, squish it with her hands and magically it became dough. She'd take her wine bottle and roll out the dough between pieces of wax paper and then cut it into strips and then large squares. She would have already boiled a whole chicken until it fell off the bone. Then she would take the stock and use it to cook the dough into dumplings. She never mixed the chicken with the dumplings. Then she'd make mashed potatoes and fried okra, and that constituted my favorite meal of all times. Mother was very generous with the coating on the okra which she fried until crunchy. Not a low carb diet. Don't try this at home unless you live near a medical center. Incidentally, it's also my daughter's favorite meal. And no, she's not fat because she doesn't get it that often anymore. And her two three year old twin daughters are excellent aerobics instructors.

No matter what the food, it is the atmosphere in which you eat it that adds to your fond memories. The little yellow kitchen in our house in Hogansville was cozy and warm in the winter. We closed the cafe curtains and shut the door just behind where mother always sat. Then we enjoyed our meal while the windows steamed over. In the summer it got pretty warm in that kitchen, mainly because we had no air conditioning. I then welcomed the opportunity to go to the garden and get my daddy's pepper and tomatoes which he had conveniently forgotten until he sat down to eat. The breeze on the way to the garden cooled me off from the hot stove that occupied space just across from my chair. Of course no one lifted a fork until mother said grace.

Mother stopped cooking back when she gave up her apartment for assisted living. The memories are still there though, and occasionally I get my wife to duplicate some of mother's recipes. Now-a-days, I'm used to our house and I get the same feelings about my surroundings and the meals. I miss mother's cooking but I have discovered a whole new world of taste with my wife's twist on food. Her Cajun lineage introduced me to red beans and rice, Gumbo, and she sometimes throws in a few un-Cajun dishes like stroganoff and lasagna. Sounds good doesn't it? Well, she can do all this and also make it healthy by reducing the fat content. Don't ask me how, but she goes to a lot of trouble. When she won over my mother I knew she had to be a good cook. In fact she has won the entire Dale's approval and some of the James side of my family like my Uncle Pete. As my friend Homer Lee says, "Life is good."

TOM DOGS: DELICACIES FROM MY DADDY'S KITCHEN

Out of necessity both my parents had to work. I never understood why they didn't work on the same shift at the mill, but they didn't. This arrangement may have been the key to their successful 50 year plus marriage. Whatever, it turns out daddy had to take care of me once I got home from school. He was faced each evening with coming up with something to feed a ravenous preteen who had endured much hardship in school learning, or fighting it, which is what some of my teachers firmly believe I was doing. His answers ranged from warming stuff mother cooked earlier in the day that didn't get devoured by her and Ruby, our twice a week maid we shared with Edna Fielder and Lois Payne, or going to get Traylor hamburgers in LaGrange. Fortunately, mother and Ruby weren't big eaters so we usually had leftovers.

There is one thing you can say for guys who have to cook, when it becomes necessary then necessity is the mother of invention. When leftovers fizzled out and the lure of a Traylor hamburger got a little stale, daddy would resort to his own devices to come up with a meal. He never disappointed but sometimes he completely amazed me with a few of his original concoctions. Like most gourmet chefs daddy kept his recipes simple and direct.

Today I found myself having difficulty coming up with something for lunch. My wife eats almost nothing, likes everything, and can make a sandwich out of mustard and onions. So being left to my own devices, I decided to construct one of my daddy's simple delicacies he used to make us when he ran out of ideas. There was one bratwurst hotdog left in the refrigerator and no buns. Is it just me or do those folks who make hot dog and hamburger buns deliberately package them so we either have too many or not enough for the meat we buy? Well anyway my daddy never messed with buying hotdog buns when we could use Colonial bread. Besides, as he said, "Buying hot dog buns might run the well dry." When he didn't want to spend money or buy an appliance he considered superfluous, he used running the well dry as a reason for abstaining. Mother never got a washing machine due to this logic and we never got a toaster oven either.

I took out an onion and minced it using a paring knife. Then I took a huge slice of Sunflower bread (we don't eat Colonial anymore) and cut it in half. I squirted both halves generously with mustard and ketchup and spread the onions across them. The next step in the recipe was to take the dog and cut it in half then take both halves and split them sorta butterfly shape. Sounds pretty gourmet so far, huh? This is where my memory began to fail. I took the dogs and put them between the bread slices and firmly mashed the dickens out of them to conform them to the bread, and then sliced the bread in half again with each dog in its own blanket. I should have considered this done and eaten them cold as we used to, but you know me, I have to add my own little touch. My touch was to heat them in the microwave for a minute. I don't know if my daddy would have done this since we didn't have microwaves back then, but sometimes if he really wanted to go all out he'd fry the hot dogs. Anyway, I now know heating this recipe means you can't eat it because it's too hot and most importantly it falls apart when you lift it. Well, maybe next time I'll remember to strictly follow my daddy's recipe. If you liked this recipe, I can give you another from my daddy's kitchen.

TRAYLOR HAMBURGERS

Once in a while when my wife is not looking, I dream of things to eat that would destroy my health with one bite. She tells me now that she doesn't understand how I managed to live my fifty something odd years when I relate to her all of the things my mother cooked and my daddy "created" in the kitchen of that little ranch style house on North Highway in Hogansville. Although, of all the horrifying tales of that kitchen, nothing could have been worse for us than the cafeteria food we ate on Sundays after church at the Plantation Restaurant in LaGrange. We're talking good southern and fattening. Well, there was something even worse than the Plantation and it was DELICIOUS. My daddy agreed too, and we ate at Traylor's three nights a week. We weren't thinking about saturated fat and cholesterol in the fifties. Good thing, almost everything we ate then was full of it. It does bother me a lot we weren't more health conscious then because I lost my daddy to a heart attack; his third and final one got him at seventy-two.

My folks worked on opposite shifts in the Old Mill. Daddy worked the first shift and mother worked the second shift and they were never at home at the same time, except maybe on weekends. Mother would always cook something for dinner, don't confuse this with the night meal supper; whatever was not eaten by me, mother and Ruby was left for supper. Sometimes nothing was left, such as the time Yank ate dinner with us – lunch to you.

It didn't have to be a day when the dinner was all gone for daddy to up and decide to go to LaGrange. There were all sorts of reasons he came up with that would require a trip straight from the mill to LaGrange. My daddy was a fastidious man who was extremely self conscious about his appearance. The first thing he would do when he got home was take a bath and shave. Shave at four thirty in the afternoon? Yep, he never failed. So whenever he suggested he must go to LaGrange straight from the mill he got no argument out of me. I knew the real reason was a Traylor hamburger. Bet you thought I'd forgotten my original train of thought? I wanted to savor it just like I did those hamburgers. However, I'll have to admit I savored them for about two seconds when I got them. I rarely made it back to Hogansville before they were gone. I'm getting a bit ahead of myself here so let me go back some.

  Before starting her shift, mother would pick me up from school in the '57 Pontiac along with Mike Eason, Kenny Hines and at least three more guys, and make the rounds to deliver them home before going to the mill to park and wait for daddy. Sometimes during the trip the radio speaker, the designers forgot about until they had already assembled the dash, would get kicked in a new direction providing a different sound every day while I waited for my daddy to come out of the mill. Mother would park just outside the gate under the oaks that lined Green Street. The oaks would meet over the street to form a canopy and I guess that's why the street was named that. Anyway at about a quarter 'til, mother, Mary Alice Huff, Dena Arrington, and Avaline Hooten would all file into the mill and I would be left alone for 15 minutes to listen to Clarence Frogman Henry, Sam Cook or who ever was on WTRP. Then my daddy got off work and took me over for the rest of the day.

  When daddy announced we were going directly to LaGrange, I would briefly interrupt the rock-n-roll to give him a big broad smile of agreement and a hello. The twelve mile trip down took no time at all and because I was usually busy trying to learn the latest lyrics to a Bobby Daren or Neil Sadaka song, I didn't pay much attention or remember much about the drive. When we started to get close to Traylor's, I suddenly forsook my music to prepare for the culinary delight that was about to befall us. Traylor's Hamburger Joint, as we called it, was really Traylor's Cafe. I can see it in my mind's eye now, but the street names don't return as easily as the pictures. The little white frame building could have doubled for Mr. Richie's Cafe in Hogansville. Mister Richie and his wife ran the cafe in a building right next door to St. James Methodist Church. It later moved next door to Boots Parham's store on Askew Avenue. Daddy and I ate there a lot too. Trying to cut down on the cooking you know, but I need to get back to Traylor's.

My mother's sister Mary and her husband Willie lived within spitting distance of Traylor's. Mary would never fail to see the Pontiac parked in front of the place. On those days our mission was Traylor hamburgers and not visiting nosy relatives. After we got the hamburgers, we had only one thought: going home and enjoying them at our leisure. And who could visit properly knowing Traylor hamburgers are waiting in the front seat of the car? When we went to see Mary on the weekends, she never failed to say, "Well, Tom and Jimmy were at Traylor's twice this week and didn't even come by to see us." My daddy's standard reply was, "Mary, they made more than one of those kinds of cars that year." And that would be that. Too bad Mary didn't sneak over and get the license plate number.

The cafe itself was not inviting. The booths were plywood with no padding. If you ate at Traylor's, it wasn't because they were trying to get you to. Most people just bought the food and took it home as we did, or in my case attempted to do. Mister Traylor's priorities were hamburgers not bench seats. He was a friendly man who always wore a white apron and a little white paper cap that most restaurateurs of that era wore. He looked like a soldier with it on. His mother or mother-in-law, an older woman who looked a lot like granny on the Beverly Hill Billys, would cook and serve. The hamburgers had a wonderful aroma that permeated the entire store and neighborhood. You knew they were full of grease before you saw the massive stains they left on the wrapping paper and the brown sack. The only way I can describe the two I always inhaled on the way home, making my daddy extremely nervous over his car seats, is they were heavenly. They melted in your mouth, literally, due to the immense amount of grease they contained. And washing them down with the chocolate milk was better than, well I will let your imagination conjure that picture.

Unfortunately Traylor's, like everything else in the way of progress, couldn't last forever. My daddy and I continued trying to duplicate those hamburgers long after the cafe was torn down, but to no avail. Like Richard Harris says in "MacArthur Park" (a popular contemporary song, by the way), "I'll never find that recipe again". And it's too bad since it also contained a lot of my youth.

WOULD YOU LIE TO YOUR MAMA?

"Alright, Jimmy who broke my lamp?" I was pinned down because that morning the lamp had been in one piece while I was still asleep. But now the lamp might never be in one piece again and worst of all it was one of the living room's matching set of lamps. I had galloped Trigger a little to close to that corner of the room and his tail clipped the lamp causing it to topple to the hardwood floor of our immaculately maintained living room. Actually, Trigger was my mother's trusty broom but we won't go there. No one saw me hit the lamp and Trigger sure wasn't going to talk. So I decided I'd just simply forget it happened and that way I really wouldn't be telling a lie if I said that I didn't know how the lamp got broken.

I worked hard to "unremember" what I had done. I told myself since I had already passed the lamp when I hit it (technically) I really didn't see it fall and that it could have just been my imagination when I heard the crash. That would do. "Mama," I said convincingly, "I didn't see the lamp fall so I don't know if I did it or not. Besides, I don't remember bumping it. But, I could have and I just don't remember." Then I gave her my best sweet and charming little boy look. I could tell it wasn't working when she began to ask probing questions like, "Are you sure you didn't hear it fall right after you went by?" "Well," I said, "Yes, I did hear it fall but then I was in the kitchen by then and anyone could have knocked it over." She looked at me and continued the line of questioning. I could then tell I needed to take a different tactic so I said, "You know, that lamp was already broken. I don't know if you noticed it or not but it probably wouldn't have been smashed when it hit the floor if it hadn't already been broken. Did you know that Mama?"

The questions stopped and she looked at me, not with a stern look as she had started with but with a loving look. I hadn't seen this before when in trouble and I didn't exactly know how to react. Then she began to speak softly, "Son, I thought I taught you better than this. Your daddy and I take you to church and we have tried to live our lives as an example so you can see the right thing to do and now you are telling me a story." Mother considered the word "lie" a bad word. "The punishment you get for breaking the lamp will eventually stop hurting; but the story telling will hurt you and those you are not honest with forever."

I wasn't too mature at nine years old but I did analyze that statement with what intellect I had developed in that short amount of time. Besides my conscience, that little nagging feeling I always get when I know I'm not being honest, was already beginning to work on me. I said, "I broke the lamp mama." "That's all I need to hear son," she said, and continued, "When I tell your daddy about this I will let him know you were honest and that it was an accident. Maybe he won't spank you too hard. But you know the punishment will be because you broke the lamp playing where you shouldn't and you have to pay the price for your mistake."

Now that I'm considerably older and slightly more mature than I was then, and seldom get the urge to ride a broom through the house, I look back on that incident as a time when I came of age. No, not in the manhood sense but I learned a lesson that stayed with me to this day, and that is if you tell the truth you can live with yourself and you may not be in as much trouble as you would be if you had lied, I mean told a story. So, when I know I have messed up or if something is my fault I don't try to avoid responsibility. I remember those words from the conversation with my mother even though it has been over 40 years ago and I know I'm doing the right thing by telling the truth. The last thing she said before we put the lamp incident behind us was, "You must always tell the truth. After all, you may grow up to be President one day."

RUBY

My mother had an unusually difficult day around forty-eight years ago that she won't forget and I can't recall, the day I was born. There was one more person in addition to my daddy that didn't forget, either. Ruby maybe didn't know it then but she was my designated second mama. When mother brought me home for the first time Ruby was there to take me. She was probably the only person outside my parents to hold me for any length of time. Of course, I wasn't too keen on being held by anyone if my actions were any indication. I was a lot like my present cat, Smut. She doesn't take to being held by humans much either.

I didn't notice Ruby's skin color was not the same as mine. I did notice she had on some really good wire-rimmed glasses I felt needed closer examination. I could never examine them enough. So when it came time to feed me or change my diaper, Ruby took off the glasses. I often wondered in later years if she ever really needed those glasses at all. Well, by now you are asking what was so special about Ruby. Lots of kids were tended by people other than their mothers and most of them were probably as good, and in their own way, as special as Ruby. That may be true but I wasn't raised by them.

Ruby put up with my colic, as well as my generally obnoxious nature as an infant and later as a teen. She tolerated well my growing years and managed to gain a few scars from falls taken over toys I neglected to put away after play sessions. She covered for me a lot too when I did something I shouldn't have or didn't do something I should have done, although she was not one to be taken advantage of. I knew just where my limits were with Ruby. If what I did or didn't do resulted in someone getting hurt, I knew I had to admit it because Ruby wouldn't go along. I can talk forever about her goodness and taking guff off me over pieces missing off my model cars just after dusting, but her true worth was measured in devotion to me and my family, and it was strong. It was in her values. That is what I think was special about Ruby. She was devoted to my family – working sometimes when I could tell she needed to be home in bed. She never complained and she never let anyone down.

Good as it was, Ruby's value system was sometimes hard to understand, especially to someone who had not been in this world too long. She chose not to eat with us even at our constant behest. I asked her about it one day while we were eating and she was ironing just behind my chair. Her answer was she had work to do and would eat later when she finished. I didn't buy it either. She also refused to ride in the front seat of the car with me when I took her home in the afternoons during the summer after I became a teenager. I felt like Nim Childres, Hogansville's premiere taxi driver. I was driving a four door '61 Chevy similar to Nim's with Ruby sitting in the back seat. Regardless of my incessant pleas she steadfastly refused to ride up front.

After Ruby retired, she and her husband, Charlie, settled down to a less hectic life. There were times, just as it was with mother, when Ruby decided retirement was too dull to tolerate and she resumed her job. That is until she realized why she retired in the first place; she was getting too old to keep up with all that work. But Charlie was instrumental in getting her to quit for good. He didn't have to have that heart attack; I think a mild palpitation would have worked just as well. Anyway, he needed her more than we did, and as always Ruby knew her priorities.

  Retirement didn't stop our communication with Ruby and her family. There were those days when mother carried her things we grew in the garden, or when someone in the family canned preserves and gave us an over abundance. Ruby and Charlie couldn't have their garden anymore as failing health wouldn't permit. I could tell each time we went to see Ruby she was not getting any younger and her arthritis, like mother's, was steadily getting worse. Probably the thing I noticed most was Ruby and Charlie had very little; the small house was heated only by a wood burning fireplace and they had no electricity. It didn't matter to them that they didn't have these things. They were proud and kept the place spic and span. And now that I'm older, I realize having only a few earthly possessions doesn't mean you have very little. They had each other and they were happy. That's a lot more than some people today will ever have in their lifetime, regardless of their material wealth.

  When electricity finally came their way, Ruby and Charlie were able to have a radio. They were not ones to take charity. They had always worked and took care of their own, raising their children to be prepared for meeting the challenges of a not-so-friendly world. When she worked for us, Ruby loved to watch the twelve o'clock news with Gloria Lane and Ray Moore. She managed to do the ironing or something else that would allow her to continue to work while she watched the news. Now that Ruby was retired, she didn't have our TV to keep up with the news and the radio wasn't the best with a lot of static to fight. Her hearing was beginning to fail and wasn't any better than mine is now.

  I talked with my wife often about how much Ruby had meant in my life. When my wife suggested we get a TV for Ruby and Charlie, I balked at the idea saying they wouldn't let us out of the car with it. I was wrong. They accepted this gift in the spirit it was given, with love and respect. She knew it came from our hearts. We all spent the evening experimenting with the rabbit ears so we could pick up the best reception of the six o'clock news. It came in clear and without static. The volume could be adjusted so that Ruby could hear.

That evening when we left, I had a feeling I might never see that family as happy again. It wasn't a feeling of foreboding or tragedy, just one that said I should savor the moment and enjoy the friendship we developed over my lifetime. It wasn't long before mother called to say Charlie had gone. He just couldn't fight that final heart attack. And it wasn't too many years after that Ruby joined him. The last of her days were spent in a nursing home.

I've spent a lot of time telling you about Ruby and her family. Now let me tell you something more about her that is eternally enduring, her spirit. A day didn't pass that I learned something about Ruby's outlook on life. It was based on two words, self respect. Built into that was discipline. If it was worth doing, Ruby did it right and she did it regardless of how difficult it might be. She was honest. I remember her finding a half dollar in one of my daddy's pants while she was ironing them. She gave it to mother, when she could have just as easily slipped it into her pocket. How many people today would do that? Ruby's perspective looked for value in the person regardless of sex, race, or whatever. So many people ignore those precepts, forgetting them in the scramble to promote their own selfish ideals.

Being proud of who you are and where you come from is a good thing. But in today's world it seems to be becoming a basis for hate that has led to polarization between people and their races. Ruby took her share of this kind of stuff, being a black in the fifties and living through the violence of the late sixties and seventies. She never lost her objectivity and never hated anyone I could ascertain. She didn't have much use for the behavior of radicals, both black and white, during this trying time. She relied on her faith and practiced the moderation it taught.

FIRE! WHAT FIRE?

Last week we were visiting the granddaughters who seem to have some kind of new toy every time we are there. This week they were displaying their new fire hats. The things were made of light plastic and had a sticky decal on the front for the Cobb County Fire Department. I think these were promotional toys the kids got at their church school when their class was visited by firemen. Boy did the memories flood back when I saw those hats, especially when Madelyn put hers on my head.

Possibly because Hogansville was a small town, it seemed every kid had a chance to get promotional toys from various businesses. I remember getting bunches of them all the time. This made my parents happy since they didn't have to pay for them. My first fire hat came from Bad Eye Cardin's Texaco gas station. Texaco promoted their "Fire Chief" gasoline by giving away aluminum-foil fire hats with red cellophane paper around them and a big "Texaco Fire Chief" sticker attached. I went through about a dozen of those. The first real fire I remember was when our high school burned down in 1954. I was about eight years old then and my daddy took me out in our front yard on Marshal Avenue to see the horizon lit up red. Of course, Hogansville's one truck fire department wasn't able to do much with that big fire until after LaGrange sent several of their trucks. By that time that school was a total loss.

It took a while before our fire department won back the hearts and minds of our citizens. They certainly made an impression on us when one day, my mother picked me up at school early and decided to go by our house to get something she forgot before going to the mill to work. On the way home we thought Williamson's Junkyard, located just down the hill from our house, was burning cars again. But no, the smoke was coming from further up the hill and we arrived just in time to see the entire back side of our neighbor's yard engulfed in flames. Their house was in imminent danger and flames were moving toward ours. By this time I was old enough, about twelve, to be aware I could lose all my stuff. Mother was in panic and so was our neighbor. They began trying to beat the fire back with their brooms. Not smart since brooms are made of straw and even not smarter since they were wearing very flammable print dresses that could have easily caught fire. But this time our Hogansville heroes got there in the nick of time, kinda like Roy Rogers getting to the bank just as the robbers were mounting their steeds.

I think this was the first time our heroes got to use their brand new 1955 Ford fire truck so they were careful to keep it out of harm's way. Heaven forbid they get it dirty while putting out a fire. We didn't have a fire plug since we lived outside the city limits so they had to use onboard water and they were thrilled to say the least. They managed to bring the blaze under control and still keep their gleaming truck safe, they thought. I sorta hated to tell them they'd dented their rear shiny chrome bumper when they accidentally backed over mother's swing, so I didn't. Why spoil a good time for everyone except my daddy when he came out of work to find no car, no wife, and obviously no child waiting for him.

THE DAY THE TRAIN STOOD STILL

About a month ago at work, I stopped by the desk of a fellow collector friend. Hanging above his head was a beautiful print of the *Southern Crescent* passing through a snow covered ravine. It brought back memories of those pretty, old, streamlined diesels passing our house during the fifties, taking passengers to exotic stops.

Our property line ended at the railroad cut just down from our garden. I always looked forward to seeing the six o'clock train pass as I helped my daddy tote water for the vegetables plants. Remember, he wouldn't use a hose as our well was always too low and might go dry. My imagination wandered to the far away destinations of the waving passengers from the still slow moving train, which was picking up speed and heading north out of Hogansville. As I watched it go by, my mind slipped into those outlaw days when Mike E. and I rode the length of my backyard chasing that train on our Western Flyer bikes, waving threatening six shooters and wearing black cowboy hats with red kerchiefs over our faces. The engineers, who got a big kick out of it, waved back with their red kerchiefs. One day, realizing our steeds were a little too slow and we kept getting flat tires, Mike and I gave up train robbing and decided to see if we could get the train to flatten a penny like those our classmates were always showing around at school.

If a penny looked good flattened, we surmised a dime would look even better. So we slid down to the rail-cut one afternoon while my mother caught a few winks before work. Using some thick Johnson and Johnson cloth tape mother always kept handy – because I was so spastic as a kid that I needed taping up almost daily from war wounds – we attached the dime to the tracks. Then we scampered to safety a few minutes before the three o'clock daily flyer was due to pass. We found a place with a good view and settled down to watch our dime get flattened to smithereens.

It wasn't long before we heard the diesel's horn blasting away. It blasted and blasted, and blasted. The rotating light on its nose was in sight as the train slowed and just sat there right behind the neighbor's house exactly where we taped the dime, and continued to blast away on its horn. Mike and I looked at each other in mortal fear. Had we put too much tape on the track and caused the train to derail? Did all those men walking around the tracks find our dime? What are we going to do when they finally catch us? I could see me serving life for attempting to derail a passenger train and putting the lives of gosh-only-knows how many people in danger. The Herald's headlines would read, "Two Boys Nearly Responsible for the Train Wreck of the Century."

Our first inclination was to fess up to my mother, but we thought better and decided to wait until the police came for us and then plead for our lives. Meanwhile, we sneaked down to the rail-cut in our best WWII infantry fashion to get a closer look at the train as it sat there blowing its horn. Fear freezing our hearts, we couldn't run the risk of being caught at the scene so we went back to my house to await the inevitable. My life, all twelve years of it, was over. Would they let us share the same cell so we could at least know who slept across from us and talk to each other over those lonely years? I could see it all in my mind's eye, getting out of jail when my hair would be gray and I'd be too old to work. How would I live?

Sitting on the side porch waiting for my mother to wake up, we suddenly heard the unmistakable sound of the train's engines revving. Soon it slowly passed the house and picked up speed. It was moving and it seemed all right! No one was dead and better yet the police had not shown up. Not wanting to take any chances though, we waited until the train was out of sight to rush to the rail-cut and retrieve our dime. It was gone, tape and all. Evidence, maybe? It took a while before we realized the police wouldn't show up at our door steps, and the fear finally subsided. To my knowledge neither of us has ever taped another dime on a railroad track nor a penny for that matter. I don't even get the urge today. And why did the train stop and all those men walk around it? No one except those folks will ever know, and I definitely won't ask anyone why such things happen.

LITTLE LEAGUE (GLORY IS FLEETING)

I was thumbing through some loose pictures to find out if any of them were worth putting in the more recent photo albums we keep in the wall unit, when I came across an envelope with a bunch of black and white photos crammed inside. There were pictures of me at three years old with my cousins, as well as my mother and I standing in front of the trusty '61 Chevy Bel Air (the first four-door car she would let my daddy buy as I was sixteen and likely wouldn't accidentally open the back door and fall out of). There was also one of me in my Little League uniform pretending to field a ground ball. It was one of the few views of me in a Little League uniform not trying to protect my face from the fury of a baseball that could change directions in a flash.

The date on the baseball picture was May '58, and it probably was my last year of eligibility for Little League. I always belonged to the "Braves." That was the team managed by Don Howington. Don probably thought it his civic duty to pick me as I was always selected ignominiously last, after the really good ball players were already spoken for. For some reason I have never been athletically outstanding. Come to think of it that probably applies to a lot of other things I do too. But being slightly below average does have its advantages, as you are not expected to do wonders; when that does happens it's icing on the cake. That was the case with my Little League career where I can recount only one moment of triumph.

I remember spending a lot of time on the bench. You would think I would remember my co-bench-warmer partner's name, and I do, Warren. On occasion they let us alternately play left field. I specialized on left field and an occasional third base if the coach was desperate. For reasons unexplained I never felt comfortable playing the other two fields (center and right). It just felt natural in left field and I caught better than my co-bench-warmer whose batting average was better than mine. I was best known for my agility at catching flies that were seemingly uncatchable. But that did not outweigh my ability to swing and miss anything that remotely came near the plate.

I was that "out" all the pitchers dreamed of. When I stepped up to the plate they would pretend I was as serious a hitter like Butch or Noel, or Mickey or Bobby; I don't have enough paper and time to go on. For the pitcher, I was like the ten minute break in the middle of a tough workday. I had an abnormal fear of being struck in the head by a bullet or some similar object that was passing within a hair of my batting helmet. These things were not like the sophisticated helmets of today. They weren't full caps but looked like a red leather band that wrapped around the side and back of your head, and were held together over the top by elastic straps. It was hard to wear your cap with one on. If you did wear your cap, you couldn't hear the umpire or your coach yelling signals to you. And the batting helmet didn't do anything about deterring a pitch that was determined to hit you full in the face. My reflexes were never quick, so by the time my brain said, "Move out of the way of that pitch," I was hearing the dull thud of the ball against my leather helmet and finding myself surrounded by adults and uniformed midgets with startled looks of their face; at least it seemed that way from the ground. They all were concerned I might never come out of that coma and if I did, would I be more retarded than before?

The Braves were just one of the teams in our league. I remember we had the Cardinals. They were coached by Mr. Hartman and had green, white and grey uniforms. Yep, that's right. I never understood it either, but Mr. Hartman didn't mind, and most of the players never questioned it. So they stayed the Cardinals with green uniforms. There was also the perpetual league leader, the Tigers, who were managed by Mr. B.C. Granger. This man was the Casey Stengle of Hogansville. He lived and breathed baseball and could get his players up, even for a rainout. We always had teams named the Yankees, Dodgers, Pirates and White Sox. There were enough teams to occupy three games a week of doubleheaders.

We played on the Johnson Street field which was later named for Mr. Granger. It was adjacent to Jap Keith's Store. Just like the Cardinal's green uniforms, I never understood the store's name as Mr. Keith wasn't Japanese and the war had been over a good ten or twelve years. In fact, the store was just behind the left field fence. I spent a lot of time within feet of the Coke sign on the side of the store during and after games. Between innings and after games we would run to the store and fill up on soft drinks and candy, necessary nutritional highs for growing baseball players. And it didn't hurt to pick up a few pieces of bubble gum, the kind with baseball cards in them. Mine would be worth hundreds now if only I had saved them, which I did not.

I hated to play under the lights because you could get hit easier than in the daytime. You couldn't judge the ball's speed that good at night even though it was easier to see. The only time I got hit by a ball was when I practiced. I got whacked on the arm, on the shoulder, and once in the face. My daddy was hitting flies to about three of us kids in the side yard of our house one afternoon. I was trying to judge the ball and avoid running into the apple tree at the same time. The tree was our permanent short stop on the designated playing field. I was too intent on avoiding a collision with the tree when the ball went right between my outstretched hands, glove and all. When you get hit in the head with a baseball you don't have time to make noises and let people know you are in trouble, especially when you are automatically knocked out. But somehow my mother sensed it just as she sensed all my injuries, even till now. Before I hit the ground she was there with a wet wash cloth and a chunk of ice. When my vision seemed to be returning to normal and the pain set in, I tried to speak and thank her. Then I saw my daddy staring down at me saying to mother, "Sara, let the boy get up and catch another one. If he doesn't do it now he may never do it again." That was sound advice because if he had not made me catch another fly, then I likely would have hung up my cleats forever. This, by the way, would be considered classic child abuse now-a-days.

Mother always starched my uniform. It could have stood up by itself after she finished. I didn't especially like the uniform anyway because it was a dull gray and I wanted a white one like B.C. Granger's Tigers, or the Yankees' striped ones. The green Cardinal's uniforms looked better than ours. At least theirs had green piping and ours was a hideous orange. But our orange-billed and blue caps were the envy of the other teams which was some consolation. Usually I never played enough to get the starch completely worked out of my uniform, so next starching it got even stiffer. It was obvious in the picture from '58 that the uniform looked like it was cracking. My pose was not one of fluid grace but more of being trapped in a space suit.

Don't worry, I'm not about to forget my hour of triumph. It was an afternoon game and we were down by one run. I had spent my only other at-bat stepping back and swinging at air every time the ball crossed the plate. I would always step back to get an early start on moving out of the way. With my slow reflexes I needed all the head start I could get. Don tried constantly to get me to stop doing that saying, "You lose power every time you step back to take a swing." I don't understand why he was so concerned since I never hit anything anyway. We had a man who by some weird twist of fate was on third. Why Don didn't substitute someone for me so that we could get him home will never be known. But he didn't, and I came to bat with two outs and only one left for the Tigers to claim the game.

Dick Austin, the pitcher, was a strong thrower who burned them in close to the plate. He did this on purpose because he knew I didn't like the idea of being clobbered by his fastball. I think his second pitch, which was wild and almost hit me, was psychological warfare. Nevertheless, I stood my ground and vowed I would not step back. I was already down one strike and managed to dodge the wild pitch for a ball. After a long look at his catcher, Austin wound up and hurled a "blue darter" as Dizzy Dean called a fastball. I don't recall if I stepped back but I did swing and something happened that amazed me as much as the coach and players. I connected with the ball. I was so shocked I didn't even think about running since I hadn't exited the plate in this manner in such a long time. I was naturally inclined to leisurely tossing the bat aside and slowly striding to the dugout.

Finally, after frenzied yelling from my teammates, I awoke and ran for first. By this time, the ball went just out of reach of the second baseman and into shallow center field where no one was at the time. This caused the third base coach to motion me on to second base. The throw, when it was finally fielded, was wild and screamed over the first baseman's outstretched glove. He was lucky because Austin was there to back him up. Austin threw the ball to second but the guy there wasn't ready. The ball went over him and the short stop, between the center and left fields, missed it too. I ran to third base with the third base coach waving me home. I didn't look back to see where the ball was when I slid into home plate.

I accomplished two things that day which I've never experienced again. I scored my one and only home run even though it was on errors, and I broke the starch in my uniform, not to mention getting the thing good and dirty. Who says mediocre kids can't excel occasionally? I was proclaimed the game's hero and Don rewarded the team by piling us into the back of his pickup and driving over to his service station for free cokes. By the way, did I tell you we won the game?

BOY SCOUTING

I recently saw a copy of the old Scout Handbook I used to carry to the meetings of Walt Bennett's Troop. It was for sale in an antique shop in Dahlonega, GA. On the plastic cover were the words, "collector's item from the fifties." Am I that old?

I moved up from the Bears of Lena Gay's Cub Scout Pack to a full fledged Boy Scout sometime in the late fifties. I got a big kick out of shedding the blue uniform of the Cubs and getting into the khaki one that reminded me of my daddy's WWII Army uniform. I've never felt comfortable in a blue uniform for some reason even though I had occasion to wear one again about fifteen years later when I went into the Air Force.

There were a lot of us Cubs moving into the only troop of Boy Scouts in Hogansville. Walt Bennett, our Scout Master, and his son Barry who was an Eagle Scout, were anxious to make us feel at home. A stocky guy with a graying crew cut and a raspy voice, Mr. Bennett was always attired in a neatly pressed uniform. I remember thinking of him while going through "basic" in the Air Force. Maybe because my Training Instructor was a stocky guy with a graying crew cut, a raspy voice, and always wore a neatly pressed uniform. But of course, Mr. Bennett never referred to us as dinks nor threatened to do all kinds of unthinkable contortions to our bodies if we didn't get up when the lights came on.

Our scout meetings were held at the Community Building on Johnson Street. We always arrived early to lounge in the big overstuffed vinyl chairs and sofas with the wide wooden arms and watched a little TV before the meeting. Of course in the other adjoining rooms there were ping pong tables and a basketball court to keep us busy if nothing good was on TV. Located in the basement under the basketball court was the swimming pool where I learned to swim, but it was closed and off limits by this time. On the nights our troop meetings took place it looked like a USO Club during the war.

Mister Bennett decided the best way to incorporate us new guys into the troop was to have a campout. Now, camping still isn't one of my favorite pastimes, and as a matter of fact, I don't do much of it today because my wife doesn't even want to stay in a cheap motel. Anyway our troop wasn't going to be in the deep woods, only just across the street from the Community Building in the vacant lot behind Granger Field. My daddy dropped me off and told me he'd see me in the morning. I was very glad to see that '55 Ford when it appeared the next day, but then I'm getting ahead of myself.

It wasn't long after we finished roasting wieners and marshmallows, and singing a few folk songs accompanied by Barry and his guitar, that we felt a few drops of rain. Soon it fell harder and then harder still. Realizing this wasn't just a quick shower, Mr. Bennett ordered a retreat over to the Community Building. About midnight the lightning and thunder of the storm knocked the lights out and consequently the TV. Our Scout Master decided it was an excellent night to tell ghost stories, besides he needed some kind of organized activity to control us. Not a good idea. He got tired of that about one-thirty and told us to turn in. Who was he kidding?

Every time the building groaned, and it did a lot of that even in the daytime, we kids started chattering about spooks. Billy, Noel and I dared each other to check out the chains we thought we heard rattling down in the swimming pool area. I got half way down the dark staircase and decided I wanted to live a little while longer and deprive Frankenstein of his opportunity to smother the life out of me at the bottom of the stairs. Besides being scared out of our wits, we spent a very uncomfortable night sleeping in our damp uniforms because rain had soaked everything else.

When we got up the next morning, the scene looked like the aftermath of the Battle of the Bulge. Of course, Mr. Bennett never knew about what went on because like my Air Force TI, he too slept like a rock. Turns out our troop never had another camp out that was this much fun. Thank God.

THE STUDEBAKER BOAT

Last week, I went by my daughter Emily's house to take her and my three granddaughters and their daddy a few things my wife and I had gotten them on a recent cruise to Bermuda. While we were sitting at the table eating our fast food lunch, I was looking at pictures one of my seven year old twin granddaughters had drawn. She had done a good job and it brought back memories of a picture I once drew in seventh grade. My granddaughters were busy with their hamburgers so I showed the picture to my daughter and told her it reminded me of the time when my teacher told us we were going to be required to draw pictures of a theme from one of the poems from a pamphlet we had for English Literature. The winners would have their posters placed in the hallway for everyone to see. By the way, I still have the remnants of that pamphlet of poems. I've always been interested in history and especially military history so it was easy to choose my favorite poem from the pamphlet, "Old Ironsides" by Oliver Wendell Holmes.

Unlike my peers in seventh grade who read "Batman," "Green Lantern," and other superhero type comic books, I read the historical ones such as the exploits of the U.S.S. Constitution and her victories against British ships during the War of 1812. Because cannonballs bounced off her coastal Georgia Live Oak sides, the Constitution gained the nickname Old Ironsides. When she was about to be broken up for scrap in the 1830s, there was an effort raised to save her, and a poem by Holmes was the catalyst that did the trick. So there was no doubt "Old Ironsides" would be the subject of my poster submission. I spent a lot of time studying my collection of historical comic books to get the lines of the ship just right, making sure I had the right number of gun ports, the quarter gallery windows accurately drawn, and the mast and yardarms as well as the bowsprit and rigging as close as I could get to reality. Emily asked me to draw a picture of the ship as I had done for the poster in seventh grade. So, I set to work drawing the best rendition of "Old Ironsides" I could remember.

One of the kids in my class was a tall thin good looking guy and not very into academics. Truthfully, he also was a bit of a ruffian to boot. Don't get me wrong, I liked him and still do because on more than one occasion he was my salvation from being beaten to a pulp in the boy's bathroom by bullies. He too decided to draw "Old Ironsides" for his poster. The picture he came up with was one many people of the times would have compared to a '50s Studebaker, a car many people couldn't tell whether or not it was coming or going. The ship had one mast, one yardarm and huge portholes. There were no bowsprit or gun ports, nor was there any rigging to speak of. Now we all know the U.S.S. Constitution didn't have portholes, don't we? Neither did it have just one mast nor did it look like it was coming or going because in reality it had a sharp bow and a blunt stern. That's front and back, for you non-nautical folks.

I also made sure I had the white checkerboard stripes down the sides where the gun ports were located. That's the same checkerboard pattern made famous by Lord Nelson of the Royal Navy. Any seventh grader knows that too, doesn't he? Of course we Americans couldn't let the Brits tell us what to do, so our stripe was white while theirs was yellow. Emily was trying to hold back a laugh while I went into all this extraordinary detail which she knew I would when I got really wound up telling my story. Then I sprang the finale on her. My poster wasn't among those chosen to hang in the hallway for display to other classes. The kid's poster of the Studebaker ship was chosen to represent "Old Ironsides." Good grief! I still haven't totally gotten over the rejection as you can see. So I went into an animated explanation to my daughter of the situation and of the teacher who I considered not to be too much smarter than the kid whose picture she chose over my historically correct drawing, the one I spent hours to perfect. Finally, unable to hold it back any more Emily began to laugh and said, "Dad you gotta put that story in your book." So now I have.

TWO OF A KIND

It wasn't too long ago I re-established contact with an arm of my family I thought I would probably never hear from again. I won't go into the whys and whatevers of what caused the separation but suffice to say it was beyond my control to influence.

The renewed contact thanks to the Internet put me back in touch with my cousin Jenny and her daddy, my Uncle Howie. Of course, my uncle immediately e-mailed me a message containing jokes. He hasn't changed since we sat in that Mimosa tree for our portrait in nineteen sixty. You see, my Uncle Howie and I have never really grown up. Every year or so, my Aunt Dot and her family from Florida would travel to Georgia to visit us and Aunt Mary who lived in LaGrange. Mother and Mary didn't travel much, never, if they could avoid it. They felt if they were supposed to be in another state then God would have had them born there. Daddy used the occasion to crank up his trusty barbecue grill to cook steak. We never used the grill unless we had company. You see, mother felt cooking was meant to be done on a stove. Well you get the idea. Daddy was elected to do the grilling.

My daddy loved to talk men stuff while he cooked on the grill since the women folk were always in the house making potato salad and other things to have with the steaks. Only problem was daddy had to cook the steaks alone because my Uncle Howie, my cousin Jenny, his step-daughter whom he loved as much as his two natural children, and I would be target practicing with my BB rifle. My uncle's other two daughters would be our responsibility. What can a six and four year old do to deter target practice? My uncle and I usually managed about a half hour before we were missed. Then we all would be in trouble with my mother and Aunt Dot.

All I can say is Howie must have been a saint, or at least a difficult man to make angry. My Aunt Dot might have been little in stature but she made up for it with her spirited temper. She was a good soul but always truthful and out-spoken. Howie always laughed it off and as a matter of fact I never saw him frown. Eventually he and my daddy would end up talking about sports, one of the few things they had in common. But it wouldn't be long before Howie was back talking to me about my model cars and racing me up the old Mimosa tree in our front yard. Daddy would eventually give up on the conversation and check the steaks. However, evidence shows daddy did manage to take a few snap shots of me and my uncle in that Mimosa tree. Seeing those photographs again is how I guess I began to remember all this stuff.

I found them in a cookie tin that survived mother's move to the "Home." There I was sitting on a limb wearing my plaid shirt, cut off shorts and a sailor cap. My uncle, perched on a limb opposite me, was wearing his usual garb, a T-shirt and long slacks. We were both grinning up a storm. If he ever took life seriously then, I don't know about it, but he did take us kids seriously. Kids in the fifties were cute and then you sent them out to play. Uncle Howie didn't do that; he never let us think we were just in the background. He talked to us about things we were interested in and showed interest in what we had to say. I sent those pictures to him and he e-mailed me right back letting me know that he hasn't changed a bit in the thirty odd years we haven't seen each other. I can tell you without hesitation I haven't changed much either.

So, now-a-days when I look at those pictures I see someone who genuinely was a friend. And when I read those e-mails from him I get just about daily, I see someone who still is a friend as well as an uncle.

DADDY'S CARS

If you ask the average man how many cars he owned over his

lifetime, what do you think the answer would be? I'd be willing to say no less than ten. However, having had some experience at car trading for more years than I care to discuss here, I want to offer some insight into what really drives a male's quest to own one of every kind of legal/illegal automotive conveyance. Before I get started, let me preface this story by saying I'm not a psychologist and what I say shouldn't be considered therapy or suggestion. The Surgeon General couldn't have put it better. Boys are taught from an early age to emulate their fathers and generally most of them do. My daddy was a good example to emulate. The first recollection I have of his life long love affair with cars came with the 1947 Pontiac. Daddy was a definite Pontiac man. That long black two-door fastback (actually humpback) Pontiac straight eight was beautiful when it was clean. I could always tell when he was within a block of home because every time he geared down to take the intersecting street to our house, the down shift caused the transmission to whine like a muffled air raid siren. It was only when he shifted into a higher gear that the unmistakable announcement ceased.

I remember the first wreck of my up to that point brief life. Daddy had just a little more beer than he should have (before mother rehabilitated him) and was determined to go to Jap Keith's store for something mother just couldn't live without. When she discovered he intended to take me, she suddenly decided she could live without whatever it was she had wanted. It was too late as we had already negotiated the driveway and were proceeding on schedule with the mission. That is until he forgot to stay in the road and at a whopping fifteen miles per hour he aborted the mission by crashing into the giant oak tree that stood on the border of the street in our yard. I had been standing up on the front seat. Being the three year old I was, well I just went with the flow. I tumbled over into the massive floor board, missing the chromed iron that passed for a dashboard. I don't want to linger on my physical agility too long but I only got a small bruise on my cheek and one heck of a short but fun ride. To give a little drama to the thing, I decided crying should not be left out of the scenario. Thus ended my first experience with what was to become a long and interesting relationship with the automobile.

Well, it was hard to see the Pontiac go but the time came when the itch was too much and we sold it to Boots Lankford. Since Boots lived close to us, I could never get rid of the ingrained notion that every time the Pontiac rounded the corner I had to immediately stop what I was doing and go see. My parents mistook this for loyalty to the car but for me I just couldn't break the habit. The next car was to my daddy what my Prelude is to me. This was his one and only true love of all the cars he owned. I still have pictures I know he made of the car and not of us even though my mother and I were there in the pictures. There are pictures of the car with its doors open so the interior can be seen, with me and mother and sometimes even daddy himself in various poses just to give the impression of pictures of the family. It was the Super '88 bechromed white-side-walled big V8 black 1950 Oldsmobile. This definitely was my father's Oldsmobile, but it was also the envy of every teenager on our street. It was flashy with its fender skirts and twin exhaust. It had a hydromantic (automatic) transmission, something of a novelty at that time and even more so in Hogansville. And above all it was fast. Mother was grateful because daddy never drank anything before driving this one. He cared too much.

The year 1955 was a major redesign and also a leap forward in technical advancement for cars. The changeover was tantamount to a ten year leap in everything. Daddy was like some kid that had just discovered peanut butter for the first time. Some of my best memories are from visiting the two dealers in Hogansville when October had come and they finally stopped teasing us with shots of fenders, tail lamps, and covers that were pulled back just enough to stimulate the imagination. Needless to say with all this hoopla over the new '55, daddy overcame his deep abiding love for the Olds and succumbed to the lure of the seductive lines of the new Ford. He was definitely infatuated, but that was all, as the love that had been deep for the Olds was never there for the Fairlane.

My memories of the Fairlane were the first clear ones I had of a car. I remember the dash was in the same two-tone colors of the car's outside, aqua blue top and a white bottom. The speedometer sat in an arch just above the straight line of the dash and the back was smoked glass to allow sunlight inside to make the digits seem illuminated, even in daylight. The heater, radio and clock were encased in chromed rings. My fondest recollections were not specifically of the car so much but what we did with it, going to Traylor's Café for hamburgers. The '55 finally gave daddy his excuse to move on to something else. He tolerated mother spilling preserves on the front seat (yes, the car he watched so carefully when I ate on the way back from Traylor's), but he couldn't tolerate the Ford not steering.

Mother decided to go shopping in LaGrange and also visit my Aunt Mary. She invited some lady friend of hers to go with us that Saturday. We were cruising along down Highway 29, a lovely drive on the two-lane that was to be replaced later by I-85. The large 16-wheelers were zooming past us at an incredible speed. You see, daddy was no slouch at keeping these dragons at bay, but with my mother and her friend along he was every bit the gentleman including his driving manners. He got an ulcer later from this kind of activity. Anyway, the car decided it wasn't listening to a human anymore and stopped responding to the steering wheel. Needless to say, we were all quite a bit disturbed but the low speed helped us retain our civility while daddy continued to beat the wheel, turn it in all directions, stomp the brakes, which did work, and cut off the ignition. The car rolled to a stop just off the road.

The next question was how to get the thing to the dealer. The Ralls dealership was ten miles back and the Ford dealer in LaGrange about the same distance when you consider the turns and traffic in the booming metropolis of 10,000 people. After a while of tinkering and cursing under his breath, daddy decided to resume the trip since the steering wheel kicked in a little better. He made it to my Aunt Mary's and deposited mother and her friend. He told them Uncle Willie could take them to town or that they could walk as the square was only a couple of blocks away. Mother was under the impression daddy was going to take the Ford for repair at the dealer. He had no such notion, the Ford was dead meat. It was fortunate that on earlier trips to LaGrange he had been able to break away from mother and visit the local dealers just to see what else they had available.

The year 1957 was another windfall for good looks and style. Fins were just beginning to be attractions on cars. Daddy had already decided the error of his ways was leaving General Motors. We made straight for Johnson's Motor Company. After slowly negotiating the hill into the dealership, the Ford suddenly decided once again it didn't want to steer anymore, but daddy adlibbed and just told the salesman he always parked parallel in straight parking places. All was considered fair in bargaining. We immediately spotted the car we "needed." It was on the showroom floor. This was my first experience at the negotiating game. I didn't pay much attention because they deposited me in another salesman's office.

There were no cubicles back then, so the other salesman decided the best way to help his coworker sell the car was to divert my attention from total destruction of his office and nerves; he gave me something all little boys wanted, a model of the very car my daddy was interested in buying. There was a condition though, I must try very hard to get my daddy to buy the car. This sounded like a fair deal for getting the promo model but what the salesman didn't know was that daddy needed no convincing and I wasn't about to tell him the Ford didn't work anymore. After about three hours of nonstop arguing and my token pleas to buy the car, just to hold up my end of the deal, the bargain was struck. I wasn't looking forward to this part of buying a car when I went on my first forays a few years later. However, I do believe it was an experience that set the tone for every negotiation I've made since my car buying career has blossomed.

When we returned to Aunt Mary's with the new Pontiac, mother became violently ill. Not to worry, because this was to become a regular happening every time daddy bought a new car. It was temporary and when the time came to go to work again she suddenly got better. Mother would always say buying a new car was going to break them and they could never retire or save enough money to send the kid to college. That reinforced my endeavors to support daddy in getting any new car he wanted. If we didn't have enough money for me to go to college that meant I wouldn't have to spend the rest of my natural life in school.

The Pontiac was the car I eventually learned to drive. After getting my feet wet, so to speak, I had the bug for sure. I wasn't old enough to get a license yet so I couldn't take it out on the highway but daddy let me drive on side roads and occasionally back streets in town. Daddy had other cars but these were the ones that created my mindset, the mindset my wife thinks needs to be overcome by events such as prices, environment, and unimaginative car design. They all look the same to her, especially the white ones which she claims look like refrigerators on wheels; she doesn't understand what drives men to buy the cars they drive.

YOU'RE DRIVING ME CRAZY

My first experience at driving came when my daddy thought it was about time I learned how to point the armored personnel carrier our family called a '57 Pontiac Chieftain in a straight line and hold it there. The monster had a pig iron grill with two large blunt bullets protruding at least one and a half feet in front of anything else on the car. Thank God Pontiac had seen fit to remove those hideous chrome strips from the hood and trunk or I'd been blinded by the reflection. Ours was a two door, as had been every car my parents owned after I was born. My mother believed a four door was too dangerous because as she told Tom (my daddy), "He'll open the door and fall out." I don't know how she figured that since I had never had the opportunity. It must run in the family? Although, when I was allowed in the front seat not sitting between the two of them, I was never prone to open the door at speed. Maybe my daddy didn't care because when we went to Traylor's Hamburger joint in the evenings while my mother was at work he never made me sit in the back. And worst of all he never locked the doors which mother always did. I'm convinced the reason their marriage lasted fifty years was they worked opposite shifts in the Cotton Mill and never saw each other that much.

The Pontiac had a radio speaker that wasn't really part of the car because it appeared to me to be a sort of afterthought thing. The designers worked hard to style a really spiffy dash. It had a speedometer consisting of a red ribbon that stretched across the dash to 120 mph. The clock sat in its own little contoured curve, and every surface that could accommodate it was chrome plated. After they finished, one of the designers probably said to another, "Where did you put the speaker?" "What speaker?" asked the other designer. "You know, the radio speaker you idiot!" "Oh that speaker. Well . . . " And the conversation went on until one of the guys grabbed up a parts box and cut a hole in the bottom, inserted a speaker and proceeded to lodge it between the dash and the transmission hump. That's where it stayed even into production. Something like that today would get someone suspended since no one gets fired anymore. But this topic can wait another day for examination.

Our speaker finally got dislodged by all the kids mother usually collected for home delivery when she picked me up at school each afternoon. It hung by the wires and as we turned curves it would shift from one side to the other. There was no use to try and fix it as the thing was determined to either get kicked by a kid, or on occasion dislodge itself. So we may have had the first car stereo radio in existence since it would play on one side and then the other, eventually giving a somewhat stereo effect.

The '57 Pontiac had fins too, but not as sharp as Plymouth's, Chevy's or Ford's. But if you weren't careful, you could still impale yourself or get a nasty bruise. The car had a large V8, and no, I don't know the displacement. I do recall it was blue with white stripes on the side and had duel exhausts. Since it had been an oil burner from the start, the exhaust tips which were part of the bumpers stayed sooty even after a good spit and polish wash job over at Bad Eye Cardin's Texaco Station. Daddy had it washed at least once a month. He seldom washed it himself. I really didn't get into washing cars until I realized those people with dresses and long hair weren't guys. Cars came in handy for dating.

It wasn't long after I turned fourteen that my daddy asked me if I wanted to learn to drive. Since I was not good at little league, I guess he felt he might be able to help me learn something. He decided we needed to be on a road that was fairly remote but close enough so that if I did some serious damage to either of us or the car, we could get help. There were no cell phones in those days. The logical choice was Ralls Road. It was a good choice because it was just past Keeble's Store and Keeble's Pond (the Keebles owned a lot of stuff). Besides, we could use going to the store as an excuse to make sure mother wouldn't find out what we were up to and insist on having me drive from the back seat where there were no doors.

Ralls Road ran by the Power's Dairy Farm, and its pond was made famous by a wild story of Jim Keith and P.L. Cliett killing a renegade alligator over twenty feet long. Since we were only two hundred miles from the nearest swamp, the Okefenokee, it was perfectly logical to everyone who told the story that such a creature could be inhabiting a dairy farm pond. Funny, I can't recall any cows going missing and none offered any complaints about intruders. The pond lay right in the massive curve everyone said you could meet yourself on. I pondered that statement a lot. Being a kid in the fifties and early sixties I took everything adults said with extreme seriousness, including the alligator story.

The drive started where Ralls Road dead ends into another road. The only recollection I have of that particular road was later on when Larry, James and I would periodically test James's father's '58 Biscayne for possibilities as a drag racer. Our times were never recorded, and a good thing because that car was not fast by any stretch of the imagination. It looked wicked enough because of the unintentionally raised back end, compliments of a miffed job at replacing the shocks.

Daddy turned our car around at the intersection with this road and pointed it down Ralls Road, then gave me the wheel. I was just barely able to see over the red ribbon of the speedometer to a view of a hood as long as a football field and chrome Indian heads on either fender that looked like the wind had blown them till they stretched back to the windshield. I immediately became aware of the power of this car when I dropped the column mounted shift lever into "D". I pressed the accelerator with care and we began to move forward at a breathtaking twenty miles per hour. I noticed my daddy's breathing increase rapidly and then after a few minutes of perfect guiding he began to return to normal. We were having a great time cruising at thirty-five. The spring day was clear and not a glint of too much sun or any other inhibitor was in my way.

We were coming to the big curve, Deadman's Curve, you know the one where you meet yourself and also the one where the notorious 'gator had met an untimely end. Daddy leaned over and said, "GO UP." I immediately pushed the accelerator hard and the Pontiac fairly jumped ahead without hesitation. His face looked drawn as if he had just taken the sound barrier. It felt good to me and I didn't have enough experience (I bet you thought I was going to say sense) to know any better so I stayed off the brakes through the curve. In those days I didn't know a big, bulky, soft-handling American sedan didn't possess the cornering agility and tight suspension of a sports car like a Jaguar or Porsche. The Pontiac apparently didn't know it either, because it just hung in there and listed heavily to the left all the way around the curve never once offering to come unglued or change direction.

After a mild seizure, possibly the beginning of heart problems that my daddy developed in later years, and after we had negotiated the curve, daddy grabbed the steering wheel and jammed on the brakes at the same time. The Pontiac hauled up in the back end and blue smoke emitted from the rear tires as the red ribbon slowly receded from sixty miles per hour. "What's wrong with you boy? You don't go around curves on two wheels," were his first words. "But just before we got to the curve you said GO UP and I thought that's what you wanted me to do?" was my response. "What?" he said as he fell back in the seat to catch his breath and try to understand why I wasn't diagnosed as mentally retarded at an earlier age. "I said, SLOW UP," he related to himself under his breath. Perhaps I should have recognized this as the beginning of hearing problems for me, inherited from my mother's side of the family, that would later rear its ugly head in my life.

The driving lessons didn't resume for several months. Eventually, I would get my license and my daddy got his first prescription for tranquilizers. Oh yes, the last time I asked around Hogansville, no one had broken my record for Deadman's Curve and stayed out of the infamous alligator infested Powers Dairy Farm Pond.

LOOKING BACK ON AN EXCITING DAY

 Last night I lay in bed half asleep, contemplating having spent the day doing some of my favorite things, like preparing a special gumbo recipe for my brother-in-law and his wife, overeating and watching a movie until late. Whenever this happens, which fortunately isn't too often, I have nightmares; but this night I slept well, dreaming of another exciting day when I was a kid.

 Mother always picked me up after school and we'd drive to the Reid Mill to wait until my daddy got off from work on the first shift. She would go in as he came out because she was on the second shift. I remember it like yesterday, doing my homework in that aqua and white nineteen '55 Ford Fairlane while waiting for the shifts to change. I also remember one late September day when my daddy drove us straight to Traylor's café in LaGrange for the best burgers I've ever eaten. I listened to the Platters and Buddy Holly on the radio while devouring two hamburgers and swallowing a pint of chocolate milk on the way home. After he cleaned up, daddy and I headed straight to Hines Chevrolet and Ralls Ford to see the new cars that were being unveiled that afternoon.

 I was about to turn ten in the late fall of 1956 when my daddy took me to see the new cars that had just been introduced. Back then all the car ads on TV and in the papers showed them with covers on them, and the commercials counted down the days to when they'd come off. Sometimes we'd be enticed by a fender or tail light showing. When that long awaited day arrived, it was a major event in Hogansville and everyone would turn out. We kids would fill our complimentary bags with free balloons, gum, pencils and pens with dealer logos on them, key chains and anything else not fastened down. All the literature was crammed into those plastic sacks for viewing later at home. It was all the salesmen and our parents could do to keep us from spilling coke and dropping mustard from our free hot dogs on the new car's upholstery. The expensive convertibles and hardtops were on the showroom floor and the other models were out on the lot. We'd have to walk around and look at each one and sit in them to smell that heavenly scent only new cars have and still do today. That was a time when you could tell one model year change from another. Talk about a three ring circus; that's what the Ford and Chevy dealers were in our small town when the new cars arrived.

If you don't know, let me tell you that 1957 was a watershed year for car design, so on the weekend we'd go to LaGrange to see the other makes like the Pontiacs, Buicks, Chryslers, and even a Cadillac we knew we couldn't afford. Naturally when daddy got exposed to new cars he came down with a severe case of new car fever and I knew it wouldn't be too long before we'd have something else to ride in. I'd always put in my two cents worth about what he ought to buy but mother would pinch me and tell me to leave him alone. She knew it wouldn't take much for him to get the idea on his own. Well it didn't take long before daddy on his own discovered the new Pontiac. You guessed it. We left the Ford with Johnson's Motors and drove a new Pontiac home with that heavenly new car smell. Of course mother went to bed sick for three days – her usual reaction to daddy's buying a new car she was convinced we couldn't afford. It's a shame nothing that exciting happens anymore. Now-a-days new cars are released with no fanfare or notice, it seems, and sometimes a year before the actual year of the car. Then, we're a bit more cosmopolitan in our "too much information" age and that's too bad since it leaves us with nothing to surprise us and make us feel like a kid at the fair.

JIMMY'S DREAM

It was cold and all I wanted to do was to get warm. I had gone to bed that night thinking about summer days in Hogansville. Did I mention I was also delirious with the flu? I eventually drifted off.

The breeze blew through the big old pecan tree that sat at the end of the driveway next to Hwy 29, the super slab straight from "Hotlanta." I couldn't have been more than fifteen years old, making the year about 1963. My daddy and mother were sitting with me on the side porch as we watched the traffic flow across in front of us. We saw trucks to beat all forty and then there was Katie Mae in her '62 Nova. She slowly passed, and passed, and passed until I thought she was going to be a permanent fixture in front of us. The Nova was capable of speed but not with Katie Mae at the wheel. She never took it more than fifteen or twenty miles per hour anywhere around town. Her husband, Herschel, drove a transfer truck, one of those sixteen wheelers. Once in a while he would send Katie Mae to Keeble's Store in the semi to get cigarettes. It seemed Katie Mae pretty much kept the Parham's bordering plants crushed into smithereens as she was bad at steering, so the Nova was bought for her. It was cheaper than all the transmission work on the truck was costing Herschel.

Shortly after Katie Mae passed by we heard this AWFUL crash. I jumped from my seat and beat mother and Luby, the neighbor, to the scene of the noise. There was smoke emitting from Katie Mae's car, and its hood had its grille smashed to bits with a big Lincoln sitting in its engine bay. Katie Mae was sprawled out in the middle of the road and this guy climbing from the Lincoln was singing a hymn.

Mother immediately ran back to the house and called the State Patrol as well as McKibben's Funeral Home. McKibben's hearse doubled as an ambulance and picked up accidents too. Luby and I moved Katie Mae to the side of the road just in case someone should come around the curve and accidentally run over her. She wasn't quite conscious yet as the State Patrol car drove up. It was a big Plymouth with a hemi engine and a tail fin that for the world looked like a shark's. The trooper that got out was about 200 lbs and had a crew cut. He put on his hat, spit out a wad of tobacco and said, "Which one of you boys was in this wreck?" Luby had just finished pulling the engine on his truck so he told the trooper he was dirty from working, not from an accident. I said I was too young to drive, so that left the guy singing hymns and walking around in a daze. The trooper handcuffed him to a mail box and said he would deal with him later. About that time McKibben's hearse drove up. Seeing the ambulance/hearse, Katie Mae decided her condition was worse than she thought and passed completely out. The guys from McKibben's loaded Katie Mae into the hearse and lit out for LaGrange Hospital.

Now it seemed this accident happened close to the city limits of Hogansville; Otis was the local cop on duty and so he was notified. He had been in hot pursuit of Joe L., a kid who worked with my daddy in the mill. Joe L. was a good boy but he loved his fast '55 Chevy and kept the hood locked with a chrome chain to keep people from finding out what kind of engine he had. Joe L. had never been successfully pursued by the State Patrol, and of course at about forty-five miles per hour, Otis' maximum chase speed, he was never caught by the Hogansville Police. But, Joe L. was in danger of being caught this time because he had just slung a rod and the Chevy was about to give up the ghost. Since it was Sunday and Ralls Motor Company, the local Ford dealer, was closed Joe L. decided to duck in behind the place to avoid Otis. He hated worse than anything to have to pull his Chevy into a Ford place but this was no time to quibble as he was close to having his streak of not being caught broken.

Eagle eyed as he was, Otis fumbled on his glasses just in time to see where Joe L. was going. He wheeled the '61 Biscayne cruiser in behind Joe L., and the streak was history. Joe L. surrendered peaceably, embarrassed by having Otis of all people break the streak. Otis said, "Now, Joe L., I ain't got time to question you as I been notified Katie Mae had a wreck. I ain't been to see her and Herschel this year and I'm kinda feelin' bad about it. So if I get to the wreck quick, maybe I can see her before McKibben hauls her off." Joe L. perked up. He might get to see a really good wreck. He liked wrecks, especially when he wasn't in them. So Otis told Joe L. if he would get in the back seat and behave himself he wouldn't handcuff him.

When they got to the wreck, the state trooper told Otis he had things in hand. Otis didn't take too kindly to this so he pulled his revolver and told that state cop to hit the road. Only thing was Otis had gone off and left his belt, the one with his bullet in it, at home. Even though the state trooper knew Otis was allowed only one bullet he left peaceably. The drunk cuffed to the mail box began to sing louder and Otis yelled, "Boy, you got thirty seconds to git yourself over here and answer some questions or I'll shoot you on the spot."

Otis was pretty occupied with the drunk who was still cuffed to the mailbox, so Joe L. got out and examined the scene closer. After checking out the damage to the Lincoln and Chevy he walked over to the porch and spoke to mother and daddy. They just had a good time talking as mother hadn't seen Joe L. since his sister ran off with Duck Lawrence's boy and went to the Hemi-Fair in San Antonio for three days. She wanted to catch up on all the goings on from that. It took Otis about a half hour to separate the two of them and he thought for a while he might have to take mother in too, because she wasn't about to quit talking to Joe L.

About the time McKibben turned in at the hospital, Katie Mae came to. She looked around the interior of the hearse and decided she had already gone and with this she passed out again. It seems that Katie Mae would have lots to talk about too, when she finally realized she wasn't dead.

Suddenly I found myself in the floor and wide awake. It must have been when McKibben took that turn into the hospital.

Anyway, I didn't get to see how things turned out in just another one of Jimmy's dreams.

A DE-LIGHTFUL CHRISTMAS

Up on North Highway the entire month of December was spent in the Dale household getting ready for Christmas, and then getting over it. My daddy was the sergeant in all these tasks and my mother was the general. The Christmas boxes and assorted paper and ribbons were always in the very back of the closet in our little ranch house. Where else would they be since Christmas only came once a year? I was a bit smaller than my parents so I was sent in to pull the stuff out and push it back in. Mine was a dangerous job because I could easily smother if those blankets and bedspreads mother never used and stacked on higher shelves fell on my little body. They probably couldn't have gotten to me in time; it was a deep closet.

Well, putting up the tree was easier than taking it down. After Christmas mother would remove all the trimmings and carefully pack them away for next year, but it was daddy who had to take the lights off the thing. I've been around for just a little over half a century and have seen planes go from prop to jet, offices switch from typewriters to computers, a man land on the moon, and the invention of telephones you can carry in your pocket, but no one has improved very much on Christmas tree lighting. Yes, today bulbs are high tech, smaller, more reliable and not likely to blow up or set your tree on fire. Then, now-a-days Christmas trees aren't usually real anyway and are mostly fire proof. Oh, and if one bulb burns out the whole set doesn't stop working, sometimes. But I noticed this morning when I was taking the lights off our tree, they are still on a string of wire that is even more complex than what my daddy had to deal with.

My daddy was a pretty mild mannered man most of the time until he started taking lights off the tree. He was reasonably intelligent too, but you'd never know it once things started to get out of hand. "De-lighting" our Christmas tree turned him into a raving lunatic, capable of hideous acts of violence against Mother Nature's creation (tree) and the lights my mother had warned him to handle with care so they would burn the next year. Give him an E for effort, but when the lights turned into an anaconda and wrapped around his legs and ankles and the small child at his feet (who was only trying to help), he turned into King Kong. He'd growl and start ripping strings of lights off his body while the kid was hopelessly lashed to a chair by the green vine. Once we were free of the lights, daddy would find he had to get them unraveled from the tree stand. The easiest thing to do was to take the tree down. We never got that done without spilling the sugar water on mother's hardwood floor. After she mopped the floor, daddy would put the string of lights away and begin to slowly calm down

As a matter of fact, this still happens with me today. I'm calm now since my wife heard me talking to myself and came into the room and pointedly stared at me in disbelief as I wriggled around the floor entangled in a vine of lights and wire. Now, our tree isn't real so I finally had to take it apart to get the wires off the stand. I didn't remember until I folded all the branches where the thing came apart, so next year maybe she won't notice the tree is now in three sections instead of two. This is one thing my daddy never had to deal with but I'm sure he'd have eventually figured this situation out, too. At least there was no sugar water to mop up this time and no kid to get unlashed from a chair.

CHAPTER III

LIFE CHANGING EXPERIENCES

We all have to grow up one day, even little Jackie Papers who played with Puff the Magic Dragon. The first milestone in this process is graduation from high school. Frankly I never thought I'd live that long so I didn't do a lot of long range planning for the future. High school graduation is probably the happiest and the scariest occasion of one's life. When handed that diploma, you know you're not a kid anymore and college is just around the corner. There wasn't much thought of leaving home for the first time, but college meant it had to happen. It was done reluctantly, but done, and it eventually led to a degree as well as a wife and a date with Uncle Sam.

There were a few years before all this would happen, and they are without a doubt among my fondest while living in Hogansville. This chapter chronicles the story of how the two academic accomplishments occurred in spite of some things I and my friends did to put the doubt in our parents' minds we had the intellect to find our way out of town. It also gives one pause to think parents deserve a rest after eighteen years.

PART ONE:

EARLY TEEN YEARS

Teen years, need I say more? I suppose I should, and tell you I was a reasonably well behaved teenager, but I can't. I was nearly impossible to get up in the mornings; did things just to make sure my parents were on their toes; avoided responsibilities like house and yard work; and spent time in my room alone wondering why I had girl furniture. There was also time spent with my parents when there wasn't anything else to do. I managed to learn a few things about life, family and love from those episodes in spite of my lack of attention which still plagues me today.

It seems just about all teens of the 60's had delusions of being rock stars. Never mind the lack of musical talent you will read about from the high school band fiasco. My best friend's mother discovered he had a real musical talent for the guitar which I hoped was catching since we were nearly inseparable. As I learned, talent unlike childhood diseases isn't transferable.

GETTING UP IS HARD TO DO

When you think about it, why do we get up in the mornings? Well, usually it is because we have to do something; and that something is something we really don't want to do in the first place. That is unless you are a workaholic. I have no concept or knowledge of what constitutes a workaholic personality.

When I was a wee child I slept in a bedroom with no heat. The house was new but we just didn't have central heat; my parents never did until I moved out. I still wonder if that wasn't done on purpose. Anyway I didn't like getting up any better then than I do today. I wasn't much of a studentaholic either. In fact there isn't a lot of difference to me between why I had to get up then and why I have to get up today. School and now a job are places that tax my faculties more than I think necessary. What they amount to is a four letter word that has had bad connotations for me all my life, and I try not to say it in polite company. But you won't understand why I have a hard time getting up unless you know what that word is. It's WORK.

On those cold mornings back in the sixties when I was bundled up in my electric blanket with three pillows strategically placed for comfort, it would happen. I'd hear it out of the corner of my ear, noise. It began with banging of pots and pans coming from a distant part of the house. Low voices and indefinable kinds of sounds alerted my almost sleeping consciousness that it wouldn't be long before I would have to go on the defensive.

After what seemed like a short time, but probably was at least a half hour, I would sense that awful sound of the door to our den opening and see the half-light that signaled someone was coming into my room.

I knew who this would be as I unconsciously clutched the cover, getting ready to hold on for dear life. I never looked because if I did I'd compromise my position under the covers. Usually his first try would only net the disguised pillows. Then he'd hunt for my feet. He found most of the time a good tug on the toe would do it when I was really little. As I became a teenager the toe thing was just an annoyance I could overcome with sheer strength of jerking it back under the covers as he pulled me toward the floor. So he was forced to come up with a new tactic. The new tactic was the ultimate in callousness, uncaring and meanness toward one's offspring. My daddy would grab the covers at the top of the bed, regardless of whether it was me or the pillows that got uncovered first, and in a split second there was no cover left to grasp. Exposed for the world to see, worse yet to freeze in the subzero temperature in my unheated room, was my fragile body. Well, I'm not correct there, my body wasn't that fragile and I didn't freeze for long. His tactic worked extremely well but it did cause him to have to replace a few electric blankets over the years. I guess it was worth the cost as I never heard him complain.

I'd make for the warmth of the den and kitchen which were nice and cozy from the heat of the propane space heater. Of course, my daddy's new tactic only worked in the winter. When spring and summer came around, there had to be other methods of attack employed to wedge me from my cocoon. The bed stripping was still used but opening the curtains did it in the warmer climates when the sun was up sooner. I can't sleep in a room totally lit by sunlight; nature doubled-crossed me on that one. In fact I have a hard time sleeping where there is any kind of light in the room. When we are on vacation, my wife leaves the light on in the bathroom so she can navigate in unfamiliar surroundings. It takes me forever to get to sleep under those circumstances, but she has never fallen while on vacation. Well, at least not at night in our room.

When five thirty in the morning rolls around these days, my body is conditioned for what is about to happen. I'm partially awake when I hear out of that corner of my ear, the one that still works, a little a faint noise. This time it isn't pots and pans and low voices from the kitchen, it's a radio alarm blaring so loud it wakes up most of the neighborhood dogs, but to me it's still a faint noise. It still causes me to go on the defensive and I subconsciously grasp my sheet. I know he will be there soon. Then, right on cue it happens; I'm awake. I'm exposed to the world again. And so I get up to start another day of WORK. But this time he who jerks the covers off me isn't my daddy, he's me.

WRITER'S BLOCK

Here I am wanting to write something, but no subject comes to mind. I knew it would happen sooner or later, but I never prepared for it by filling computer disk with stories while the creative juices were flowing. It could be I haven't treated myself to a break from work to sit out in the back yard and do some serious day dreaming. It's been rather hectic at our house this summer and I haven't had much time to just sit and do nothing. Just like the race cars I watch on TV, I need to come in for a pit stop occasionally or else I'll run out of gas.

When I was a kid, I managed to find time to relax no matter what the situation. Things didn't appear as life threatening then as they do now. For instance one of my main summer jobs around the house was cutting the grass for my daddy while he worked. I dreaded that chore with a passion. Our yard up on North Highway was the size of two football fields, if you count the back. As a matter of fact the Gays, Bobby, Sidney Michael and I used to play football on the front lawn. The front yard amounted to a practice field in comparison to the backyard which matched Bobby Dodd Stadium in acreage.

Now that I look back on it cutting the grass wasn't that bad, as I got to do it with a riding lawnmower. Considering I was too young to drive the family car, the lawnmower was a real thrill. There was one small problem though – well, it wasn't that small. Getting me out of bed required a couple of charges of dynamite and a threat to cut off my allowance until I reached college age. Even then it was a struggle for my mother to pull me physically from the sheets in the summer after daddy had gone to work. After all the preparation necessary to get psyched up to begin grass cutting, it would be around noon. By then I knew I'd better begin if I wanted to make it look like I had a go at trying to follow my daddy's orders.

Once I got the lawnmower cranked, after coming close to doing permanent muscle damage to my arms, I would grab the shift knob and pretend I was Fireball Roberts. Running at full throttle I'd hit the track, I mean the yard. My pre-race preparations included pouring a half bottle of Coppertone on my shirtless body, grabbing my baseball cap and sun glasses, and a coke. The riding lawnmower was a Sears and Roebuck special our neighbor Luby was kind enough to haul back from Atlanta on his truck for us when he bought his. It had a steering wheel like a car so I could do my balancing act with the coke and drive at the same time. Lawn mowers of the fifties didn't come with cupholders. It's also a good thing we didn't have cell phones then, or I might not be here to tell this story.

The mowing process in spite of my cutting edge (pun) driving was painfully slow. About three o'clock I'd break to cool off in the house. Needless to say when daddy got home he had to pitch in. My response was, "I saved you some to cut. I knew you would want me to." He was very grateful to say the least. Daddy would grab the push mower and trim around the house. If I still hadn't finished the back, he would start on that too.

We were a team, me and my daddy. The grass cutting brought us together more than any other activity, well except hauling water to the garden. Then that too is another story. And when it was all over with and we got cleaned up, we'd sit on the side porch to cool off, relax and watch the cars on Highway 29. We had just as much to do then in Hogansville as I do now here in Kennesaw; nevertheless we made time to relax and communicate. So from now on I'm going to treat myself to that break in the back yard after a long day's work. Just sitting with my wife, relaxing, and watching the world go by no matter how hectic things may become. It might not cure my communication problem (writer's block), and things might get slightly off schedule, but it's a pit stop that might see me through to the end of the race.

IN MY ROOM, THEN AND NOW

If you are my age, then no doubt you've heard of the Beach Boys. Maybe even if you aren't my age, you've heard of them. I think they still perform on occasion when they have good days at the home. Actually not too many of the original group is left, but I have the CD of their greatest hits in both cars. And on a sunny warm day, it's good to put down the windows and listen to a little of my youth. That youth of mine was spent mostly in two places, school and my room.

Having your own room in those days was tantamount to having a BMW or Mercedes in the school parking lot today. Of course I know only a few who can afford these cars in their garages, much less buy them for their kids. But you just weren't on the "cool" register in the 60's unless you had your own room. Of course when my parents built the small ranch house up on North Highway, they made sure to designate one of the bedrooms as specifically mine. I'm afraid even though it was my room it got repossessed for guest and relatives on a regular basis. This meant I didn't have my own furniture or curtains and mother chose the pictures on the walls. I did get to put the uneven bookcase built during my freshman year of shop in the room to display my model cars and airplanes. I'm still jealous of Frankie Bryant who had real guy furniture and curtains, and could put up posters and place his models wherever he liked in his room.

About the only thing masculine in my room was a square light fixture that had colorful parrots on it. Or were they Parakeets? But it wasn't the contents of the room that made it mine, it was as the Beach Boys say in their song, ". . . a place where I can go and tell my troubles to. . ." There was nothing like going into that room on those days when things didn't go so well at school or when my parents "just didn't understand." I'd stretch out on the bed and play forty-five rpm's on that little record player that looked like a small piece of luggage when it was shut, and drift off into another world. If only I had had a desire to write, then I might have been a famous novelist today. I took trips and had adventures that only came about in an adolescent mind with no worries. My wife says I have the capability to write those novels today. Huh, we'll see.

There is a time, I believe, when we all need "our room" to get away from life and its problems only if it's for a short time. The Simon and Garfunkle tune "I Am a Rock" talks about having ". . . my books and poetry to protect me." Well, I'm not the intellectual type but I had, and still have, things in my room that make me feel protected and sustained. As I sit here I get the same good feeling I had in my room forty years ago. All my stuff is here, even the model cars and books, but unfortunately no poetry save that English pamphlet from seventh grade. All this in one room where I can just come and shut the door to recharge so I can go out later and face whatever life brings. I still have to share my room though, but I don't mind it at all. My wife's art table is here but at least I have pictures of my own choosing on the walls, desk and bookshelves. The most important part of having my own room again is I can come here anytime I want and dream at my computer instead of on the bed, and be in my own little world much like the Beach Boy's song implies. Wonder if I can squeeze a decent forty-five rpm record player in here?

BRUNSWICK STEW

What! Did someone mention L.B.? Well, they may as well have. Those initials are synonymous with Brunswick Stew. If you don't know the L.B I speak of, then you haven't lived in Hogansville and you've missed the treat of your life. To deliver some news to you who never tasted his stew, I'm talking about L.B. Jackson's. You can eat Brunswick Stew forever but you'll never taste the real thing until you've put a spoonful of that delectable stuff in your mouth. I believe I heard L.B. took his stew making talents to a better place a few years back. If this isn't so, then there's still a chance for you laggers. If it is, then let's hope someone still has that recipe written down somewhere.

What brought all this to mind was a short stay at my uncle's in LaGrange. My cousin and uncle live in the same house and neither of them are in good health. In fact, my cousin is so diabetic that he can't be left alone. So when my uncle went into the hospital for surgery, I went down for a few days to watch after my cousin. Those two bachelors were pretty set in their ways and even though my cousin was very sick, he ate what he wanted to eat. And one of those things was Brunswick Stew. Unfortunately he never tasted L.B.'s stew, but he did know where to get some that rivals, if not nearly equals, it. Just looking at this stuff told me I might once again taste L.B.'s touch. I wasn't disappointed in the stew, but I was disappointed even though its taste was heavenly, that it didn't bring back L.B. or those days that just "made" the stew.

What did bring back those days was my memory of occasions that called for such things as Brunswick Stew. The Sportsman's Club was the number one purveyor of L.B.'s culinary gem.

They always had a barbecue on weekends just off the Blue Creek Road at the lake. I can't remember the name of the lake but I can remember it was big and there was supposed to be a lot of alligators there. Now that I think back on it, all I can remember seeing was a cottonmouth in the little branch that ran parallel to its shore. You had to cross a small bridge over the thing to get to the lake. But before you got to the lake there were shelters with concrete tables and large barbecue pits scattered about a cleared off area; I was still leery of snakes and those ever quick 'gators even through that area. There were a lot of guys like my daddy: Boots Lankford, Buck Smith and Jackson from Belks who helped out. Naturally L.B. was there and so was the delectable stew. It came in three sizes: pint, quart and jumbo (a gallon to you). We always got the quart as it lasted about a week. Why? Because my mother worked the second shift and daddy didn't like to cook. "Besides," he would say, "if you have L.B.'s stew, why would you need to cook?" It was good with a slice of Colonial bread and coleslaw. Well okay, potato chips for me. But even if I didn't have the chips, it went perfect with just the pint of chocolate milk I always accompanied it with. Don't try to envision this as it will only do things to your mind I can't be responsible for. You could gain weight just reading about it.

   The other big event where L.B.'s stew was always prevalent was the annual F.F.A. Barbecue Chicken Grilling. It used to be held on the little street that ran by Jap Keith's Store and Granger Field. The cinder blocks were arrayed in long parallel lines and the charcoal briquettes spread generously in between. Then the grill master Mr. V.R. Stephens and his helpers would grease the huge metal racks and pin the chicken halves between them. The racks would be placed over the white-hot coals, and the aroma permeated the whole town. I don't see how the Martins, Artleys and all the other people in the nearby houses kept from drooling to death over the eight or so hours that the barbecue lasted. The old baseball field would be covered with people and the feasting went on into the night, creating one of Hogansville's rare traffic jams. I remember it doubled Keith Brother's grocery business. They sold a lot of dessert stuff (candy) to both adults and us kids. Of course as I grew older, I found myself being a worker more than an eater. Nevertheless, I always saved room for L.B.'s stew and took a little more home too.

The Brunswick Stew was so good that after a while L.B. didn't need an excuse like a barbecue event to make the stuff. He just did it when he felt like it, and no advertising was necessary. There was always someone asking when L.B. was going to make another batch of the stuff. It was more popular than "moon" and it was legal too. I miss those white cardboard tube cartons and moreover I miss L.B. He was a mountain of a man who was loud and friendly and never forgot to speak. He seemed to enjoy life and us kids, as well as making stew.

Remembering my brush with greatness-in-stew-making, renewing the feeling with a taste of the stew my cousin would buy, and just today talking with a colleague about what to do in retirement all culminated in this thought. If I can find that recipe of L.B.'s, and there aren't any copyright infringements involved, I'll make more money in retirement than I ever made working. And making stew, as with L.B., will be a labor of love instead of work.

TELLING CIVIL WAR STORIES

This weekend I attended a Civil War Symposium at Kennesaw State University, a place I haven't been since I was Assistant Registrar there when it was simply known as Kennesaw College. I got lost trying to find the visitor's parking lot. When I worked there we had visitor's parking spaces, two of them. Needless to say, it's not the same place I left and probably a good thing because the room where the symposium was held is bigger than the gym during my tenure.

There were four professor/historians at the symposium that

spoke and then discussed their topics with those of us who came to listen. During the discussion one of the professors said something that probably went over most everyone's heads except mine, and it's because it hit a familiar note. He said the Civil War is receding in the collective memory of Americans because they do not live as family groups anymore and therefore do not get to hear stories that are passed down from their elders. He went on to say more Southerners are leaving home and living in other cities and states. Well, I can't argue with that since you know where I live, and I haven't been in Hogansville fulltime since 1964. But I did have the benefit of some of the stories passed down because the generation before me and those prior to it, that all the way back to "The War Between the States" as mother called it, lived within miles of each other all their lives.

Mother was the storyteller of the family, and rightfully, since no one in the Dale family can trace further back than the late 1800's. They aren't easy to find but I am still diligently on their trail. She told her stories to me and daddy while we sat on our porch on summer weekends and waved at neighbors and acquaintances passing on Highway 29. She mainly reminisced about her Grandma Hines. She told the story of her grandmother just before the war when she began walking through woods to take food to an old neighbor lady and was stopped by a run-a-way slave who threatened to cut her throat if she told anyone she saw him there. Fortunately he was apprehended and Grandma Hines was later able to relate the incident to the family. Then mother would get my full attention when she told the story of Grandma Hines hiding her pony in the woods for three days until the Yankees passed through. Her daddy came home from the war and told her they were not far behind him and they were taking all the crops and livestock from the farms.

I often wondered why Grandma Hines' daddy came home from the war before it was over. I feared he may have deserted, but it wasn't until later when I did research I learned he was wounded at The Battle of Jonesboro and was sent home to recover. Fortunately for him, the war was over before he was well enough to go back. Mother says Grandma Hines's mother made him take off his uniform and bathe in the creek to get rid of body lice before allowing him in the house. Also, he had to boil his uniform in a black cast iron pot in the yard. Life wasn't easy then and I've made sure to pass these stories and others down to my daughter who I know will do the same with her twin daughters. Maybe we have lost a bit of our past by living too fast today, as there are fewer porches to rock on and more people talking to each other on cell phones than in person. Maybe there are family stories you know, so think about writing them down and passing them on before they too become lost forever from our collective memory.

WAGNER ON WAGNER

Bands have always intrigued me because in war movies armies had musicians marching up front playing stirring tunes while leading troops into battle. My childhood dream was to be a military officer carrying a saber and wearing a uniform with a big yellow stripe down each leg, while riding a white charger. But I needed an alternate plan just in case Cavalry wasn't needed anymore. That alternate was, I thought, the ability to play a musical instrument. I didn't know then that officers were the directors and not members of the band.

So I began to think about what kind of instrument I wanted to play. It was obvious from the start, since Cavalry always blew bugles. But bugles were not in the band at school. Then I remembered I had gotten a genuine plastic gold painted trumpet one Christmas. The thing worked just like a real one. It had a little music stand attached just behind the valve taps and even a little relief valve for, well you know. I could play things like "Red River Valley." Well, I can't think of anymore tunes I could play but I was good on "Red River Valley." It seemed to me playing the trumpet would be a cinch and I'd have it licked in a week or so. I was in sixth grade when I signed up for band. The junior high school was not part of the high school, so band gave us a rare opportunity to mingle with upper classmen who could actually play their instruments. I constantly watched the band trumpeters at their work and didn't know if I'd ever have that much wind. I'm not a politician today, so that might give you a clue.

High strung is the way most creative people are described and that was used in the book I read about Wagner, Richard that is, and not Leonard our band instructor. I remember Leonard was also high strung to the point any sour note or miscue would put you in dire straits. He was a short thin man with very little hair on top. When he didn't wear a white shirt and black tie and pants, he wore a checked short-sleeved shirt and black pants. I don't think he ever had pants any other color. He liked to compose, similar to Richard who could have been his ancestor. I got the impression he fancied himself quite an original composer, and I personally liked some of his stuff. He did a great job on "The Boys from HHS." It turned out to be a pretty good football fight song but it really didn't suit his classical style. He never let us practice a real song, something with a tune. It was always a classic by some writer who I now know to be Beethoven or Brahms, or whoever. Mister Wagner, like his namesake in classical music, demanded strict attention and impeccable behavior from his students when giving lessons.

So this is the situation Lamar, Franklin and I found ourselves in when we decided to join the band. Lamar and I were dead set on the trumpet and Franklin, looking something like "Our Gang's" Froggy with the round wire rimed thick glasses, decided the trombone was his instrument of choice. We religiously attended practice even though it was after school. Being in that building after everyone except those incarcerated for talking, chewing gum, and general nuisance had left was really troubling to me. I knew it wasn't punishment, but I didn't like staying after school for whatever reason.

We usually sat for fifteen or twenty minutes waiting for Mr. Wagner to appear, as was the case on almost every occasion of our practice sessions. Being rambunctious, we three decided to improvise in a highly original fashion while awaiting our teacher. Lamar and I discovered the trumpet has a much louder and shriller sounding tone if you take the mouth piece off. So being former cavalrymen in another life we decided to learn to blow "charge" without a mouthpiece. This never failed to bring Mr. Wagner earlier than his finicky feet dragging arrivals. I think finally having had enough of us, he politely, as politely as his high strung personality would allow, advised us to seek a new interest. Needless to say I never learned to play trumpet and neither did Lamar. Franklin was able to control the trombone and play a few things but his heart was never in the instrument. It's hard to explain why Mr. Wagner tried to make us into classical artists, but whatever his reasons the band was always impressive at our football games.

PART TWO:

HIGH SCHOOL AND COLLEGE:

A DECLARATION OF INDEPENDENCE

What is the one thing you can think of that is synonymous with teens and independence? Well, in today's world there are more than a few things to choose from but in the mid-sixties it was without a doubt driving a car without your parents present. Getting a real license to drive combined with a radio blasting out groups like The Beach Boys, Jan and Dean, and Ronnie and the Daytona's singing about GTOs, shiny red super stock Dodges, Little Duce Coupes, T-Birds, and 409's was an explosive combination when a teen was climbing behind the wheel for the first time. But before driving, there were a few other adventures, a couple that would prove I should not seek carpentry or farming as a profession, and definitely not a musical career.

All right, yes, there is just one more major thing synonymous with teens in the evolving "let it all hang out sixties" and other times as well, and that would be the opposite sex. From first to last love, emotions ran high on the hormone indicator ranging from complete euphoria to deep depression. When you are young, recovery from heartache is much quicker when one realizes there are others out there who may have been overlooked while you were occupied in a long term relationship. If you believe that I have some land in Florida . . .

I recall high school graduation like it was yesterday. Considering my mental maturity, it could have been yesterday. I'm still not too sure I survived college. To use a phrase popular today, "What happens in college stays in college." Glad it does because there aren't too many of those stories I can safely relate and hope one day to run for elective office. Nevertheless, I eventually buckled down and earned a Bachelor's Degree.

J.B., LAMAR, AND ME

Shortly after the fiasco with none other than Leonard Wagner, chief bandmaster and worshiper of the classics, the three of us decided that perhaps music was not our destiny. I mean Franklin, Lamar and myself. I don't know about Franklin, but Lamar was definitely not displaying the latent musical talent that lurked beneath his tough skin. Me? As I've said before, not a musical bone anywhere. I didn't know that at the time we all signed up for band. I did have an inkling it might take a little additional effort on my part to find talent after I was summarily dismissed by Mr. Wagner. So one very expensive musical career came to and end.

My daddy told me if he ever paid money for another musical

instrument he would murder me with it if I didn't learn something. I knew no court would find him guilty for preserving his sanity. It wasn't long before Lamar, sitting at his mother's piano, suddenly began to play Ray Charles. Neither he nor I understood why he could do this. So if Lamar could do it, then why not me? Of course, Lamar's mother knew a special gift was there and she set out to develop it.

Elizabeth, Lamar's mother, picked up the phone and called the Hogansville resident musical guru, none other than J.B. I had my mother do the same. At the risk of desecrating those no longer with us, I won't tell you J.B.'s last name. He was a natural guitar player who started back in the forties. He even got to Hollywood and starred with Don "Red" Barry in "Jesse James' Women." Well he really didn't star. He just got shot by Red Barry. J.B. was the bartender who went for a shotgun to get Jesse. You know the rest, don't you? I saw the movie and thought J.B. did an admirable job falling all over the bar and through the mirror before he died.

J.B. lived with his mother on International Avenue. I never figured out how he made a living since he was dedicated to practicing guitar eight hours a day. I suppose he earned his keep by giving guitar lessons to folks like Lamar, me and a few others. He did have some cool runs and always put his cigarette in the strings at the end of the neck next to the tuning keys. It was wide enough there to hold the filter and not squash the tobacco. He said musicians in Hollywood jam sessions always did that. The smoke obscured some of the chords he tried to teach me and maybe that's why I never learned them all. J.B. kept me on a year before he decided that eating had too high a price.

True to his word, my daddy was ever vigilant of my success. He was alright with buying me a Sears and Roebuck special Silvertone electric blue and cream flat top box. It was much less expensive than the trumpet he had to buy for band. It was beautiful and played like a champ for those who could play it. Even Luby, my next door neighbor and another talented musician, lusted after that guitar. As I recollect he eventually got it and saved me from an early grave, because my daddy got his money back. However I had learned enough to be dangerous and I needed a serious weapon for the sixties, an electric guitar and amplifier. Once I got these monsters using my own money, and benefiting from a year's worth of J.B.'s knowledge, I was on my way, but I didn't exactly know where. My daddy said anywhere but our house. That was okay with me because that house had bad acoustics anyway. But as I would find out a few years later, Mr. Stephen's cabin didn't.

HOWLING AT THE MOON

It got pretty laid back in Hogansville, especially in the summertime. Living out on North Highway even with the traffic from Atlanta, evenings were soothing until some hound decided he had to let his presence be known. Hounds howl at the moon for different reasons and I've never quite understood their primeval need to do this. But when a man howls at the moon this needs to be investigated further.

Our neighbor Luby, back in Hogansville, was a jack of all trades. Not only did he have one of the best restored '50 Ford trucks in the county, he built a garage he never parked it in, a room on his house, and a screen porch on the back where he did a right smart of howling. Luby was a real good singer but this sound had definite sad undertones. The reason for this howling I thought was due to Luby's marriage ending and leaving him sad and lonely, missing family life and his son.

Luby had been in a country western band where he played guitar and drums on weekends. After he was left alone, he took to sitting out on the back porch that faced our side porch where my family and I sometimes sat in warm weather. Every once in a while my daddy and I would hear this low moan and eventually it developed into a longer one that sounded something like one of those hounds. We suspected it was something more when we heard a guitar accompaniment. Since it was usually about dark when this would start we couldn't be sure what it was. All we knew was it was coming from the direction of Luby's house.

The guitar was Luby's weapon of choice to assist his howling as he figured the drums might be just a little too much for the neighbors. Besides, it wouldn't do any good to howl if you couldn't hear yourself. If howling is to be done properly it must be done where it can be heard with real hurt, the right frame of mind and the right accompaniment or you are wasting your time. And if you don't know all the words to the songs or when to change chords, you can absolutely ruin a good howl. Well, that was no problem for Luby as he knew all the chords and words to every Hank Williams crying song ever written, not to mention quite a few others. His repertoire was long and included such lyrics as these:

"Once a day every day all day long
and once a night from dust till dawn,

I'm missing you since you've been gone,
once a day every day all day long."

This stuff could depress Norman Vincent Peal. Just writing the lyrics again almost brought me to tears, and it's been close to thirty years since I helped Luby howl them. If that wasn't enough, when Luby really got going he brought out the heavy artillery, George Jones. George could sound like he was crying in his beer even when he and Tammy were on the up and up. But he didn't hold a candle to Luby when there was Patsy Cline's "Crazy," "Sweet Dreams," "Walking after Midnight," and the big one "I Fall to Pieces." He could really hit the high notes on those and sometimes they were better than when his truck engine broke loose from the mounts and fell on his chest.

Luby had a chain pulley that was hanging over a limb of the big old Pecan tree next to the driveway. What really happened was when Luby climbed under the truck to loosen the motor from the mounts so he could lift it out with the pulley, the limb cracked. The engine dropped and the chain pulley caught it just in time, but Luby was trapped under the truck. This caused him to release a really good combination rebel yell and howl. Pain or not, it was good enough to bring my daddy out of the house where he stopped two cars on the highway to get help with the pulley so Luby could crawl out.

One time my daddy told me, "You ought to go on over there and keep Luby a little company and maybe you might learn how to play your guitar." My guitar was a thirty five dollar Sears Silvertone flat top box. That's the kind of guitar that doesn't have a hole in the center. It has two little slits in the body on either side of the strings that looks like an S. I remember it being a pretty sweet blue and cream instrument, and it had the thinnest neck of any guitar I've owned before or since. This did not go unnoticed by Luby either. When the howling started I grabbed my guitar and headed over. Luby showed me chords and told me to make them on his guitar as I had to be able to play any of them and not just my own. Then he'd take mine and go at it, howling Willie, Waylon, George, Patsy and whoever else he felt could convey his morose and melancholy mood. Luby always told me to remember him when I decided to sell that Silvertone.

As luck would have it Luby wasn't always to remain lonely. When he met, fell in love with, and married Ethyl the howling stopped. However before that happened I learned a bunch of good chords, runs and songs. Above all I really learned how to howl. We had gotten so used to all that howling and when it stopped, my daddy told me he was gonna get a hound to take up where Luby left off. Oh, before I forgot to tell you, it wasn't long after that I woke up to rock-n-roll. You don't need to know how to play guitar or howl with that kind of music. All you need to know is how to make noise. The flat top box Silvertone couldn't make enough noise, but a Silvertone single pick-up I managed to get with a modest increase in my allowance and my job at the mill during the summer could do the job. Luby got the Silvertone flat top box and I got the electric and we went our separate ways musically. Now that I've gotten older and gotten over rock-n-roll I'm back to playing an acoustic guitar. So I guess I need to practice howling at the moon, but just now I don't have anything to howl about. I wonder if my cat would mind if I supplied her with a hound dog companion. Nah, she likes her quiet.

HAVE YOU BEEN TO THE ROCK HOLE, JIMMY?

After I passed Calvin Hipp's swimming course at the Community Building pool, I was ready to take on any body of water. My mother wasn't as sure as I was, so she was careful to monitor my swimming activities. I was an only child and she didn't want to lose me just yet.

Mother knew it wasn't an option to take Tony along to save my life every time I swam. You remember Tony? He rescued me during swimming lessons. So she decided she and my daddy had to accompany me every time I got into the water. It wasn't such a bad idea when we went to the ocean. Although I didn't get a lot of warm and fuzzy feelings about my life guard parents' capabilities after Preacher Webb had to drag me and daddy from the surf at Myrtle Beach. Why didn't he tell me he couldn't swim? It took a while to get them to understand I might swim better than at least one of them and about as good as the other. It took awhile but they finally got the message and let me go without them. Glad we didn't have to do it this way when I started dating.

My parents lost their fear of my swimming alone at the Grantville and LaGrange pools but always warned me about the one place I was not allowed to go, "The Rock Hole." My daddy took me there once while mother was at work and gave me the complete rundown on the place. According to him, legend has it the place is bottomless. It was once a granite quarry. One day the train that was being loaded there was swallowed up by a massive earth slide. All that was left was a pristine lake that now stands at the bottom of a shear rock cliff.

By the way, the cliff made for a great diving platform. Don't tell my mother about this, okay? When we were around twelve, my friend Lamar and I made a few expeditions to the Rock Hole just to check the place out a little closer. It was always spooky and dark in the shadow of the cliff. The jet black water also added to the eeriness and every time I looked at its mirrored surface I remembered all those tales from my daddy about divers looking for the train and not being able to go deep enough to find it. There was also a story going around about a lady who committed suicide by driving her car into the dark waters. They found the car but never found her. So how did they know it was suicide?

You have always heard about the impossible teenage years? Well, in the early sixties there were sixty two of us in my high school class. We had our own logic and swimming had to be done dangerously or not at all. We, I mean they, would go up every weekend and swim in the cold water. You had to be careful when you dived from the cliff because there was a place just under the water where some of the quarry didn't choose to sink with the rest of it. Someone would always stand on that part and invite us on the shore to wade out and join them. I found, I mean they found, out differently when they tried to wade out to the clown standing on the rock.

If diving from the cliff wasn't scary enough, it beat falling from it as one of my classmates discovered. It took a long time to recover from the broken back she sustained. I saw her at the homecoming reunion last year and I'm glad to report she is still doing well. This episode kinda spelled the beginning of the end for the Rock Hole. T and the boys from the city police began to patrol it a lot more after that incident, and it could be us, I mean those, kids learned something from our unfortunate classmate. Whatever the reason, the Rock Hole began to lose its attraction.

My favorite route into Hogansville is down HWY 29 from the Grantville exit off I-85. Each time I make the trip down to see mother I look for the pull-off to the Rock Hole. The good times there are not forgotten nor are the bad ones. It might be someone's private property now but it will always belong to us kids, if you know what I mean.

OH PIG OF MINE

A remembrance of mine from the movie "State Fair" was when Tom Ewell sang "Oh Hog of Mine" to Blue Boy, his spoiled swine which he hoped would win him a blue ribbon. Well, Tom didn't get the blue ribbon because Blue Boy acted just like Custer Elizabeth, both of them being cut from the same mold. They bit the stick carried by their loyal and much abused owners. The judges didn't take too kindly to that lack of discipline and it cost everything.

So begins this somewhat dismal tale, or tail may be more appropriate for this one. Now Hogansville could be considered country by someone from Atlanta, but it was city as far as I was concerned. Country to me was south of LaGrange at Abbott's Ford which currently resides at the bottom of Lake West Point. Looking at it from that view point, I wasn't a country boy, I was somewhere in between that and a city slicker. At Hogansville High School you had to choose between two vocational subjects to take in order to graduate. Since I wasn't big on home economics and cooking then, I chose vocational agriculture. Strange, today I watch cooking shows on TV and help vacuum floors every other weekend. What's worse is I'm beginning to look forward to both of them.

I really didn't want to be a farmer either. But to appease Mr. Stephens, our local shop teacher and Future Farmer's of America (FFA) advisor, and also to pass the subject I reluctantly joined the FFA. It was, I guess, similar to 4-H since I stayed away from that one too. Being in the FFA provided the benefit of buying a blue corduroy jacket with your name embroidered in gold on the front left breast and a giant FFA symbol stitched to the back. I believe it also had the name of your chapter on it too. Anyway we got to wear these to show our membership. Believe me, they were nowhere near as appealing to girls as the green football jackets with the big white "H" sewn on the left front breast.

The second benefit to being in the FFA was getting to do a project. You can imagine how thrilled I was to hear I had to do a project. I didn't realize the project had to breathe and be fed and watered. Since my dog didn't qualify as an FFA project, I was forced to consider some kind of farm animal. We couldn't afford to fence the whole area behind the house that went to the railroad track, so a cow was out. My mother refused to let me raise chickens because our dog had a real taste for them. That left one thing we could afford fencing for and the dog wouldn't eat. It was a pig. The only thing "pig" I had ever had much contact with was what was served for breakfast at the Bowen's when we went to Abbots Ford. I knew what pigs looked like, and I remembered they like to get filthy in mud and usually ate something we called slop. That stuff looked as bad as the name sounds. But the dye had been cast and my daddy and I began in earnest building a pig pen right next to the two cedar trees that could be used as scratching posts, and just before the drop off to the railroad track. It was far enough from the house we would avoid any obnoxious odor, and yet we could see it to make sure everything was all right. What kind of trouble can a pig get into anyway? Well, I think my daddy had the idea of it escaping and that's why we needed to see it.

The little Poland China pig was cute when it was a baby. It

looked like a little Panda bear with osteoporosis. I never understood the connection of Poland China with black and white. Maybe there is no connection at all. It seemed to like its surroundings with the exception of the three times a day and two at night passing of trains. It made weird noises after the trains got by. The first order of the day once the pig was settled in was to name it. Since it was female it was going to be hard for me to pick a name, all my heroes were guys. Remember this was the early sixties. I decided since my neighbor's daughter and I got along so well (ha!) I would honor her by allowing my pig to receive her name. But just the same I was going to give that pig a guy's name too. So the little pig became Custer Elizabeth. Custer, for none other than George Armstrong of the Little Big Horn Massacre that happened somewhere in Montana.

Soon after we adjusted to Custer Elizabeth, whom I called Custer for short, I found her taste in slop was changing. She rejected her food and this meant money spent on a vet. The vet found nothing wrong with the pig and gave no relief as to solving her non-eating problem. Mother, feeling sorry for it, decided to take its wheat and bake it in an iron skillet similar to making corn bread. Feeding this to Custer was like bringing back the sunshine, meaning she really took a shine to this food. In fact, she refused to eat any uncooked food again. This meant mother cooking a pone of this stuff daily and me feeding it to a now spoiled pig. Custer was definitely high strung. She demanded her mud hole be continuously filled with fresh water. This meant I had to carry tubs of water to her daily. My daddy was still having war with the city water department, so we still depended on well water. This meant a hose for watering wouldn't work.

The pig got bigger and more defiant as time went on, but Mr. Stephens was very pleased when he visited and saw how well shaped she was. Is this man all right? It looked like a pig to me, and they all pretty much are the same shape. I was glad because he was glad. I never figured out what I was doing right. It must have been the cooked slop. The problem was that Custer, like her namesake, never took well to discipline. I tried in earnest to get the pig used to the stick to guide her for competition. But she thought the thing was tickling her and so she always bit it. After turning red in the face several time and banging his first two fingers into his forehead very hard, Mr. Stephens would say, "Jimmy, Jimmy, Jimmy, you've got to work with her to get her to mind you." I wondered sometimes if Mr. Stephens didn't give himself headaches from that; or perchance I caused him to give himself headaches by making him do it. Either way, I think he enjoyed it or he wouldn't have done it so much.

Finally the day came when we were to go to the Southeastern Fair in Atlanta. Obviously Custer couldn't go on the bus with me, and just as well, as she probably would have bitten Robert W. for turning our brand new Dodge bus around in the middle of the interstate highway because he went past the exit. Can you imagine that today on I-20? I can because I drive the interstates every day, and I don't want to think about it. It was almost easy to forget I had a mission at the fair as I rode everything and saw tons of sideshows. I guess eating the corn dogs and cotton candy was the most fun.

I could never get the competition of that afternoon completely clear of my mind though and my jumpy stomach was evidence. It came sooner than I wanted it too. I had just eaten one more corn dog than my stomach could handle. Just as I opened the gate to greet Custer, I lost my lunch. She seemed to take it as an insult. This was not a good sign and from that point on the pig and I gave the worst performance of our lives. She bit the stick and I couldn't stand up straight or I'd throw up again. Mister Stephens had about burst a blood vessel with those two fingers, and I wasn't sure Robert wouldn't turn the bus around on the interstate going home. That evening lasted two years, and after I had managed to herd Custer back into the stall (she liked the open area in front of the judges), I collapsed in misery. I frankly don't remember if the bus turned around on the freeway again or not. I was spared from knowing because God granted me the grace of sleeping it off on the way home.

Project or no project, after what she did to her litter of piglets, I decided to let daddy sell Custer to our neighbor Luby. A few weeks later Luby was kind enough to offer us some sausage, but we didn't accept. It seems to me as I now look back, if you are endowed with the name Custer you meet an untimely demise. Perhaps that part of the name was the problem all along? Oh pig of mine!

TED AND LARRY JOE

Every time I pass the Mobley Bridge Road intersection with Highway 29, I can't help thinking of Hogansville's checkered past with fast cars and the kids that drove them. Of course, the Mobley Bridge Road was once known, in the 50's anyway, as the ultimate road course and possessor of a stretch known as Deadman's Curve. I can't say with certainty but I believe it was the late Max C. that provided the legacy for that title. You see, road courses are curvy roads that require an agile car with quick and accurate steering like a sports car. The American cars of the 50's and 60's were long on styling but short on agility, and that's where Max made his fatal mistake. His cream yellow and white '55 Ford Victoria couldn't negotiate the curve, and it and Max wound up in someone's stand of hardwoods. Neither survived the crash.

That incident was the awakening of speed in my life. I was probably about eleven or twelve then. But again it may have started at the age of six standing in the front seat of our car (don't tell Ralph Nader) going to LaGrange every Saturday. I could identify almost every car we met. By the time we lost Max, I could not only tell you what kind of car but the trim line of the car, you know, like the difference between a Bell Air and a Two Ten. Anyway by nineteen sixty the dynamic duo, to steal a phrase, was beginning to make the scene in the Hogansville annals of speed; and the stylists at Ford and GM blossomed.

The classic battle between Chevy and Ford was at its peak between Hogansville's two car dealers: Hines Motor Company (Chevy) and Ralls Motor Company (Ford). This competition was personified by Ted and Larry Joe. Ted drove a blood red '60 Ford Starliner and Larry Joe a jet black (white stripe) '60 Impala two-door hardtop. Now, both these guys came from well-to-do families, at least by Hogansville standards. Ted's daddy ran a service station and taxi service. The taxi service was the same one that employed the famous Nim Childers and his always slick Chevy Biscayne. It seemed like Nim washed it after every fare, and the custom hub caps and white walls set it off perfectly. Anyway, Ted was the exact opposite of Larry Joe. He was blonde haired and thin to Larry Joe's black hair and slightly stocky build.

The two guys did share some things in common: their ducktail haircuts, jeans with white socks, and checked shirts. But then again who in the late 50's and early 60's didn't dress like that? They also had no trouble with the girls, and having the fastest cars in town didn't hurt either. Speaking of girls, wasn't I? Well, I don't recall Ted having a steady but Larry Joe and Luanne were definitely the couple during that time.

Larry Joe and Ted usually made their presence known on Main Street most Saturday nights. The really big thing in Hogansville then was for any kind of "hot" machine to park uptown in front of the Rexall Drug Store at about dusk. Some of the guys even brought dates. The idea was to stand around and look cool, make bets as to who had the fastest car, and chew tooth picks. Sometimes someone would get in their car and rev the engine to hear the sound made by a slightly loosened muffler. This didn't sit well with T, the chief of police, who was quick to appear on the scene to keep down the noise. Naturally the kids didn't like this and a few would usually throw "fireballs" under T's police cruiser's tires to make him think he had a flat. Fireballs were little round balls you got at Jap Keith's or Boots Parham's stores. They had a cap inside and when you threw them down on pavement they exploded making a popping sound. T could never find out who did it because no one admitted to the blame. Would you?

Then right at eleven o'clock, just when most of the guys were so sleepy that being cool was overcome by efforts to stay awake, Ted and Larry Joe would whistle through town in a mock drag race with their dates beaming from ear to ear; and the sounds of pure power would bring everyone back from the brink of sleep. I don't know why they would always wait so late but it seemed to coincide with the ending of T's shift. The appearance of the two local celebrities was well worth the wait. By the way, no one ever got hurt. That is until Larry Joe got the infamous Corvair Spyder. Where was Nader then? Oh well, that's another story.

GIVE ME FIVE GALLONS, DOC

That's the amount of gas I always asked Doc McVey to put in my daddy's car when I stopped at Bad Eye Cardin's Texaco Station. It sounded good because that was also the amount daddy would always ask for when he took my mother to visit relatives in LaGrange. I can't figure why he just didn't have Doc fill the car up because he could afford it. I knew five gallons never amounted to more than a buck ninety five and that left me with over five dollars for my date. So that was my reason for never exceeding the nice round number I requested with authority.

We didn't have credit cards then but we did have credit. When my funds ran low and my romances high, daddy would authorize Bad Eye to let me charge to his bill so I could make that date. I'd walk into the office and sign the little ticket book like it was my own account. Bad Eye would open his big metal ledger and put the signed ticket in one of the little wire clipped pockets, and once a week daddy would go by and pay his bill. The station was immaculately cared for and I always got a kick out of the pin-up calendar that hung over the desk. While Bad Eye was filing my ticket, I took a little peak at the month's layout.

When Doc wasn't pumping gas and calling me "Tommy" Dale, he was repairing a tire or changing someone's oil in one of the two service bays. The bays were stocked with crates of Coca Cola, all kinds of motor belts, lubricants and tires. The tires were hung overhead just out of the way of the lift. If your car needed a quick repair, you didn't have to go to the dealer because Doc fixed it while you waited. You'd put a nickel in the coke machine out front and watch a few cars pull in and out, and then Doc would be there with your keys. Sometimes while we waited for repairs daddy and "Bad Eye" would chew the fat and I'd get a better look at the future months in the calendar, or go back and watch Doc run the hydraulic lift.

It wasn't always fun for the guys at the Texaco, especially in winter. I never had to leave the car when it was cold because Doc was always there wearing his Russian style cap with ear muffs, ready to pump my five gallons, clean the windshield and check the oil. In thirty degree weather he performed with the same efficiency and courteousness as if it were August. Doc was a big man, not fat but stocky. His hair was gray from the first day I remember him, and he always had a crew cut under that Texaco saucer cap. In his later years he took to wearing horn rimmed glasses but he always sported that gold tooth when he smiled. I liked Doc. You saw what was there with no mask. I don't know that he ever retired but one weekend when I returned from a hard week at college he was gone. Daddy went to the funeral.

Life goes on, and today as I lose another good friend, I remember that changes are inevitable. You think things will go on forever when you are a kid. I did. I missed Doc badly when I stopped at the Texaco; but once "Bad Eye" retired, so did the Texaco home my daddy took me to since I was able to stand on the front seat. There was a friendly new owner who took up where Bad Eye and Doc left off. He was always helpful and quick to please. Oh, and the station stayed the same clean green and white Texaco it was under Bad Eye. But for me the atmosphere was never the same without Doc's friendly greeting, "Five gallons today Tommy Dale?" with me watching him clean the windshield of my daddy's Chevy as he smiled to reveal that gold tooth.

HEAD EM UP, MOVE EM OUT

The year was 1964 and two lonesome cowpokes were sitting on a fence, wondering what they were gonna do when the weekend rolled around. Yep, it was a lazy and laidback time in the wild, wild, West Georgia that is. The two guys I was daydreaming about were me and Mike (Yank). We were actually at his house and the fence was the fender of his daddy's brand new Malibu Chevy. So much for my imagination.

What were our weekend plans? They were going to be closer to my daydream than I could have imagined. You see, Yank had a baby bull in that pasture next to the Malibu's parking place. It was a Black Angus, and mean was an understatement concerning his personality. He was using the bull as an FFA project. On occasion he would let Yank feed him but usually it chased him into the barn. It just so happened the bull was also smarter than either Yank or I had anticipated.

On that Friday the bull executed its well thought out plan for a bold daylight escape. Since there were no hostages to take, the bull decided swiftness was his only ally. He jumped the fence and continued on up the Corinth Road from my friend's homestead. Yank knew immediately what had happened when he arrived home and there was no bull charging the fence. His first thoughts were to call me and enlist another body in his search for the bull. We took off about five o'clock with three hours of daylight left, late in the spring day. There was no sign of a bull anywhere and as evening crept in we gave up the search.

Early next morning the phone rang. It was way too early to contemplate getting up but my daddy was overjoyed when he called me to the phone. He was really excited to see I might actually get up before noon on a Saturday. Unfortunately I didn't share his joy, but I got up just the same. Yank wanted to know if I could bring our car for a renewed search effort. Being happy about my arising so early, there wasn't anything my daddy wasn't going to do for me. He turned those keys over so easily it seemed almost worth getting up while the sun still wasn't so bright. Nah, but he did worry a bit about me still being sleepy and also that he and mother were house bound until I got back. In those days not everybody had two cars.

I took the trusty '61 Bel Air, four doors and all, over to Yank's house. We formed a posse of my '61 and his '64 Chevies. The plan was to patrol a square area of the Corinth Road, the connecting road to Ralls Road, and back down Highway 29 to the Corinth Road, basically a square where we figured one of us would spot that rascal bull likely at either Frank Powers' Dairy Farm or Keeble's Pond. It had to eat and drink water, didn't it?

Yank took off in one direction and me in the other. We figured when we met we could share information. We met somewhere near the end of Ralls Road and Highway 29 with no success. We were convoying down Ralls Road toward Yank's when out of the blue was a streak of black against the far horizon at the Frank Powers place. It was the bull, or we thought it was. The only way to make sure was to turn into the pasture and check it out.

The gate was not locked so we brought both cars into what we thought was a smooth grassy area. Come to think about it, perhaps Mike and I were the first folks to use car-like vehicles for off roaders. Maybe the two Chevys were the first SUVs in the USA. They did well and the little bull decided cars in motion were a lot scarier than when they stood still. We finally herded him into a corner with the green sixty four and white sixty one beasts. But we made a mistake when we stopped the cars to put a rope on him. Suddenly without moving cars and realizing he had only one way out, the bull charged. Mike and I ran for the cars making it just in time; but not in time to save the new Malibu. It took a serious blow causing Mike to land on the horn. The little bull had never heard a car horn before and thought he had really riled up that beast. After the horn surprise and having run for half an hour escaping cars, the bull was too tired to do anymore. We finally roped and tied him to a fence post.

When Mike returned from home with a trailer it was past six o'clock and too late for our usual Saturday night cruise. Besides, I had noticed the 61's grille was bent and the front license plate doubled under from my off-road experience. Funny thing, I was too tired to worry. It seems things turn out all right when you're a kid. The next week, having never noticed the damage, my daddy ran over a chicken while going to LaGrange. He thought the chicken had done all that damage to the grille. So while he was in town he traded it for the nineteen '64 Chevy Impala Sports Coupe. It was the one with the 327 engine he and I had looked at the week before. I promised myself I would never drive that car in a pasture. It was about a month old when I stripped all the chrome off the driver's side. But it wasn't in a pasture, and it's another story.

FIRST LOVE

It was one of those Fridays you know God worked overtime to create. The leaves had just begun to change color. The sun reflecting off all the bright red and orange foliage signaled it was about to be fall. I was ready for a trip down to see mother at the Home in LaGrange. This wasn't our usual weekend trip and my wife had to work and couldn't accompany me. We had planned to go down over the weekend as we usually do, and come home via Hogansville stopping off to enjoy an evening with friends from the Class of 64 on the way back. But my wife's family had a serious medical crisis we needed to make time for on Saturday. So I took a day off to go down early to visit mother and take care of a few things I normally do on the weekend visits.

  I hopped into the car at first light Friday morning and made short order of the Atlanta traffic. On the trip down, my thoughts began to wander back to my high school days as I imagined the party I would miss with my classmates on Saturday night. Finally, I gave in to listening to tapes of vintage fifties and sixties songs. One thing led to another and the gentle growl from the four cylinder Honda engine under my hood slowly developed a little deeper and raspier V8 sound. The black Honda transformed into the white Impala sports coupe as my mind raced back to 1964. Hogansville would cooperate too, since it has changed little from those carefree days.

  Approaching Hogansville, I passed Angela's house. I looked back to see if I could spot her on the front porch swing. Reality is Angela hasn't lived there since the early sixties but by now that fact wasn't a consideration in my daydream. During my four years of high school, Angela was my steady girlfriend. Well, most of the time. I remember her red hair and milky smooth complexion. I also remember her little brother Barry who tried, no he succeeded, in making the courtship difficult from the start.

  Angela and I met at church where our parents were members at St. James Methodist. I recollect first noticing her at the Christmas pageant. She was dressed as an angel, halo, wings and all. I'm not sure about the halo though, I mistakenly got her Irish up a few times over the years. But the rest of the costume befitted the image I maintained of her. I recall school breaks being well worth the run from one end of the place to the other to spend a few minutes with her twice each day.

   The car tape began to play, "This Time We're Really Breaking Up." I listened and don't mind telling you memories of that spring of 64 made me feel a little sad. After four years Angela and I "split," a term we kids used in 64 for ending a relationship. And what's worse, it came just as summer was beginning. It happened because Uniroyal transferred Angela's family to South Carolina. That wasn't all either, I had been accepted at West Georgia College for the fall term and not only was Angela leaving Hogansville, so was I. We promised to keep in touch. Now I was hearing Bobby Vinton singing "Roses are Red" in my mind.

   Suddenly, I realized I was still driving a Honda and clearly did hear Vinton's song droning on my tape player. Reality slowly begin to set in somewhere around the outskirts of LaGrange. It's a good thing because traffic didn't cooperate well with my daydream. Anyway you know how the story ended. Despite one last ditch effort a few years later, Angela and I went separate directions and lost touch, well just about.

   Recently I heard she was married, had a couple of kids and was living in Chicago. I finally graduated from college and went on with my life. There are still a few pictures around from that spring. They're stored "Among my Souvenirs" as the tape started to play when I rolled into the driveway of the "Home." It seems you don't forget your first love or your last one. By the way, I'm married to the last one and I have a date with her on Saturday night, if the sick folks are better.

CAROL'S CAFE

It would be shortly before midnight when I rolled up in front of Carol's Café. It's in LaGrange so if you don't recall the place, I'll forgive you. It was located in an area I think is called Three Points, where three roads I can't remember the names of all connect. It was a convenient stopping off place for us guys in the mid-sixties when we were dating girls from LaGrange.

There was a season in 1965 when a few friends of mine from Hogansville and I were making weekend trips to pick up our dates in LaGrange. Larry and I had a habit of visiting Carol's Café after we left our dates, and that usually was about eleven thirty or midnight. Since Larry was dating the owner's daughter, I guess he had his reasons for patronizing the restaurant. Whatever the reason, for the rest of us the food was welcome and the company even more so because we ended up comparing notes and eating hamburger steak and fries smothered in caramelized onions with gravy. It wasn't like we had not eaten because we usually had popcorn, coke, and candy at the movie or a hamburger later in the evening at the Brazier or the Chicken Treat. Anyway, by the time I got Barbara to her house on Greenville Street and drove back to Carol's, my stomach would be ready to digest some great grease. Instead of a romance movie with John Travolta and Olivia Newton John, "Grease" could easily have been made about Carol's Café. We were growing boys and needed energy especially after a night of being with what we then considered the best looking women on the planet.

In fact when I look back on it, those girls could still hold their own with the modern day high school sweeties. At least they didn't have black fingernails and hardware hanging from their ears, noses, cheeks and tongues, and tattoos in places where not many folks were allowed to view. Don't ask me how I know about the tattoo thingamabob. The sixties girl's dress for a date would be considered high formal by many of today's standards.

Our girls also had curfews, so if we wanted to continue seeing them we had to have them home at a certain hour somewhere in the eleven o' clock range. Wonder if parents require that now?

The worst trouble we could get into during those days was occasionally losing track of time and staying out a little too late. Although some of what you have heard about the sixties era drive-ins is true. But wait a minute, we weren't totally irresponsible and the girls were class acts, so forget all that stuff you were about to think. A night of stress trying to impress her so she'd be sure to keep that class ring one more week took a lot out of us so we needed replenishment. That brings me back to Carol's Café. I don't know how long they stayed in business after the LaGrange girls told us to find a new venue, but I still remember the place when I go to LaGrange and occasionally drive by to see what business is occupying the building. Oh, by the way, I still think about stopping for hamburger steak and fries smothered with cooked onions and gravy after a hot date at the movies with my wife. But these days I'm trying to eat a little better, so I usually settle for a salad. I guess like the girls and the times, food preferences also change.

ADJUSTING TO COLLEGE

Have you ever thrown a cat into water? Well, now that I'm a cat lover I would never consider doing it. But when I was the soulless, not to mention the heartless, child Attila, I did things like that. The affect is horrifying and startling for the cat; such was my first experience at living away from home. Topping it off was a notification that my application and acceptance was later than most, and this resulted in my being assigned to an off campus dorm. Off campus was my lot because the school had accepted more students than it had room for and had to contract dormitory space. My dorm was part of the First Presbyterian Church's facilities. I don't know why Presbyterians designate their churches First, as is the case in so many small southern towns, when it's the only Presbyterian Church in town. They were thinking ahead I guess. The building was constructed of plywood and pressboard and had scars of previous boarders, most likely from indigents with efforts to penetrate the walls with their bare fists. The holes were worthy communication systems as we didn't need to go next door to speak, we just used the convenient hole in the wall.

I was fortunate getting to live in one of the two basement rooms. These rooms were entered from the outside rear of the dorm. They were not directly connected to any of the upstairs rooms. My room was large and encompassed a line of iron bunk beds looking much like a military barracks. The furnishings were early junk. Tables, chairs (non-padded) and desks that were all salvaged as furniture store rejects. There were no pictures on the wall, short of the Playboy posters attached with straight pins or whatever sharp instrument was available to hold them in place. The paneling was thinly covered press board, providing that plush cheap look. Imagine your Mercedes with genuine hand rubbed pressboard paneling.

It had a kitchen, something I was familiar with at our house as my mother's domain. Apparently from their looks the other guys felt the same way about the place as I did. But in this case I was expected to make my own meals or starve. I bought a meal ticket for the campus dining facility. I didn't join the others to heat up cans of spaghetti and Vienna sausages on the gas stove. I had always been warned by my electric stove loving mother that gas would blow you up, even if you did everything right. That didn't explain our propane space heaters at home. But I never tried to reason with adults as it wasn't worth the time. Buying a meal ticket had its obvious advantages, but it also had drawbacks too. Staying to eat dinner, especially in the fall and winter quarters, meant having to get from the campus to the dorm at night. This was at least a mile, and more like two.

Freshmen weren't allowed to have cars even if they lived off campus. But my friend and only roommate from Hogansville, Frankie, had his hopped up '50 Ford clandestinely stashed just off campus. This sounds like a perfect situation, but my and Frankie's schedules weren't the same and there were more days than not that I didn't connect for the ride home. This meant a half hour walk or, if lucky, a hitch. Hitches were surprisingly easy to find on that route but being an only child and raised without benefit of want, it was difficult for me to ask for a ride with a total stranger. So between my teen metabolism and walking four miles a day I managed to eat anything in any amount and stayed slim. There was some advantage to this after all.

I wish I could say that it was good for my grades. The two quarters I spent in that room with four other guys didn't allow much time for study, and I had little self discipline. The whole time spent in this dorm amounted to a B rated beach movie without the girls. My mentor and a junior with a solid B+ average, Ed Chandler, tried to lead me in the ways of right. He allowed me to ride to school with him each morning in his somewhat matronly '61 Chevy Biscayne, but it beat walking. This was a Godsend during the winter.

Life and grades improved in the spring when I moved on campus. I can't begin to explain the wonderful feeling of a freshman without a car getting to live on campus. The two-mile hikes were over and when I finished a class I could go to my own room with my own stuff, change clothes, leave my books, go to eat and do all kinds of things. I was living in that little self contained world where nothing was too far away, the campus.

I found living in the "Rat Hole," as Aycock Hall the freshman dorm was known, involved a bit more self discipline. No more wild parties, noise of all sorts or late lights. We didn't have to discipline ourselves about sneaking girls in and out, because at Presbyterian Hall none would be caught there, dead or alive, and the same went for Aycock Hall. Worst of all there were room inspections. We had to keep our on-campus rooms reasonably clean. The payback was worth it though, as I had only one roommate and we were both from Hogansville. Although Frankie and I were never the best of friends, we tolerated each other knowing we both could have done worse. He finally had to start leaving the '50 Ford at home because on campus he really didn't need it.

Sunday afternoons in Hogansville were the depths of depression, especially if it was dark, cold, or just dreary. Staying in Hogansville would not have been so bad, but anticipation of going to Carrollton the next morning to begin another week was the cause of deep dark depression. When I think of it now, I'm reminded of Monday mornings and waking up to a single solitary light from the barracks in the window across from my bunk during basic training. I knew when that light came on, it was only seconds before ours did too. But basic training is another story. Because we freshmen could have no cars, our parents rotated picking us up on Fridays and returning us on Sundays. Regardless of whether it was Terrell's, Frankie's or my parents, I felt like I had been sentenced to a week in a concentration camp.

Fortunately, over the four years my attitude softened into accepting that life was not going to change, so I had to change to accept what it gave me. Dinner was forced and I looked forward to going to sleep more than anything else. But there was the inevitable homework or test to prepare for on Sunday nights. It seemed the demented professors spent the entire weekend before that week trying to find ways to torment us. And you thought it was just the Vietnam War that produced student unrest, protest and weirdness.

RED, BLONDE, AND BRUNETTE
(NOT MY SCHOOL COLORS)

It all started when I heard from a co-worker friend that "Hogan's Heroes" had been featured in the Atlanta Journal entertainment magazine culinary section. He used words like "gourmet" and "one needed reservations" on some nights. My friend was confused that reservations were needed at all in Hogansville after I revealed its size. So I explained that, at least to my knowledge, Hogan's Heroes was the only restaurant in town and maybe everyone decided to go to supper the same night. It could happen, you know.

Of course, any mention of Hogansville immediately brings back all sorts of memories including past romances, which I felt obligated to relate to my co-worker since we were at lunch and not on the clock. I really can't explain how I made the connection between the restaurant and my love life. It might have had something to do with a friend from home who has an office near the site of the restaurant. I'm not at liberty to identify this friend but he and I dated the same girl, albeit not at the same time. She was a class ring basher. I don't know if she bashed my friend's ring but she definitely didn't get mine. I need say no more about Candy the "ring basher" as it wouldn't be beneficial for her or me. I'll just let bygones be bygones. This turn in the conversation increased my listener's interest about life in Hogansville so I had to explain a little bit about my romantic adventures.

Like any good story, I had to back into the explanation. It started when I was ditched by a cute little blonde with a devastating smile and a slight lisp that gave her an innocent little girl quality. She definitely had me wrapped around her little finger. In fact I had to ditch another girlfriend, a redhead, to get this one. In retrospect I should have and could have been much better off dating Jenna, the brunette. However, Jenna was dating Larry who had just broken it off with Callie who was also a brunette. This might have created problem with Larry, you know. Do you not see? I only considered Jenna a confidante but as I later learned she harbored a real liking for me. She had always been there just two doors down from my Aunt Mary's house. There were many summer days during visits to my Aunt's that Jenna and I spent enjoyable afternoons swinging on her grandmother's porch and talking. Somehow it never occurred to me she could be more than a friend. Like all good soap operas, this one has a few more twists.

You see, my buddy Mike and I attended summer school in LaGrange the summer before college. It was a slightly bigger town than Hogansville and only twelve miles away. Yes, I had to take a class the summer after I graduated high school to satisfy a college entrance requirement. Mike decided he needed to learn to type so he joined me at school. We met a bunch of LaGrange girls who were in our classes. He met Mona there but that's another story entirely. He and I also made a mutual friend, another fellow at summer school. His name was Larry but not the same Larry in the previous paragraph. Confused? This Larry introduced me to his cousin Belinda, of a higher social order in town. Belinda was nice but had no personality to speak of except maybe a matter of fact attitude that might have served her well if she had gone to Law School. There was never any chemistry but I didn't have anything to do much that summer so I continued dating her.

One thing led to another and Belinda decided to have a party to introduce me to her friends. I made the mistake of bringing my guitar, which as you no doubt are already aware I can't play. I didn't realize one of the guests was going to be a girl I knew from my MYF days who could play and sing. We were requested to entertain and fortunately she covered my bad playing with her beautiful singing. The entertainment attracted the attention of the pretty blonde with the little girl qualities I mentioned earlier. She asked me to play several numbers I had no idea how to play, but I made the effort. At any rate the guitar did the trick and she was paying attention to me. I was fascinated by her innocence and smile. I was in love and didn't even know her name. Worse, I had to start college the next week and there was the possibility I might never see her again after the party.

There were two problems, how to exit the Belinda relationship and how to win the blonde away from Dougie, the rich preppy she was with that night. I found Dougie was history anyway in spite of the new Pontiac Grand Prix he had just been given by mommy and daddy. Ending the Belinda escapade was another matter altogether. I had never had two girls interested in me at the same time. It was fun and I thought perhaps I should make hay as long as the sun was shining. Don't try this at home, or better yet in two small towns. I don't have time here to go into all the intricate details of this balancing act but suffice to say, it didn't and couldn't balance, or last very long. Like us guys, girls compare notes, especially if they are already friends. It ended, naturally with hurt feelings and bad karma which would one day would return to haunt me.

I may as well tell you I did finally learn the blonde's name. It was Haley and we dated for over a year. It seemed pretty serious to me but what did I know? I learned from my friends she wasn't very loyal, while I was working those summer weekends in the Reid Mill so I could finance the relationship and also put some money away for school. I decided I needed to be the one to end it; however, one should never try this on a double date. The four of us spent a very anxious evening hunting all over the Callaway Monument grounds, the local popular parking spot, for Haley's class ring which she flung to the seven winds when I gave it back. She then had burst into tears asking me not to break up. It made things worse, when this happened at nearly eleven o'clock at night and she was supposed to have already been home. When we finally located the ring, I let the better part of valor win and my southern gentleman tenor forced me to ask for it back, and to give her back my ring.

It was only a few weeks later at a most inopportune time for me that it happened again, but with an exchange of roles. It happened on the way back from a college function where we double dated with none other than Belinda, (Remember her, the girl I ditched for Haley?) and another Hogansvillian West Georgia student. I wondered then if all this was karma returning to massacre me. I still wonder. My heart dropped to the floorboard of the backseat of that car when she handed back my ring and asked for hers. I felt like ". . .", well, I felt bad. On top of that, I had to go to work when I got home that afternoon. I forgot the one lesson I had been taught in the cotton mill, never cry at work. Cotton lint sticks to wet places and halfway into the shift my face looked like it had been tarred and feathered, but as I've said before, that's another story.

The war was lost and so was the relationship. Later that summer, I met a former high school buddy working near me in the mill. He was there for school money too, and was a natural rock-n-roller I would soon form a band with. From there, he eventually introduced me to the ring basher. So now you have it. What did I learn from all this? Not much, as you will see in later confusing episodes of this soap.

I BOUGHT MY BRAIN OFF THE DOPE WAGON

Some years ago I was attending a college registrar's convention when one of my colleagues got up to perform a little comic relief, but I didn't realize it at first. I just thought he was another one of the boring speakers that had just about accomplished what Nytol could never do for me. His first line was, "How many of you folks ever worked in a cotton mill?" I raised my hand. Of course, he didn't expect a response. It destroyed his opening line and the monologue collapsed.

Needless to say the speaker and most of the folks in that room were transplanted Yankees who probably thought a "cotton mill" was a place that made cotton. In fact, that was the punch line for the opening joke. For you Yankee readers, a cotton mill refined the product into a usable material. The Reid and Stark Mills in Hogansville made duct for the tires U.S. Rubber Company produced in New York, pretty much like before the war, the one between the states, where we supplied the raw material and Yankees made the finished product. Where is General Longstreet when you need him?

I spent several summers working in the cotton mill and I won't soon forget a single one. I worked on the second shift from four pm 'till midnight with my mother. My job was creeling, and it's an art form. You have to be in good shape physically to do this job. I wasn't. The first step was getting a long metal cart. Then I went back to the stack of about two thousand pads of spools, filled up the cart, and pushed it ten or so miles back to the twister room. I had to climb the twister and put a spool on each little protruding axle and pull the string down so when the twister ran, it twisted about ten spools of string into a heavy yarn on a big bobbin. Got all that? I didn't think so. Anyway, you had to do this fast or the person running the twister would lose valuable time, and time was money for them. They got paid by the number of bobbins they filled.

In my first year, my physical shortcomings and affinity for being slow did not endear me to those running the twisters. In addition to being slow, I found reason to pay a lot of visits to my fast and efficient warp-tying mother that first summer. And no, I'm not going to explain what warps and tying ends involves. She and her friends Elmira and Corrine would shoo me back to my job, telling me I didn't need to be halfway across the mill visiting when I should be creeling. I hated creeling. Did I mention I was afraid of heights too, not to mention being spastic? And those twisters almost reached the ceiling. The ceiling was higher than I want to remember.

Well, my most favorite time was lunch break, although on the second shift it came at about eight o'clock at night. I got half an hour and most of it I used actively involved in eating. Mother always packed us a lunch so there was no need to buy anything; but being eighteen and not always liking potted meat, I opted for using some of my hard-earned money for college to buy a hamburger off the dope wagon. Now I know this was the sixties and I know what you are thinking, but the dope wagon wasn't what you think. Dope was the nineteen thirties name for Coca Cola which people in the area still used at that time. So when you bought a dope, you actually bought a Coke. They had everything on the dope wagon including all kinds of sandwiches, drinks, chewing gum and candy. They also had cigarettes and snuff too, but they wouldn't let us kids near that stuff. I usually got a candy bar whether I brought a lunch or not, and chewing gum.

I found out pretty quick you don't need something to keep your mouth open when you work in the cotton mill. It's not fun to chew Wrigley mixed with cotton lint, and you also try not to sweat, or especially cry as I did when Haley broke up with me. That was an exception, as she had done the dirty deed about two hours before I had to report to the twister room. I was still crying at six thirty when I went down to see mother. She wasn't too worried about my heartbreak as she was the fact I might suffocate from the cotton lint stuck to my face, in my nose and in my ears. It got in my eyes too; in fact it was in every opening not covered by clothing. I now know how tarred and feathered folks in the last century felt. I eventually got over Haley and learned a very valuable lesson at the same time. Never open your mouth, or get wetter than you have to in the cotton mill. Sweating will cause your body to get covered in lint quick enough without any help from other sources of wet.

In my second summer I became faster, stayed at my job and kept my mouth shut. I'm proud to have been a "linthead," as we were called by the Yankees who produced the tires in New

York. I guess they probably thought we bought our brains off the dope wagon too.

This is an aerial view of the Reid Mill known to Hogansville residents as the 'Old Mill', circa 1930's. My parents worked there when I grew up in Hogansville.

IN-BETWEEN

There are times in life when you are dealt a hand that is beyond recovery, even if you could draw and discard an unlimited number of cards. This occurrence was more than occasional for me in high school and college, especially when I got jilted by a particular girlfriend. Question is what do you do when you're nineteen years old and in between girlfriends?

When it finally sank in that the last relationship was irretrievably broken, to use a legal term, I set about trying to find another girlfriend. However, that took going to some of the places that could easily end my short life, like the skating rink or even more dangerous places like dances. Why were the dances dangerous? Well, even at your home school there were bullies, but hopefully enough of your friends would be present to make these guys think twice. The old "safety in numbers" rule was a very necessary requirement to survival in the sixties. The real problems occurred when you went to dances out of town.

So on Saturday nights, a pack of us guys would head out to West Point, home of the Red Devils and Hogansville's arch enemies in football. Going into the enemy camp required a special group of friends, those with whom you have spent most of your life and trusted with your best lagging marble. Of course the primary mission was always to locate potential female companionship, but usually the results were just the opposite. We tended to attract half the opposing football team and unfortunately not a single member of their backfield was ever in the group. Some of our guys could never figure out that the problem might have something to do with them wearing Hogansville letter jackets. They figured girls would be attracted to their sports prowess. They never considered guys would too, but for different reasons.

There came a time when it was necessary to sit back and take stock of what I was doing, especially after several failed attempts at attracting anything vaguely resembling a female and succeeding spectacularly in attracting the enemy team's line backing corps. In my current day job, the Army, we call these sessions analysis. The analysis I engaged in during the sixties resulted in getting together with a few close friends and cruising the various hamburger joints for the more genteel, and rarely less attractive, female species, those that didn't go to dances or care much for guys at the skating ring with tattoos all over their anatomy. The main cruising haunts were drive-ins like the Chicken Treat or the Dairy Queen Brazier in LaGrange. Also, we were relatively safe in a car and it gave us some time to discuss our strategies.

When strategy, money and gas all ran short the same weekend, we went to the drive-in, stuffed on popcorn and hot dogs from home and took in a B movie. Because of limited funds, we always took advantage of the drive-in specials. Once, when it was two-for-one night, even though the ticket taker probably wondered why two guys were going to the drive-in together, we didn't tell him there were four others in the trunk. Necessity ruled we temporarily stop on the last row in the darkest spot, close to where Larry Joe and Ted always parked with their dates. That was the only place where we could unload our excess cargo and get them into the car without being seen. Then we'd set off to find a speaker that worked. Most didn't, especially those on the back rows. But with six guys all eating and talking at the same time, no one expected to hear the movie anyway. So much for honesty.

Resourcefulness like that used in the one-time drive-in caper and a few draws off the bottom of the deck when no one was looking eventually led to my winning the hand of another yet charming maiden. Once again I could go to the Callaway Monument and park, and hold hands with someone at the show on Friday night. Oh, and on occasion I would go to the drive-in with an empty trunk. Sometimes we would find a speaker that actually worked, not that it mattered then either.

MAYBE THE LAST TIME

That's a song lyric and hopefully not an omen to my writing. Actually it is from a rock-n-roll song played by a band I was a member of in the sixties. You see, during my freshman year in college I was a budding rock star in spite of my lack of a musical ear. What reminded me of this episode was the Hogansville High Homecoming and Alumni Reunion held a little while back. It was pretty good fun and the thing about it was, not only my class but everybody else's classes were there too.

While I was wandering aimlessly though the crowd trying to get my bearings and identify all those familiar faces I couldn't match with a name, I saw him. Boy, did he look familiar but the name just wasn't there. I let him pass because I just didn't have the courage at that moment to walk up and read the name tag, feeling he would certainly recognize me on the spot. But it happened anyway, as he came to me and without hesitation said, "Jimmy Dale, do you remember me?"

I should have recognized Tommy on sight because it all began in 1965 when I was a freshman at West Georgia College and he, Charlie and Chuck were still in high school. We decided to form a band. It was more than kind of Mr. Stephens to let us use his cabin to practice. He knew it was secluded, and with our combined talents it was the most benevolent thing he could do for Hogansville. We practiced relentlessly, sometimes three and four evenings a week until midnight. Tommy and Charlie have inherent musical talent. Charlie could sing and play guitar, and Tommy was the most natural lead guitarist I have ever had the pleasure to play with. Chuck was good on drums. My rhythm guitar provided just enough noise, but it fortunately was drowned out a lot.

Tommy and I had a prolonged reunion discussing the band and our guitar playing. I learned he still played and he found what I called "playing" in the sixties wasn't even practiced by me now. The next day at the reunion I ran into Charlie. My wife was with me when Charlie told his two sons how I had inspired his musical talent. He also told me he and his brothers were planning a music park near their home in Tennessee and invited us up when it opened.

It wasn't apparent to me until after Charlie and I had parted that my wife had this really puzzled look on her face. She said with a puzzled look, "You don't have a musical bone in your body. You can't carry a tune in a bucket and you have absolutely no rhythm. On top of that you don't play a guitar." She's right on all counts but there it was, two of my former band members remembering me as a bona fide part of their group and even giving me some of the credit for helping realize their musical talent. Maybe they liked the way I looked holding a guitar? All I needed then for a clean sweep was to run into Chuck but that was not to be. So I'll just accept my role as the senior member, age of course, of a once very good rock band thanks to Tommy, Charlie, and Chuck.

It felt good to get those tributes even if I thought my efforts were a might inflated. I've since pulled my two old guitars from the depths of the closet and wiped the dust from their worn cases. I'm a bit afraid to look inside. Maybe I'll just be content to remember the band that we once were in the sixties and let that be "The Last Time" I play my music.

DEATH IN THE AFTERNOON

Late June in 1966 was the closest I have come to being referred to in the past tense. No, I wasn't in the jungles of Viet Nam; although I would have stood a better chance of survival there. I was in Hogansville. Not to say Hogansville was a more dangerous place than Saigon, it wasn't and isn't. My problem was not hostile people but a hostile friend, my daddy. He wasn't prone to getting mad enough with me to commit a violent act. Lord knows I had given him too many opportunities to do this my first twenty years and he had not taken advantage. But in those first twenty years I hadn't damaged his car either. The car wasn't new, as he had bought it that way two years before, but to him it still was new. Even if you aren't wondering how this started, I'll tell you anyway.

It seems the Hornsbys, Parhams and Dales all plotted that their rotational pilgrimages to take us back to West Georgia College every week should eventually have an end. I was working in the mill during the summers since I started college and had saved a fair amount of my wages at the suggestion of my parents. So my daddy figured the sixty mile round trip to Carrollton every three weeks could stop if I had my own car. To solve this dilemma he offered to add a few bucks to my account and let me look for my first wheels.

It couldn't have been a better day to car shop. It was bright, sunny, and visibility was unlimited. Joel and I were on our way to LaGrange to check out all the car lots. Joel was one of the guys who worked with my daddy. He was a car expert if there ever was one. His customized '55 Chevy with its 409 was the crowning glory of his expertise. Joel was going to make sure I didn't get a bomb. After visiting about a dozen places, we found one, an aqua and white '57 Chevy Bel Air two door hardtop. Immaculate was an understatement. We took it for a test drive and stopped at a friend's house where Joel started his examination. It didn't take long for him to announce that it might make it to Hogansville before the engine blew and the bondo fell out of the doors and fenders, but he doubted it.

I couldn't get my mind off that car the whole trip back home. Even when I slowed to wave at my neighbors, the Portwoods, as they turned into a driveway to drop off a friend, I was still thinking of the '57 Chevy. That's when I let my daddy's car go just a little across the line into the other lane. Joel's uncoordinated attempt to intervene and pull the car back across to our side partially failed and we sideswiped the oncoming vehicle. The driver turned out to be a very upset and outspoken Yankee. The State Trooper didn't care for the Yankee's tone when he turned it on him, so he took the Yankee in and sent me home with a warning. This didn't fix the chrome ripped from the left side of my daddy's car.

I was careful to park the damaged side of the car away from the mill gate. I had wanted the extra four hours before my daddy got off work to make good my escape to Alabama, but mother made me go tell him about the wreck. When he came to the gate, he sensed there was a problem with the car even though he couldn't see the damaged side. Mother must have called ahead to soften the blow. "How bad?" he asked, and I had to turn it around. I can't repeat everything he said but it amounted to the fact my life was spared only because he couldn't get out that locked gate. You see, the mill was surrounded by a storm fence and the watchman who was on rounds had the only key. By four o'clock daddy had calmed enough to decide it wasn't worth spending the rest of his life in another place where he couldn't get out. That's when he made the decision next time to take me car shopping himself. It was the only way he could keep "his" car in one piece.

WHAT A REVOLT'N DEVELOPMENT THIS IS

One lazy summer Saturday afternoon, an unusual Saturday on which I didn't have to work, I decided to drive downtown. The mill had been running six days a week that summer, all the better for me to save up for the coming fall, my junior year in college. It had been raining up to then and I had been cooped up in the house with my folks, not a fate I would wish even on a West Point Red Devil fan. So I thought I'd just cruise around Hogansville hoping to see another friend home from school who wanted to drive down to LaGrange and hit the Chicken Treat for lunch.

The trusty '63 Corvair Spyder sat just behind my daddy's '64 Impala. I liked my Corvair even though a future wife had torn two of its four forward gears out. But as long as I kept the cinderblock in the front trunk to hold the car on the road, it would give me a thrill from time to time. So I strapped myself in the Corvair and proceeded toward Hogansville. When I got to the red light at the New Mill, I slowed down to stop. This is one of the favorite haunts of our hungry Hogansville Police and their one and only cruiser. Sure enough, he was there waiting for some foreigner to run the light.

What the policeman and I didn't realize was the very big Mercury behind me had not yet seen the stop light change to red. And the old cast iron Volvo attached to the Mercury's bumper hadn't noticed anything, since it had no driver at all. Filling my rearview mirror was this massive brown monster with an ironclad in tow. I watched and wondered how much his ticket was going to be as the police cruiser began to roll. It finally occurred to me this guy was sliding at an alarming rate of speed on the wet pavement. I popped first gear realizing too late it was one of the one's I didn't have anymore. Then I hit second and found it, too, was no longer available. Why didn't she leave me just one fast forward gear? Third was there but it didn't exactly move the Corvair in enough time to prevent the big brown Mercury from giving me a shove right through the light.

I managed to bring my smoking, smoldering car to a halt and detached it from the chromed monster that now was looking something like the Bismarck shortly after being bombed by the Royal Navy. Not only had he creamed my Corvair, his Volvo had broken loose and joined the shoving match rearranging the Merc's rear end. Otis, the seventy-nine-year-old policeman still serving proudly, took off his hat and scratched his white hair, removed a pipe from his mouth and asked the fellow if he had ever seen a stop light before. Without giving him time to answer, Otis asked me why a sixteen-year-old kid couldn't pop a clutch and peel out of the way. I tried to explain about the two missing gears and tell him I was nineteen but he turned off his hearing aids to write out a ticket to the Air Force officer who was now examining both of his almost totaled automobiles.

I looked at the rear of my Corvair. It had oil all over it but very little physical damage. I later found the motor had been knocked off its mounts. Otis moseyed on over to my car and said, "I reckon I'm going to have to call Tom to come after you. If you drive it that thing'll put so much oil on the road it won't be safe for the funeral due here in half an hour. I just can't let that hearse slide around on this stuff 'cause he might lose his passenger."

It turns out I got my car fixed by the Air Force guy's government insurance, but it continued to sling oil and I still only had two forward gears. What happened to the Air Force guy who hit me? Well, Hines & Ralls Motor Company wreckers were each hauling off one of his cars and Otis was hauling him off. What a revolt'n development this was for everybody, except maybe Otis, the Hogansville City Treasury and our only two car dealerships in town.

THE BIRTHDAY PARTY

My dorm, Row Hall, is steeped in history but not the kind you repeat to your parents. Nevertheless we were all proud to be "Row Men." Of course today this would be considered chauvinistic. But in good ole 1966, it was just plain pride. It was great to walk back from dinner with a group of your colleagues and approach the good ole dorm. That is if you made it inside. Problem was you usually got intercepted by a welcoming committee ready to help you celebrate your birthday whether you wanted to or not.

That reminds me, I need to give you some background before I introduce you to the subject of this story. To be more specific I belonged to the third Floor East of Row Hall. This is like belonging to a regiment of a brigade of a division of a Corps of an Army. If you didn't follow that, you probably are still in better mental health than I am after having worked ten years for the Army. We didn't have a flag but we sure had the esprit de corps that went with one. There were guys like Bear, Bubba, Dooley, Stan, Terrell, Frankie, Tony, Noel, Warren, Wolfy, Bentley, Crawford, Hal, Mote and a guy whose name no one remembers. Our Dorm Chief was Mr. Tom I. He was really Woody Allen pretending to be a Sociology Professor, but he would never admit it. Several of us hung out in his room and listened to his stories about the Navy, women he had known and loved, and his wild Chapel Hill days. He would always show us his naval officer's hat and tell us he wished he had never left the Navy. I'm not at all sure it didn't leave him. He was an easy going guy who lived in the dorm because it was cheaper than renting and was the only way to make sure his ex-wife didn't try to murder him. I don't know what he did to her. And there was no better place for a celebrity to hide than Row Hall. Not too many reputable people wandered into it.

Oh yes, getting back to the story. Well, if anyone even suspected it was your birthday, you would never get home that night. I was convinced no one knew when my birthday was, and of course I didn't broadcast it either. It was a breezy November day and after my last class I was wandering the hall looking for someone to go with me to supper. I found my friend Noel. He never was hungry, but that night he said he would join me. The meal wasn't bad and when we started back, I confided in Noel it was my birthday and I appreciated the dining hall having provided us with an unusually good meal. I figured by this time it was too late for anything to happen. It wasn't, and what I didn't know was that a plan had already been put into action. Worst of all, Noel was part of it. We were approaching the infamous back door of the east wing of Row, the site of the majority of birthday abductions. The sidewalk was clear and when we reached the door I gave a sigh of relief. When I opened it to go in, completely confident I had successfully run the birthday blockade, there stood Bear.

Bear and Bubba were graduates of Roosevelt High School in Atlanta where they had both played football, and were by any standard larger than the average college sophomore, me. Bear was as wide as he was tall and Bubba could double for the Empire State Building, except he had hair. These two were friends but unlikely roommates. Bear insisted on sleeping with the window open, even in thirty degree weather. Bubba, liking normal temperature, had to sleep under an electric blanket. Does that tell you anything about disagreeing with Bear? I didn't. He grabbed me and I offered no resistance. I was instantly thrown over his right shoulder.

During my abduction, I saw the grinning face of Terrell and the vile mixture I knew he would dispense from the fruit jar he carried. His personality was wry and he had a cynical sense of humor. He was still suffering withdrawal from working too many summers with the local pharmacist turned land developer, Jim L. Terrell was responsible for mixing up the concoction that was supposed to never wear off the skin. This horde of Row riffraff dumped me in the middle of a path just behind the pond and proceeded to disrobe me, over my objections. Once in a position I was only comfortable in while showering, I had the India ink based gunk dumped in an area I will not divulge here. What was worse, when they finished laughing they took my clothes with them.

I decided to wait until it was completely dark. I got up and looked around just in time to encounter the dining hall staff, mostly black females taking their usual route home. I did the only thing a "Row Man" would do under those circumstances, I said, "Good evening ladies" and proceeded to walk away as if nothing was unusual. It didn't work and they laughed and giggled until I was out of sight. I only regret I didn't have a top hat to tip.

If you think this is over, then you also have another thought. I'm not the only one who had a birthday. Smiling Terrell had the option as "Doctor Death," the mixer of concoctions, to be excused from the birthday dunk. So he made doubly sure he would not fall victim to the Row ritual. But I knew when his birthday was and I made sure it wouldn't be forgotten. What was so good about that time of year was that it was getting really cold outside. About eight o'clock, after dinner and settling in, Terrell dropped his guard. I tried to remember his formula to the best of my knowledge. I did get most of the ingredients right including the main ingredient of India ink. Just for a little kicker I threw in some rubbing alcohol.

What a very dumb thing to do, trust your roommate. Terrell's roommate Mike was a budding minister but not quite there yet. Mike intentionally unlocked the door to their room, and shortly after eight the door was flung open and there to Terrell's total surprise stood none other than Bear. Terrell tried to sluff off what he knew to be inevitable, and he made a trivial statement which he never had time to finish. Bear made a charge and Terrell found himself in the same over-the-shoulder predicament I had struck a pose in not two months earlier. About the time we reached the door to go outside, he begin to kick and scream. I think he knew if he started to bite, Bear would eliminate his weapons.

Once we got to the trusty path, we all joined in the defrocking ritual. But he fought like a tiger, which I might add allowed Bear to exercise his old football skills. Terrell still partially clothed decided to make a break for it, but Bear's excellently executed flanking tackle placed him flatly on the ground gasping for breath. I hated to have to empty the contents of my fruit jar on a helpless and semiconscious friend, although he had shown me no quarter when he anointed me with the same mixture not two months earlier. But I overcame my momentary touch of human kindness for my fellow man, and I poured it directly in the same place I got it. My suspicion of having used too much rubbing alcohol was confirmed not a split second later when Terrell became fully conscious. I felt better when he roused because I didn't want to leave him until I was sure we weren't all going to be held on a murder charge. Hope he didn't meet the ladies on their way home.

CHAPTER IV

POST VIETNAM:

A NEW AND DIFFERENT SOUTH, AND WORLD

Over the years attitudes, demographics and technologies have changed the South. A majority of these changes occurred while many of us were off fighting a foreign war we had little understanding of why we were not trying to win. Upon returning home the ideological terrain was almost unrecognizable. The wartime economy was winding down and it was hard to find work with so many people being discharged into the public sector. When a job could be found it wasn't in those small hometowns we left behind.

Occupations have changed over the years and the career I chose definitely isn't as exciting as being an assassin for the CIA, although there were times when I would have happily volunteered for that work over what I was doing. One particular colleague who didn't always get the response from me he anticipated would say, "Close, but no cigar." I came very near using that quote as this chapter title; however, it doesn't apply, since I don't smoke.

PART ONE:

WHAT'S A SOUTHERNER TO DO IN "THE NEW SOUTH"?

The 70's and 80's saw many of the small towns in this country lose their means of support. Companies found it more profitable to get their parts, labor and other needs satisfied overseas. Like those kids I grew up with, I wanted to stay in my hometown and work just like my parents. Only problem was there were few jobs to be had for a college graduate or a non-college graduate for that matter.

Working in the city for people who were definitely not the same friendly folks you knew who ran businesses in your hometown, or worked alongside your parents, was a mind challenging experience. However, there were a couple of bosses I would have liked to have worked for longer but circumstances and the lure of promotion didn't permit.

KENNESAW RIVER RAT

"Pilots, man your planes! Pilots, man your planes!" I jump up from the cereal bowl and grab my flight jacket to rush for my machine. The Admiral, Smut the Cat, goes outside and my wife announces as usual, "Cat off the bridge! Cat off the bridge!" It's 0630 and no time left, I must meet the enemy and run his gauntlet of shell fire and fighters in order to get to work.

But before I can launch, I must go through the preflight checklist. The executive officer, none other than my wife, begins with "contact" (for my eye) and I say "check." Then it's hearing aids, check; billfold, check; hearing aid batteries, check; watch, check; security badge, check (occasionally I forget), and finally, jacket, check. I'm ready to launch and I grab my parachute (brief case) and head for the flight deck.

The flight deck is loaded with two mid-size fighters (cars) all fueled up and armed with the latest air to air combat weaponry: tachometers, speedometers, fog lamps, five speed sticks, cassette radios and antilock brakes. They have the latest sixteen valve fuel injected in-line engines and are painted in fancy squadron colors (red for my wife, black for me). There is little room on the flight deck in the one and a half car garage. I squeeze through the cramped space between the wall and fighter. I open the canopy (door) to find my body and what I'm carrying won't slide into the seat. I must put one foot in and go head first into the cockpit, but then that isn't unusual for entering a fighter aircraft. Once inside I lower myself into the seat and strap in. My wife leans over to give me last minute instructions and a peck on the cheek for good luck and then it's time to launch.

Smut the Cat reappears in Admiral's country to assume control over flight operations. My wife calls the deck to attention, "Cat on the bridge! Cat on the bridge!" All is go, and she gives the whirling finger sign to start engines. The Honda burst into life and amid all the noise on the flight deck we revert solely to sign language. All the gauges come to life and I go through my checks. Airbag OK, instruments lights OK, fuel OK, water OK, radio OK. I make a signal to clear the chocks from the wheels, and then I slide on my helmet, (standard English driving cap). I give my wife a thumbs up, and she snaps a crisp salute and throws her arm forward in one single motion signaling the catapult to hurl the Honda into action.

I'm airborne and headed for Route Pack Six (I-75) for another mission "Downtown" on an alpha strike. I take it easy until I'm at the proper altitude (fast lane) and then go to afterburner to avoid surface to air missiles hurled by the sixteen wheelers all around me. Constantly checking my six o'clock (rear view mirror) to confirm if the flashing blue light is a bogey, I find it's a bandit locking onto my tail pipe with his heat seeking radar gun. Taking evasive action I break right into the slower lane, avoiding the bandit (state patrol) who overshoots me and breaks off the engagement. Whew! This is a tough mission today.

Soon the lights of "Downtown" flash into view. I go to the strike channel on my radio and pick up the morning news. I make my run-in and head for the friendly airfield at Ft. McPherson. My radio crackles to life with landing instructions from the Landing System's Officer, Paul Harvey, as he gives me "the rest of the story." Soon I'm taxiing on the tarmac (parking garage) at Ft. McPherson, having completed another successful mission from up north. I inspect my aircraft to find no damage, and then I debrief my commander (the boss) after reporting for duty. In twenty-four short hours I'll be fragged (ordered) to do it all again. Such is the life of a Kennesaw River Rat.

SOME DAYS JUST SHOULDN'T HAPPEN

"I'm writing this slowly, so you won't have to read it so fast," as the Cajun mother's letter said to her son in the Gulf War. Actually, I'm writing it slowly because I have no choice as my little finger is encased in metal. It is real difficult to type when the tip of your finger strikes two keys instead of one and you don't know which you hit until you see it pop up on the screen of your word processor. So if you see something that doesn't look quite right, it isn't an error, believe me! By this time, hopefully you will want to know why I have a hurt finger, or better yet why I choose to write about it in this condition. Well, there are three reasons: 1) I just wanted to see if I could do it, 2) things are still fresh on my mind as to why I'm hurt, and 3) this kind of stuff never happened to me in Hogansville and I can't figure out why I ever left.

I've always heard that when things are due to go bad you sometimes have a premonition, your "little voice" or something like that. Poppycock, I didn't hear any "little voice" last Friday as I pulled myself from bed. In fact I was looking forward to the weekend, looking way past Friday, which hadn't even started happening good yet. Well, I should have suspected something when as I drowsily brushed past my answering machine and noticed the red call indicator light was flashing with a big red "1." It was a call from my boss who wanted to know something yesterday and this AM would be too late. But even that didn't deter me from my appointed rounds with the toothbrush, shower and hair dryer. I adeptly fumbled around in the dark to silence the repeat of the message so as not to further awaken my already somewhat aroused wife. After succeeding in stopping the droning voice, I found that things fell into their usual routine.

I finished all my robotic duties and waltzed over to delight in ripping back the covers on my wife, a la Tom Dale (my daddy) fashion. But this time, as I feared, she was already up and had beaten me to the punch before I could execute the maneuver. This, too, didn't alert me to the fruitlessness of continuing the day. These two warnings should have been enough to send any slightly low IQ individual hustling back under the covers to regroup. It didn't. I ate my cereal and bananas just as if it were a normal run-of-the-mill morning, and proceeded out the door to face what I still considered a day like all the rest. Little did I know.

Only yesterday did I notice my gas tank was dangerously low of fuel. I make it a habit to never let it get below a half tank, as my drive each day is 64 miles round trip. On the freeways of Atlanta you don't need to run out of gas or you might never be heard from again. As usual my memory failed and I passed the gas station by. It was a busy corner, and to get turned around properly would have taken a chunk out of my morning timetable for arriving on time at work. So I bravely did a somewhat illegal U-turn in the very busy intersection. Having mastered this like a champion Formula 1 driver I wheeled into the gas station with aplomb. The station was just opened from being totally rebuilt. This should also have given me a clue as to an impending disaster. New stuff never works until the bugs are out.

The station used to be the busiest one in North Atlanta and you could see tags from every Yankee state in the Union there at any one time. Since it has been rebuilt it has gotten bigger and even offers Subway sandwiches to the hungry invaders. Why didn't my forefathers do that in 1864? We'd be millionaires by now. Anyway, all the pumps were brand new and the best way out into traffic was blocked for paving. This meant I had to exit just even with the light. Most of the rest of the Yankees, those that live here, won't let each other out, much less a guy with a Georgia State Flag Tag on his front bumper. I didn't realize all of this until I had entered the station and parked next to one of the shiny new pumps. After I assessed my predicament, I began to pump gas. The pump didn't have all the bugs worked out, so it pumped excruciatingly slow. I squeezed the handle tighter and this seemed to make it work a little better but the flow still seemed restricted. Another squeeze, and after what seemed like fifteen minutes, there was a massive jolt and I figured I had finally gotten the sucker to work properly.

It worked too well by gushing gasoline all over the side of the car and onto the ground. If the Feds had seen this, I would be in jail right now for polluting the entire county's water table with '87 Octane. I immediately stopped pumping and jerked the handle of the pump from the car's tank. Quickly, I replaced the handle into the cradle. When I did this, I noticed as I pulled my hand away it didn't want to come. I also noticed I was in some considerable pain at the same time. I didn't know whether to pay attention to this problem or try and locate paper towels to soak up the gasoline streaming from the overflowing gas tank and down the side of my new car. I finally decided I needed to see the source of pain as the stream of gas wasn't going to stop until the overflow had subsided.

Upon examining my finger, I discovered I couldn't see exactly what was causing the hemorrhaging of dark red blood. I only wished my mother were somewhere nearby because when I bleed a lot I tend to pass out. But I remembered mother either put toothache medicine on my hurts or took me to Dr. Harvey. At this point neither solution was a welcome remedy. I reached into the container just next to the pumps, the one that usually held paper towels, and it was empty. There was a guy at the next pump looking at me as if I were performing a tribal dance from the Shoshone Nation. I finally loped over to him and asked if there were any paper towels in his dispenser. He began to search his truck and found tissues just as I ripped out half the blue paper towels in the container next to his pump. Having stopped the bleeding, or so I thought, I thanked the guy who kindly said, "This isn't going to be your day." You would think by now I would have already figured this out, but again I proceeded to carry on as if I was going to make it after all.

I entered the station to pay for the gas and immediately attracted the attention of the guy behind the counter. He identified himself as an out-of-work Registered Nurse and grabbed up a box of bandages. After his having missed my cut with the pad of the band aid (he placed the sticky part directly over what was left of the tip of my little finger), I knew my wife was going to have to see this. So I decided to not fight to get a left into the now seemingly impossible line of traffic toward work. I went to the right and directly home to my wife. When I rolled into the garage, she was standing at the door. Somehow she knew, even if I didn't, that this was not going to be my day. After a close examination she performed the same operation as the out-of-work RN but she got the pad properly on the wound, which resembled the sickle on the Soviet Symbol.

Again I went on my way – late, but nevertheless determined to get to work. I was by then becoming suspicious that possibly this was not going to be one of my better days. But there were few surprises at work besides the pain when I hammered down on the keyboard with what was left of my little finger before I remembered it was injured. Several of my coworkers, car buffs like me, suggested I wash the car to make sure all the gas was off, as it might cause some discoloration in my paint job. I pondered their suggestions and decided it was not possible for me to wash it in my current condition. So I decided to do something that I don't like to do, run it through a carwash. On the way home I stopped at a station that I knew had such a contraption. I paid my dollar and punched in the code.

I hate cheap carwashes. I had just seen a TV news story where a woman and her child were trapped in one for eighteen washings before they were rescued. She said she thought she would never see the light of day through all the soap suds and wondered if they would ever be rescued. Fortunately they didn't charge her for all the washings, and her car had a good coat of wax. I notice that the "Big Bertha" tail of my Honda was getting nudged quite a bit during the washing, but I didn't pay much attention until I got to the drugstore where I had promised my wife to pick up her prescription and get a metal splint for my finger. Something wasn't just right as I approached the car after exiting the drug store, but I didn't know what. Finally, as I was opening the door I noticed my radio antenna looked like modern art. It used to stick straight up from the back left fender but now it was distorted beyond recognition similar to my finger. At this point I said to myself, "Why didn't you stay in bed?" But alas, it was too late.

The gas station owner, of the one that bent my antenna, said he would help with half the expense to replace it. "But," he said, "You should have read the four-foot tall sign hanging off the entrance to the carwash. It says to lower or remove your antenna before entering." Funny, we never do that to my wife's car and the antenna has never been broken off. But my wife never spews gas on her car, cuts her finger, and gets her antenna made into modern art all in one day either.

When I finally read the fine print on the four-foot high sign, I realized that getting half my antenna replacement paid for was a stroke of good luck, something I was in desperate need of that day. It seems this little bit of luck renewed the almost lost positive outlook I had started with that morning. When I finally laid down that night I was very thankful the next morning was Saturday; I could recuperate and remember better days in Hogansville where Doc McVey pumped your gas. And he wasn't even an RN.

CLOSE, BUT NO CIGAR

At one time or another we all have been under pressure to be perfect. It's been instilled in us over our lifetime by parents, teachers, bosses, friends and society in general. I don't know about you, but I was under the impression unless I brought home all "A's" I wasn't trying hard enough and I was certainly capable of it. About the only thing I believed I was capable of was getting caught by Mrs. Huggins for chewing gum in her fourth grade class, or making paper guns and holsters. It wasn't the intent of our parents to destroy our self worth by insisting on us all being a Rhodes Scholar. They came from a generation that survived the hardships of a great depression and won perhaps the greatest war in history. They were expected to excel well beyond their capabilities and they expected us to have that same drive and work ethic. I think we do, just in a sort of different way.

If your parents didn't insist on you pushing the outside of the academic envelope, somewhere sometimes you were under the gun to be perfect. In the absence of someone else expecting this, you expected it of yourself. If you are like me, and I think many of you are, you don't fare well under the horrendous competition of today. You see yourself as not being the person you are capable of being. If you didn't make the football team in high school, if you didn't get that last promotion at work or if you don't please your peers or mate, you think there's something wrong with you. Have you ever considered maybe those people who place unrealistic requirements and goals on you just might themselves be imperfect? Well, I didn't see this until I started reading books on self worth. One I'm reading right now is "Don't Sweat the Small Stuff". The book was given to me by a gifted supervisor whom I had too short of a time working for. She knew how to get the best from her employees and how to appreciate them at the same time. It's too bad those kinds of leaders aren't in abundance.

I spent years working for a micromanager perfectionist who made the work environment miserable for everyone including management itself. I let this person play serious havoc with my confidence and self worth before realizing it wasn't me with the problem. Today we are finally getting the message it's all right to be ourselves, even if we don't always meet someone else's expectations, be it parents, employers or peers. Plain and simple the "Don't Sweat" book's message is it's okay to be yourself, warts and all. There is nothing wrong with imperfection as it is part of the human experience, and after all we are human. Real success in life isn't based on how much money we make or how much success we achieve professionally, but the answer to these questions. Did I do something useful with my time on earth? Did I make someone happy? Did I carry my share of the load and do my best? And yes, did I have fun doing all these things?' We might be close and not get the cigar, but then as I said some of us don't smoke anyway.

IT BE FRIDAY

When the alarm goes off on Friday, I know it right away. My wife bounces up and the first thing out of her mouth is, "Happy weekend." Well not quite, we have to get through the day and it's still a workday. I finish breakfast, which consists of a bowl of skim milk mixed with half bran and half something eatable. Then I'm warned about the freeway and asked to try and bring myself home in one piece which today is becoming increasingly more difficult.

The drive in is usually hectic, with the maniacs who take the phrase "Death before dishonor" as a matter of fact. But on Friday mornings, things are noticeably different, traffic is thinner. You can actually keep a three car margin between you and the person who often mistakes his brake pedal for the accelerator. On Fridays I get to work early and can afford to get my coffee to sit for a moment while I try to figure out what I'm there for, before the place fills up with people that I must call, visit, e-mail, or otherwise take up my time with, when suspense and deadlines are eating away at me like sharks.

Fridays are always the days when things are due. Little things like your time sheet. You either complete it or hand it in to the secretary, who is a descendant from a family of fourth grade teachers, or you don't get paid. If there are big projects which you must coordinate or coordinate with, whose directors are never in their office when you need them, then you must politely and humbly request an extension until Joe gets back from his cruise. By the way, your cruise got canceled because you're not finished with your project.

Once the computer program which houses all your hard drive information has been recovered from its usual end-of-the-week crash and you have sent all the e-mails, made all the cross country calls, and filled your boss's file box with multitudes of paper, you have accomplished nothing more than being in a place far from home for eight hours, then you can leave. Five days of this sort of thing is enough and a weekend isn't just a pleasure, it's a necessity. You pick up the dirty dish from lunch, the briefcase you brought in and never use, and your glasses which the doctor made you swear an oath that you would always wear while driving, then you head out to the car. Getting the building's security system disarmed to get out the door with all that stuff in hand is the first of many obstacles you must encounter before finally arriving home.

The road course lies ahead and there you must pit yourself against the best and sometimes the worst of the field before you cross the finish line, the garage door. This Friday I had it easy but decided to stop and get a hamburger to save my poor wife from having to prepare dinner on her last day of the week. This has become a tradition in our house on Fridays. I don't understand how so many cars can be on the road on Friday afternoons when there are so few in the morning? Friday afternoons traditionally have the heaviest traffic. My wife says people probably bring their own cars on Friday instead of carpooling because they leave early and go places they don't usually go on weekdays. Well, how come the traffic on Friday morning is so light, don't they have to bring those cars in to work with them to make traffic heavy on Friday afternoon? Aha! Their wives, sweethearts, or loving children bring them the car just so they can jam up traffic together in the afternoon.

Anyway, after failing to get the attentions of seven kids supposedly running the Burger King, I have to go inside. The sign in the drive through said it was closed, but that didn't stop the yuppie in the Explorer from driving up to the window and getting his food before I got mine. When I drove out, I stopped at the stop sign in the parking lot and was fortunate I did. As I began to accelerate, I was promptly cut off by a blonde who ran the stop sign and wheeled in front of me. When she got to the grocery store at the other end of the parking lot she wheeled up in the fire lane, got out leaving her two kids strapped in, and went into the store. She was on isle three when I left.

I chose one item and went to the express checkout lane. Remember, this is Friday so I had to wait for senior citizens who paid no attention to the ten item limit. I watched a lady at the next register come up with a full cart. I was still waiting to be served when she was pushing her groceries out the door. But when I did finally get home, my wife greeted me with, "Happy weekend." This time I could believe it. As my friend Homer Lee says, "It be Friday!"

PART TWO:

FAMILY LIFE IN THE MODERN SOUTH

Living in the city does not always involve work, well, not the kind you do to earn a living. There are many other forms of it a modern day Southerner must deal with in our complex world. It becomes our turn to take care of parents. After all they did that for us. Sometimes we discover we aren't that far behind them, especially when a kid is getting married and you recall that only yesterday she needed your help to balance her bike. One finds little time for escapism unless it's purposely made; and I do that with aplomb and sometimes at the peril of my life. And our trusty pets remind us just how useful we can still be, even when we hit middle age. What Southerner doesn't own a dog? Me. I can explain later!

"I WANT TO BE ALONE"

It seem like this is always the case when the world gets a little too close for comfort. It happens now more than ever, since I have become a city dweller. I go out into the back yard to enjoy nature, hear a bird or two, and just be by myself. I concentrate well when the few opportunities for this are offered. But almost always I'm greeted with sirens and dogs yelping, as well as construction equipment buzzing only a few houses away bringing me unwanted urban sprawl. It won't surprise me if they build a bridge across my pool one day while I'm at work. When I drive home and cross the bridge, I might say, "Hum, that body of water looks very familiar," especially when I spot my wife leisurely floating under the bridge on her raft.

Silence is a state of mind in the city and not a state of fact. Of course, growing up in Hogansville I had noise too. There were dogs yelping there and an occasional rev up of a truck engine emanating from Luby's garage. Those sounds didn't seem harsh when combined with the song of birds and laughter of the neighbor's kid, occasionally breaking the silence. Silence: Oh, but for a day without traffic in front of the house, airplanes overhead, and assaults on two sides of my fence from juvenile delinquents trying to find a way to drown themselves in my pool. I can dream, can't I?

This morning I talked to a military friend whom I just learned has orders to Birmingham. He said it won't be a bad drive because he only lives a few miles from the Alabama border, in Franklin. He will just commute until his twenty-six months are up and he will retire. I said, "It must really be quiet in Franklin.

I remember it being a sleepy little town, where I barely slowed down for the only red light while coming home from college on the weekends." "Nope," he said, "They have made Highway 27 a four lane to Carrollton and Georgia Power is building a new plant just a few miles away." It makes me wonder if you all in Hogansville and Franklin can still hear the birds sing, and can you tell if it's kids at play or if it's just another ambulance?

I'm really not Mr. Wilson in disguise, a grumpy and soured old man. Maybe an old man, but certainly not grumpy nor soured (well not much), but I definitely want quiet. My wife will take exception to that statement on occasion when she sends me to another room to watch car races. But like Mr. Wilson, my military friend or anybody else, I occasionally need to be alone with my thoughts without any kind of noise.

This doesn't mean I want to do a Greta Garbo act on a regular basis. I need my wife and the cat around. The cat meows occasionally when food runs low or if it's in extreme need of attention, but most of the time she had just as well be left alone too. My wife doesn't talk much either, about the same amount as the cat. She would rather read a book than carry on a conversation. So in spite of my lamenting about noise, we do have a quiet time at home, that is if I leave the TV turned off, close all the windows and take out my hearing aids. However there are those times when I just need to put on my Longstreet hat and go sit by the pool. I need that time to reflect and get my bearings on life. It helps me write for you; but moreover it keeps me sane at work, which anyone employed by the Department of the Army will have trouble with from time to time.

BANDITS AT THREE O'CLOCK

Speaking of Florida, well, I was speaking of Florida, as in vacation. You possibly remember from previous writings when I mentioned when I was growing up my family never considered a vacation a vacation unless we went to Florida. We aren't Yankees or at least I haven't yet found any skeletons in our family closet, but my parents felt this urge to go to Florida at least once a year. This particular year my mother and daddy decided to visit family in Tampa. It was a major undertaking for mother, who had never been further south than Panama City. Feeling a need for support on this trip, my parents invited my first wife and me to accompany them. Mother considered it going to another country and wondered out loud if English was spoken there. I couldn't believe she would think otherwise, but she was more right than I had imagined.

Mother's sister married a native Floridian (yes there are one or two left) and couldn't wait to show us the area. She decided a day at the beach was just what we needed to unwind from the long trip down. Once rested, we drove over to Clearwater Beach for a day in the sun. Their beach was much wider than Panama City's beach and devoid of seaweed, deceased sea creatures and the wrecked boat I remembered from the fifties. There was actually enough room to walk on this beach, and the area was relatively safe from the aforementioned obstacles. There were also plenty of sea gulls, yes, hundreds and hundreds of them. As usual, mother brought her own food insisting we save money with a picnic lunch she made before leaving home. After the meal, heat became a real problem but not for mother who was attired in a print dress. She was comfortable except for her eyes. Daddy offered to buy her a pair of sunglasses but she refused saying she could make do with a paper hat and save the money. The only materials available for such a hat was a newspaper my aunt picked up earlier. Mother folded it into a huge thing that covered not only her head but half her face. She looked like Robin Hood with headlines across her brow.

There was a little over half the loaf bread left from lunch, so mother didn't want to waste it and decided to feed the gulls. Not a wise decision. Have you ever seen the movie "The Birds?" Well my mother isn't much on theaters or TV so she didn't see it, but I'll bet she could recount the plot for you now without missing a line. She began feeding a few well-mannered and friendly winged creatures that were fluttering around contently. Suddenly, without warning the few became a crowd, then a flock, and before she knew it there was the equivalent of a mass bombing raid on Dresden. Mother was under attack from all angles and the huge hat was blocking her efforts to put up a reasonable defense, but it did keep her head safe.

Soon it became clear to mother that probably her life might be in danger. She dropped the rest of the bread which momentarily distracted about a hundred of the predators. Then she took off running up the beach pursued by a white trail of bread-crazed birds. Hanging on to the oversized Robin Hood hat for dear life, print dress flowing in the breeze, she made for the safety of the palms where my daddy ran out to meet her waving the rolled up remainder of the newspaper. Thanks to daddy's slashing counter attack and mother's own blazing speed, she arrived under the palms unscathed.

Now-a-days mother doesn't spend too much time dwelling on the Clearwater adventure and I haven't seen her feed many birds since then. But one thing I do know is she may be cured of making those enlarged Robin Hood hats from newspapers, that is, unless they do it for recreation at the Home.

MAMA'S IN A NURSING HOME
(CAN I BE FAR BEHIND?)

It wasn't that long ago when my eighty-one year old mother's body and mind indicated it was time to stop living independent of nursing care. Only problem was they didn't tell mother. She disagreed when she found out what they were up to, but her mind and body decided her spirit was going to come along peacefully or war would ensue. It was war and mother didn't fare any better than her ancestors in the Confederacy.

It wasn't so much that she had lost it, but she had lost enough to make things impossible for her to go on in her own apartment without constant twenty-four hour aid and care. Unfortunately mother had just moved into a great senior's assisted living apartment building configured a lot like my old college dorm. I could just imagine those seniors on some inclement weekend frolicking up and down the halls partying, congregating in one room until all hours and pulling practical jokes, like flooding rooms, locking people out and faking a murder. Some of them were entirely up to this kind of mischief but realized it was a ticket out of the place if they tried. Mother, on the other hand, was not as outgoing as she once was, so unless they came to her she didn't associate. But when they did come, she talked their ear off easily.

This is how I knew she was beginning to show signs of cracking under the pressures of life. It was nothing for my wife and me to get a replay of a previous visit each time we saw mother. I knew exactly what she was going to say and when in the conversation it would come. One night I got a call from one of mother's companions, who like me, was used to what she heard from mother. This lady sat a couple of hours a day with her. Laura was definitely concerned with mother's conversational patterns that day. Mother was making no sense and calling people alive by names of people who had been dead twenty years ago. She was calling her doctor by the name of a doctor that had treated her as a young girl. So what was new, I thought, she's done this in the past. But after seeing her, I was convinced she had drastically dropped off mentally. She indeed was missing some grooves on the record and I felt it was a stroke. So did the doctors at first, so tests began. There were no conclusive results and mother's doctor advised I get her permanent nursing care at home or admit her to the dreaded nursing home, as her physical disabilities alone warranted it without this new development.

Who can manage a home while working for a living and

provide maintenance of a helpless relative around the clock? The Home we got was the best in the area and the care was topnotch. Mother still sometimes calls the telephone a television but who doesn't get those two contraptions confused; sometimes I call it a tape recorder. She has to stop and think about what to say next, but I do that too. She can't remember where she put stuff, ditto me, and sometimes she doesn't remember what happened the day before. So what's so unusual about not remembering what happened yesterday? Well, if you're in your eighties and in a nursing home, not much. But if you are in your fifties and working in a responsible job you should seriously start to wonder.

Things I need to tell someone, meetings I have to attend and responsibilities I need to accomplish sometimes slip past me. I can think of a few situations I must relate for your diagnosis. My first one began on a normal day when I got home and found the card in my mailbox. Since I don't get that many personal letters, I felt I needed to open this one quickly. It was a nice little card with a flower on it from two folks in Hogansville I hadn't seen in years. They were members of St. James, my old church home. They were inviting me to an Open House on the twenty-third; I felt honored and decided to go. My wife and I discussed it and I also decided to approach my twenty-year-old daughter about going, too. I put the card aside to attend to other matters. That night I reviewed my Indy Car racing schedule and found that there was also a race on TV the twenty-third. I would tape the race because the church came first. Next day at work I discovered that on the weekend of the twenty-third I also had security duty for work. This meant that I couldn't go out of town, and had to wear a beeper all weekend. But then, I had another week to be concerned with getting a replacement. On Saturday night I talked to my daughter and asked her to be prepared to go to church with me the next weekend. She promised, and we parted expecting to see each other again then.

Sunday morning came up with thunderstorms. They made me

feel cozy and warm while I sat at the dinner table paying my mother's bills. That's another added benefit to being in the nursing home, you can't pay bills if you can't remember them. Maybe that's why my wife pays our personal bills now? Anyway I filled out the check, except for the date which I asked my wife to supply, as she was standing next to the door with a calendar tacked inside. She nonchalantly replied that it was the twenty-third. At first it didn't register and I calmly wrote it on the check. Then after my aging brain began to translate, I realized she had read the calendar wrong because next weekend was the twenty-third. "No," she replied. "Today is the twenty third and I am sure." The pain of reality shook me and I realized that, yes, it really was the twenty third and she was absolutely right. It was one o'clock. I had missed the church open house, half of my race was gone even though I was home to watch it, and I had caused my daughter to plan for something next weekend that wasn't going to happen. Worst of all, I hadn't performed my security duty for work. Fortunately, a friend realized this and did it for me.

   I didn't really think during those times that I had inadvertently lost it, and that I really had something wrong enough to make me a serious candidate as a roommate for mother. But now that I think about it, I have done other things that might fit well with absent-mindedness. There are the three times I thought I had left work at a quarter 'til four, the correct time to do this. I looked at the clock that sits in my window at work and saw the big hand on the nine and the small hand on the three. Yes, on the three as the clock has a hash mark for the other numbers. I had left work at a quarter to three and not a quarter till four. I would not realize it until I had reached half my destination of home. I don't think my boss ever doubted my sincerity, as I handed in my leave slip for the unintentional time off. There was some snickering as I walked off, but overall I was believed. How many more times will this happen before I am suspected of having a devious or deteriorated mind? Although applying the word mind may be inappropriate in these instances.

Neon Through the Pines

My wife suggested I become more organized and I have dutifully followed this idea. Now that I'm better organized, but I can't remember where I have put things I've organized. I have gotten to the point I have sunglasses in every car I travel in and even in some I don't own. I have reading glasses in every drawer in the house, yes, and the cars too. I can't remember to take all my pills and lately I can't remember to put on all my clothes (ties are the only casualties for the time being).

I remember going to work one day and having to talk to my female boss about a serious issue. While we were conversing, I felt something slipping out my sleeve cuff. I thought I had absentmindedly stuffed a tissue up there to dispose of later. But it continued to work itself out during the conversation, until I felt something silky and not papery. Trying to talk and extract this thing from my sleeve without causing too much attention didn't work. I finally pulled the lace pair of panties out to both my and the boss's surprise. She tried not to say anything when a second pair followed the first. But then you can't talk when you're uncontrollably laughing. I didn't know what to say except I had done the wash to help my wife who was also working, and I had forgotten to check for static cling articles. I could only hope this truthful explanation was acceptable. Later in the day she passed my desk and asked if I had found anymore underwear in my shirt?

It has gotten worse lately. I constantly forget to check my electronic mail at work, only to be saved by coworkers who happen to mention things to me in just enough time to prevent catastrophe. Same is true for meetings, and I wonder how much longer it will be before I forget about bathrooms visits? There is hope though, because I don't forget to feed my cat, do fun things and remember dates of important stuff like races. Since I missed the race last Sunday, I'm beginning to wonder about those dates, too.

So far mother and I remember each other and we still talk

about things, even if we have to stop and concentrate a while on what we were saying. She complains about the Home, but it is nice having your meals prepared and someone getting you set up for the day. They are friendly, too, and you get TV and a phone. Above all, someone else gets to worry about things for you. All in all, nursing homes aren't that bad when you think about it. Since a lot of this already happens at home for me, I won't have any trouble getting used to being mother's roommate when the time comes.

ST. JAMES AGAIN, MAYBE FOR THE LAST TIME

There has always been something about burgundy carpets that causes me to think I should be quiet and sit still. I've been in doctor's offices, General's offices and some legal offices that have burgundy carpets. I've lost all of my normal urges to do dumb stuff or open my mouth when I shouldn't. In fact, I've been quite serene. I never understood it until I revisited my boyhood church, St. James United Methodist, on Granite Street in Hogansville.

Mother's only request was to visit St. James once more, and I saw to it she did. While making the arrangements for the funeral, Claude McKibben asked me if I would contact the ladies of the church regarding a luncheon they were preparing for the family after the funeral. I made the call and was invited over to discuss the details. Driving over was like a walk down memory lane, but I wasn't prepared for what I found when I got there. St. James itself was still almost the same as when I left over thirty years ago, and that isn't a bad thing. The windows on the steeple have now been replaced with wood inserts, but otherwise everything appears the same outside. I have a picture my daddy made of Tommy Whaley and Spot, his dog, in front of the church back in the 50s.

The ladies of the church are still as gracious and warm as they were when I attended on a regular basis. And, I can tell you their cooking hasn't suffered over the years either. But I guess my real "Return to Mayberry" happened when I opened the door to the sanctuary. I was offered a tour of the church after coordinating the arrangements for the luncheon, and I just couldn't resist. Everything looked a bit smaller, but then so was I when I spent most of my time there.

The burgundy, yes I said burgundy, carpets were staring me in the face as I opened the doors from the anteroom. It wasn't until then I realized why this color carpet had such a profound effect on my persona. To my right were the pews where I had sat with my friends and sometime got into trouble. There was the time when Preacher Dooling stopped the entire service to find out what was so interesting that Larry and I had to compete with him for the pulpit. Oh well, that's another story entirely. Then the next pew up is where I sat many services alongside Angela, when we were speaking. Then there is the pew where my mother and daddy sat. It was in a perfect position for mother to look over her shoulder to check to be sure I wasn't sailing airplanes or committing some other kind of noticeable mayhem that might get me a not so honorable mention from some of her friends or one of the church elders. The choir loft was still there but it was now enclosed by a wooden rail instead of the cloth curtain that prevailed for most of my tenure at St. James. I pictured in my mind Ms Lottie and Ms Mildred singing their "Special Music." They may not have always sung in the same key to my untrained ear, but I'd give anything to hear them again.

The church office still has the wall bookcases with glass cabinet doors. I won't bore you with the incident when I was convinced the noise I had created there was the breaking of at least half of those glass panes. My Sunday school room was next on the agenda where Mr. Caldwell, a dedicated and talented teacher, endured Lamar, Larry and I doing airplane pilot and racecar driver imitations with the straight back cane chairs. However, if you think I wasn't listening when I attended church, you'd be wrong. I admit it took a great deal of effort on the parts of the minister, congregation and my Sunday School teacher, but they instilled something in me I have passed on to my daughter and have hopefully influenced others with. And that something is love, honesty, compassion, and fair play. If you read the Bible closely, you will find these are things that are emphasized over and over again.

I know mother was there at St. James with me as I relived those memories. This church was a major factor in her life and I suspect she is happy knowing it served as her last residence in Hogansville. As long as its doors remain open, to me my mother will live in Hogansville; and if they should close the doors, she and the congregation will open another chapter of St. James on another plane. I'll visit that one too, but, I don't mind waiting a while.

FATHER OF THE . . . I CAN'T SAY IT!

I sat there in my recliner with the back up, and began my best Jimmy Stewart routine. By the way, the stuttering was my own this time. He looked at me like maybe there was something wrong, and there was. I had never acted this way before in front of James but he had never asked what he had of me before, either. This was not a normal situation so it called for out of the ordinary behavior on both our parts. Of course, my wife handled it as she does every crisis situation I have, with dignity and serenity. Oh yes, with sanity too.

He asked for her hand. No! Not my wife's, my daughter's. I wasn't surprised as I'd been half expecting it to happen, but I guess I was never really prepared. I can't think of anyone else I had rather have ask my permission to marry my daughter than James. His father and I belong to the same organizations, so I know he comes from a very good family. I looked over at him with my best efforts at a mature expression and answered, "Of course, I mean yes, you may have her hand, and the rest of her too if you like. You have my blessing." After my wife was asked the same question she reached over and gave him a consenting hug. Then we moved on to such things as when the question would be popped and when the wedding date would be set? He had an answer for the first question, on Valentine's Day but the second was anybody's guess. I liked both answers.

  But, back to Jimmy: Just after giving James my blessing I asked if he had ever seen the movie, "Shenandoah." You have to realize not everyone has seen a Civil War movie made in 1965, that is unless they happen to be my age and a Civil War buff. James, I found fell into the category of those who hadn't seen the movie. So it was safe to do my Stewart routine. I asked him if he "liked her." I can't describe the look but it was somewhere between a "are you for real?" and "I knew he would lose it someday but why now?" kind of stare. After a quiet and long moment of digesting what he considered to be a loaded question, James calmly responded, "Yes sir, I love her." Then I said, "Good", and stuttered trying to remember the next line in the movie, since he had followed the dialogue of Doug McClure's character perfectly. Then, I said, "You know I loved my wife when I married her but I liked her too, and that's important." "What do you mean?" asked Doug, I mean James. "Well son," I continued, "you have to like someone to live with them. You can love 'em but unless you like 'em you can't live with 'em." Vintage Stewart.

  By this time I was reaching the end of the lines I remembered; it had been close to ten years since I'd seen the movie. So I abandoned the character to the relief of my bewildered wife and future son-in-law. I know James has to wonder what kind of family he is about to associate himself with, but my wife managed to salvage the rest of the visit while I recovered my composure. Finally, James found an opportunity to excuse himself and left. I didn't hear any rubber burn but I'll bet he pushed his Honda's accelerator a little harder than usual getting out of the neighborhood.

Since then the happy couple has visited to show us the ring and my daughter Emily has set a date. It will occur in August. She's done most of the planning herself and I'm proud she has taken the bull by the horns. But, which bull? You see, the family of the BRIDE, pays for the wedding. Did I hear someone out there offer to buy my Honda? I'll just list phone numbers at the end of this page so it will be easy for you to find out how much I want for the car. Oh, and the house, too. She tells me she's keeping it as cost-effective as possible but I hear that phrase from the government every time they raise my taxes. There are expenses to be paid like the church, reception, flowers, photographer, everybody's dresses and tux's, and emergency services for me after I give her and most of my money away. Only joking about the emergency services, but just in case I'll plan for it. My wife is an excellent driver, and besides no one will buy a half restored Datsun 240 Z we will have left for transportation to the local emergency room.

I know it will be worth it, the wedding I mean. My daughter is getting an extremely decent young man who I've learned is very conscious of his responsibilities, eats healthy food, has a good job and, I hope, can deal with slightly unbalanced in-laws. And, he is getting a beautiful young woman who I love with all my heart. I just hope they wait awhile before there are any more surprises. I'm not grandfather material. My hair isn't quite gray enough, yet.

DRESSED TO KILL?

Weddings – two of them to attend! Most women would have thought they'd died and gone to heaven to have such a shopping opportunity befall them. It would send any sensible female into a feeding frenzy that could result in a complete new wardrobe, but not so in the Dale household. In fact, it's just the opposite. My wife, I must explain lives exactly three point two miles or one exit up from the largest shopping mall in northwest Atlanta, and I can count on one finger the number of times she has been shopping there in the last year. The woman absolutely hates to shop and hates mall shopping twice as much. Guys, don't you just wish?

When the news arrived that not only a daughter, but also a brother-in-law, is getting married this summer I'm thinking that maybe this isn't going to be such a good time to buy a partially restored sports car. But my wife didn't disappoint; she immediately began looking at what she already had on hand from her son's recent marriage. It looked good but since we knew many of the same people who would attend this wedding had also attended her son's, she decided there was no choice but to go shopping. But still I knew she would be frugal. I don't think the next President would go wrong appointing my wife Secretary of Treasury.

The next day started with a visit to the dreaded mall. We dodged unguided missiles in the parking lot, driven by shoppers reading sales brochures and talking on cell phones. Then there was a "chicken contest" with generation Xers for a parking spot. Surviving the trip over and getting parked, my wife spent a record three hours looking at one dress after another, refusing to wait in line at the food court, and beating a hasty retreat once she had procured the merchandise. She did manage to save three hundred dollars on her purchases but paid for it by returning home mentally beaten and physically exhausted. There has to be some deep seated problems with a distribution system where you find the same dress at the same mall made by the same manufacturer that has that big of a difference in the price tag, but she did. She found another such bargain but decided it was too short. Even though I liked it, the dress went back the next day. Before she went to sleep that night, her last audible words had something to do with being dressed to kill, or killing dresses. I'm just not sure.

Sticking straight to the mission at hand my wife now proceeded to evaluate her two new purchases. She pulled a third dress from her closet and reminded me it could work if she dyed it to match the colors of whichever wedding she decided to wear it to. Speaking of dyeing things, about a year ago I found myself eating purple mashed potatoes. It was a mystery until later I discovered my wife had previously decided to use a kitchen pot to change the color of a few items of clothing. Well, that's another story, and no, she isn't related to Lucille Ball or Gracie Allen. The dye this time was pink, so I'd know what's happened if my mashed potatoes matched our neighbor's vintage caddy.

The next step in the process was to have the bride decide which dress was suitable for the wedding. Since the other mother hadn't decided yet what to wear, we were on our own. All we knew is it had to be "T length." Now did that mean anything to me? Did it mean how far it is from the edge of the green, or does it have a Jimmy Buffett Logo on the back as in T shirt? I found it had something to do with the dress length ending somewhere above the ankle. In order for the bride to determine which T length dress was going to work, we had to make pictures of my wife in each one. It's difficult to take a full-length picture of a woman standing between a treadmill and a dresser without getting one or the other in the shot. I didn't ask why we had to avoid these objects but I'm sure there is a logical explanation. Anyway, we used the Polaroid with film that's almost as old as our cat. It didn't work. So I pulled out the old standby 35mm camera and snapped a few shots, until the film decided to automatically rewind somewhere about mid-roll. When I got the pictures back it turns out the one she really wanted didn't develop. This shot was of the dress she was hoping would be selected. So, it was back for more film.

The best part about all this is my "killer dress" wife decided she wasn't going to make it a summer long project. She basically had what she needed, and besides, as far as she was concerned the mall could wait a few more years to again be graced by her presence. If there is a need to shop further she says she'll go back to her old shop-at-home standby, the internet.

MY DYSFUNCTIONAL FAMILY REUNIONS

I am an only child who lived, while I was growing up, between twelve and thirty-five miles from any uncles, aunts, cousins or whatever on either side of my family. I blame the distance for never having gotten close to any of them. Most of my cousins have brothers, sisters, nieces, nephews and parents who live nearby so they don't really need to be too close to me. Of course, my only living grandparent was even further away than my other relatives and she wasn't even sure who I was most of the time when we went to visit. I guess being in the early states of Alzheimer's didn't help her memory out much. Then she didn't see me too often anyway.

To make up for this gap of low family communication, my parents went to either LaGrange or West Point almost every weekend. I always figured if our relatives wanted to see us as badly as we did them, they'd come to Hogansville. Apparently not, since they didn't come see us unless they were going to or returning from somewhere like Atlanta. Did I get tired of this running back and forth business? You might say if I could have figured a way to sabotage our car, I wouldn't have hesitated a Yankee minute.

After I got old enough so that my mother trusted I wouldn't get into the kitchen and burn down the house with an electrical appliance I'd forgotten to turn off, cut off an appendage with a butcher's knife or poison myself with some of the cleaning chemicals under the sink, I was allowed to stay home alone. But there was one occasion I was never permitted to miss when the entire family of one side or the other would get together. It was a sort of family reunion, actually it was a funeral. All the normal family reunion stuff was there, like lots of food, relatives and talking; everyone was dressed to the nines.

I went to an average of about two funerals a year up until I graduated from college. I got to know some of my relatives very well. When I finally moved away from Hogansville, I continued to attend family funerals and was able to introduce my family to my wife and daughter. It also helps me keep up with my cousins from time to time to find out what they were doing as adults. One good thing about funerals is everybody is on his or her best behavior and they say nice things to me, like how much I look like one or the other of my parents, depending on which side of the family is hosting the funeral and how much they miss seeing me and how I ought to come see them more often. There it is again. They never say, "Well, Jimmy, I'm going to come more often to see you now that Chester isn't around to keep me at home anymore."

I wonder if my family and I will eventually drift completely apart never to see each other again now that the generation that generated all those funerals, for the time being, is gone. I suppose future ones will be hosted by my generation? I don't want to think about that just now. Maybe the funeral reunions will have competition since one of my cousins and I have recently found a reason to visit without a coffin in the next room or some guy in a suit standing by looking somber. I like the new kind of family reunions I'm having these days much better than the old ones, even though those old ones did draw a bigger crowd and had a bigger variety of food.

A RAINY NIGHT

In 1955, I got my own room on the back left corner of our new house. The bedroom furniture that graced the room was of a vintage I still wonder about. Not typically boy, it was blond colored and had fancy bedposts that matched the ornate accompanying dresser and chest of drawers. It would have suited my sister much better, if I'd had one. But it was my own room, and that's more than I had at 6 Marshall Avenue.

The bed was situated catty-cornered between two windows, I guess to take advantage of the ventilation, but possibly because it was too big to fit anywhere else in the room. Since our new house didn't have air conditioning, that was probably the best place for it anyway. In my new quarters I missed watching a slow gentle rain fall from the porch roof, as I had experienced while lying in my bed in the front room of the house on Marshall Avenue, with street lights making it possible for me see how hard it was raining. In the summertime with my windows open in the new room, I got something I'd never had before, a cool gentle breeze sweeping across the bed as I drifted off to sleep. If I couldn't see it at least I could still hear rain dripping off our roof as we didn't have gutters.

I guess what I miss a lot today is feeling the gentle breeze and hearing and smelling the spring rain falling outside my window. Opening them isn't compatible with air conditioning. I was thinking about all this last evening when rain began to fall. My wife was watching her science fiction series, and I was reading and rubbing the belly of our trusty cat that was stretched out in front of the fireplace. It was all pretty relaxing but I just couldn't resist getting up and going to the door to catch the aroma of this early spring rain. I noticed it wasn't that gentle but a tad gusty with a little lightning and thunder to boot.

My wife called me back inside to read the red strip across the bottom of the TV screen, something about dangerous thunderstorms in the area. We live in a society where the media dramatizes everything and causes us to panic over every little thing, pretty much like old Guy Sharp did in the sixties when he predicted ice and snow at the drop of a hat. Anyhow, I wasn't worried too much as I'd just enjoy this little thunder-bumper and spend a cozy evening with my wife and cat.

Pretty soon the rain and TV worked their magic, putting us to sleep. The cat never woke up all evening. Eventually I stirred enough to put her in the laundry room where her bed cozies up to the hot water tank, washer and dryer. Then my wife and I went off to bed. When I hit the covers I could still hear a little rain even though my hearing aids were on the dresser. I could also see a little of the activity outside but not from the glow of street lights as in my boyhood days, from the neon lighting up the night sky from just down the road. Then I passed out for the duration of the evening.

Next morning my sleepy wife wandered into the kitchen, or should I say staggered in with half closed eyes. When I asked why she was so sleepy she said she'd been awake most all night. "Didn't I hear the warning sirens? Didn't I hear all the wind, hail, thunder and lightning?" "Nope," I answered, sipping coffee and watching the morning news showing the mass destruction only a few miles away from us. "All I know is I heard a soft gentle rain, a little thunder and experienced the kind of night I had not known since childhood. I almost got up and opened a window to make the remembrance complete with a soft gentle breeze." "Didn't you wonder why you heard that rain without your hearing aids?" she puzzled. Does it take a killer storm for me to enjoy a rainy night? Guess so.

FLY FISHING AND MALE BONDING

Let me begin by saying it's expensive. What? Fly fishing, that's what, and a lot more expensive than my model car collection or my Civil War books. Well, maybe not the books at the rate I'm buying them. But when you add the cost of fly fishing to my other hobbies then we are in the neighborhood of considering a second job to support the hobbies.

Such was the situation not long ago when I felt the need to do a little male bonding with my stepson. I figured as long as I was planning to become a "Mountain Man" after retirement I would learn to fish the streams of North Georgia. This would be an excellent way to spend time with my stepson too. Since he is an accomplished fly fisherman already, I decided I would ask him to teach me the art. It didn't work on the old cane fishing rod and the unmatched reel he had given me for practice. My first lesson learned is you can't cast if the rod and reel aren't compatible, something about balance and flexibility. So I passed the incompatible instruments on to his sister who immediately proved the theory of mismatched rod and reel is null and void. He advised me to get a fiberglass rod and a reel that was up-to-date and would actually send the line where I wanted it to go. Well, my rod is medium in cost and quality and the reel a little better. The whole outfit cost well north of a $100. I should have gotten my initials embossed in gold for that price.

This was only the beginning as I needed line, leader and a license. Most of all I needed flies. What did I know about flies? They are certainly pretty and colorful. So I picked out ones I thought would compliment my rod and reel. You don't want to be tacky out on the river. Well, that didn't fly (pardon the pun) when my stepson swapped my bright flies for green and black ones. He explained fish didn't have the same taste as me and if I wanted to catch something, I had to get what they liked and not what I liked. Since he ties his own flies, I followed the advice. I didn't buy waders either, or the vest that has enough Velcro to get large animals entangled on it. Wish I had.

My first expedition was to Carter's Lake in Gilmer County. We had a nice drive up and enjoyed the wonderful picnic lunch provided by his mother and my wife. So far it was A-okay. We didn't quite reach the lake, stopping at Talking Rock Creek to toss a few in the scenic little stream. Beauty is in the eye of the beholder and words cannot describe that little stream's charm, but only when you saw it from afar. I couldn't stand up on the bank, let alone in the fast moving white water. I wondered if the blood from scratches inflicted while getting to a good fishing spot would attract wild animals to finish me off. Before suffering too much blood loss, my first few casts were by the rules, stopping my swing at two o'clock and not casting with my wrist.

Then fatigue, not old age, set in and the remainder of the expedition was spent getting my line back onto the reel and standing up, as well as replacing flies lost in the trees and rocks around the stream. What can you expect the first time out! We moved up to the lake after a couple of hours with me spending most of it struggling back to the truck. We stopped at the lower lake where the dam dumps excess water. I saw bass bigger than Smut, my Rosanne-like cat. But no matter what I did these fish wanted no part of me. I was so engrossed in the effort to catch one of the uppity critters that I didn't notice my stepson starting to walk away in the ankle deep mud. He yelled something at me and motioned frantically. When I caught up he said, "Didn't you hear that whistle?" "Heck," I said, "I just thought it was one of my hearing aids going off." They squeal all the time. What was the whistle? It's a warning when water is about to be released from the dam. Why were we ankle deep in mud? Because where we were normally is the lake bottom, and in less than five minutes it would be again.

I got out in time if you don't count being covered in mud and losing another fly. Did I forget to say my stepson caught six fish including one of the haughty bass? But being the good sportsman he is, he threw them back. Me, I caught a really neat limb. Despite all this we got some good bonding in, especially when we reached the road and discovered we had to push his Ford truck up a hill to get it turned around for a jump start. And that was just the beginning of my fly fishing career.

FLY FISHING AGAIN

One can never get too much of a good thing. After the first fishing trip and the bonding experience, my stepson took a real interest in my fledgling fly fishing skills, not that he saw potential, anything but. However, he saw a way to help his mother break my weekend habit of watching Indy Car Racing and the Travel Channel. It also provided my wife an opportunity to see her child, if you call a full grown man a child. So it was off to Cousin Mary's in Cave Springs.

The Big Cedar Creek, swift water and all, awaited our high-tech fly rods and reels. I was really excited about this trip as I had honed my skills by hanging my fly in the tree lined banks of the Coosawattie River, when I almost turned over the boat that held me and my wife's uncle. We hadn't had a real successful trip that day. His dog, who loved him very much and could not stand to get more than a few feet away, ran and swam along the bank to keep up with the boat. Whenever I placed my fly in the fish-laden water, the dog swam out to retrieve it even though he had not a drop of bird dog in his blood. Needless to say the fish split when the dog jumped in, and I would jerk back my fly just in time. How could I tell the world my first bag with the new fly rod was a dog? That's how I got the fly stuck in the tree and nearly capsized the little aluminum boat. Now, having totally recovered from the fishing trip with Rin Tin Tin, I was ready for the main event.

The Big Cedar Creek was just behind the little cabin belonging to Cousin Mary. It was fed partly by a natural spring from Mary's property. There was only one way out of the creek and it was the way you came in, because the small mountain that bordered its far shore provided no place to climb out. The creek was cold even in the summertime and this was springtime. Guess what? I was so busy packing my fishing equipment I forgot to put my wading shoes in the bag. After we reached Mary's and finished practice casting, I went to the bag for the shoes I had forgotten to pack. My stepson volunteered his rubber tire soled sandals. I reluctantly accepted and we headed for the stream. His wife decided to go and take the mismatched cane rod and reel.

All three of us were in the stream experiencing hypothermia

from the knees down. He began to catch fish in an area a little ways up from me. So I thought I would walk up and join him. I soon found that was easier said than done. The creek bed wasn't a bed at all as it was a series of boulders, and slick ones at that. When my sandal-clad feet began to lose traction, I careened without being able to stop. If I hadn't careened, I would have gone down immediately. But where was this taking me? You guessed it, into the deeper part of the creek near the bank with no way out. After a few seconds weaving around like a drunk I finally found my footing but stubbed my toe. It didn't hurt, but how could it since I was dead from the knees down? But I knew it had happened and taking my mind off balancing for a second, I involuntarily took a dip in the icy stream. It's not a good feeling when you have no control over your body's momentum.

I was wet to the neck trying to hold my new expensive rod and reel out of the water. It didn't work. The reel struck a rock and I could see the beautiful black paint scrubbed from the instrument. I saw my rod get the same treatment, just as they both submerged beneath the frigid waters. I thought I would freeze to death before I could drown. I wasn't in any better shape lying on the rocks than standing up. Everything was so slippery I couldn't have gotten up anyway. It seemed that if I was going to get out, I'd have to swim. Holding my expensive and slightly damaged equipment I slowly and uncoordinatedly began to swim toward Mary's bank.

When I reached shore I found two startled people staring down at my thoroughly soaked body, doing their best to avoid it but eventually having to laugh. Handing up the rod and reel to my stepson's wife, I examined my bleeding, not yet painful, toe. I wanted to laugh, too, but the feeling was coming back and pain with it. I wasn't sure I could come up with a reason to give my wife as to why I decided to take a swim in the only clothes I brought with me. So I let her son explain it to her while I tried on one of Cousin Mary's dressing gowns for size, all of them being pink and fluffy. My wife is an extremely tactful woman who knew it wouldn't do to kid me about this so she has never mentioned it, but when I do she is hard pressed to hold back a chuckle. Okay, so maybe I'm not cut out to fly fish and maybe my rod and reel have been lying dormant in my room since that day, but that doesn't mean one day I won't go fly fishing again and this time I'll catch a fish. Heck, I'll even settle for a dog.

LIFE IS GOOD

There are a few times when everything just goes right and falls into place exactly. It happened to me this weekend. I washed the car on Thursday afternoon fully expecting the next day to encounter one of the worst storms since Hurricane Opal knocked a tree over on our house in Kennesaw. I expected, since we were bound to Helen for Oktoberfest Friday morning, that I'd encounter a caravan of little old ladies in '80 model Caddys or old men in vintage pick-up trucks driving at a snails pace in front of me on those beautiful curvy mountain roads. I love to check my Formula One skills on those roads, while scaring the dickens out of my poor wife. I also expected to see half of Atlanta in a massive traffic jam entering "alpine" Helen. At best I figured I'd have to park between two massive SUV Trucks or vans full of kids who's minds are not on protecting the sides of their, much less my vehicle. And finally I expected to have to squeeze into the fest hall amongst a throng of people not unlike those trying to leave the Titanic shortly after hitting the iceberg.

Let me explain. Please! We used to go to Helen for Oktoberfest every year until Atlanta took over and destroyed it with overcrowding. Actually, my wife's whole family used to show up: brothers, their kids with their boy and girl friends; friends of friends, and sometimes a few strangers that hooked up with us when we got there. Our German sister-in-law was the instigator and she loved having us all together to sing, dance and visit. We haven't been going for the past six years because of the overcrowding, that is, until about a month ago. While recovering from serious surgery, our German sister-in-law got the urge to go to Oktoberfest again.

We left on Friday, and the drive up to Helen was devoid of much traffic. The day was filled with brilliant sunshine so I scared my wife and myself a few times, on those curves. When we stopped for lunch on the way, I got the best place to park and we got the best table with the best view of the beautiful Dahlonega Square. We got the perfect parking place when we arrived in Helen and the family was found immediately. Best of all, the fest hall wasn't crowded on Friday night and we could hear each other talk and dance without seriously injuring anyone around us. We even managed to get a table where the whole family could sit together. It didn't rain on my car once, even though on Saturday nature tried its best with a short thunderstorm. But I outsmarted it and got one of the prime covered parking spots at the motel. So on Sunday morning with the return of the sun, I drove a still shiny clean Prelude back home. Even getting lost on the way back, due to my not paying attention, was fun. I also got to see a Formula One race when I got home. And guess what? My favorite driver won the race.

I have a friend I call Homer Lee Brown. Actually, some of that is his real name. He and I have managed to spend half our working lives together on the road for the U.S. Army. While we got kidded a lot and called salt and pepper (white and black) by our clients, they were always satisfied with the products we gave them. Homer, an eternal optimist, has a saying that my penchant for negativism hasn't let me embrace over the years, "Life is good!" Maybe after this weekend I might just be able to say it a little more often.

BUYING CARS WITH THE GREATEST GENERATION

This week has been my yearly pilgrimage to Mecca, car Mecca that is. Well, I didn't actually go there but I camped out in front of the TV set for six straight days watching the Barrett-Jackson Classic Car Auction. If I had gone, I'm afraid I'd have come home with a couple of cars worth double mortgages on the house and a detour through Las Vegas for a quickie divorce at the insistence of my wife. Since I limit my classic car purchases to promotional models on eBay, I have yet to send us into bankruptcy.

All this car stuff of late brought back fond childhood memories of my daddy's and uncle's adventures in car buying during the fifties and sixties when autos were flamboyant, and from my point of view those buying them were larger than life too. Being a kid, I never worried about where money came from to buy a car and I didn't really understand why adults got so emotional about negotiating a price. It was just fun looking at that shiny chrome and getting free key chains, balloons and brochures. And I will never forget the wonderful smell new cars emit. I have to admit not much has changed with me over the years when I buy a car. In those days cars' styles changed yearly and if your family kept one for more than three or four years, people started wondering about your finances. The cars themselves didn't really last that long either, as they were purposely not built to last. Sometimes I wonder if anything has changed except maybe the lack of annual body style revisions.

I suppose I should have paid more attention to my daddy's negotiating since I've been a dismal failure all my life at bluffing car salesmen; even when I have all the facts, they somehow manage to win the fight. In recent years though, I've walked away a few times, evidence my newest car is seven years old. I can remember my daddy spending an entire day arguing with a salesman over a few dollars difference. After several hours of hard negotiating for our '57 Pontiac, daddy had to take a bathroom break and that's when the salesman took me aside and showed me a promotional model similar to the car we were negotiating. He said it was mine if I'd help him sell the car to my daddy. Unethical business tactics were not considered bad form in those days. When we got home with my daddy's new Pontiac, I had a perfect place for my new one too, on top of the dresser in my room.

It hasn't been too many years since my Uncle Pete wanted to buy a new car. He asked if I'd go looking with him around where I lived which then was Kennesaw and for all practical purposes Atlanta. His hometown of LaGrange was auto-dealer deprived so he wanted to go to the huge Atlanta dealers he thought sold in volume and would give greater discounts. What he wanted was to argue with a salesman for a half day. Now, I thought going car shopping with my daddy was frustrating but I had to act as interpreter for my stone deaf uncle. I used up an entire notebook writing notes for my uncle to read during the heated negotiations. Finally, the salesman felt sorry for me and began writing his own notes. About six that night, several hours into the negotiation, they finally came within a few dollars of each other. Walking out for one final look at the car, my Uncle Pete suddenly decided he was finished dealing with this guy. He walked me out to his car and we went back to my house empty handed. The next week, back in dealer deprived LaGrange, he bought a car from a local dealer. Yes, perhaps it is better not being one from the "Greatest Generation."

MENTAL ILLNESS IN CATS

Actually, this story begins with humans, my wife specifically. She's a big cat lover, meaning all cats and not just the big ones. When we first got E.J. Smut and found out she was a girl, the decision was made to get her spayed. The last thing we needed was a cat farm right in the middle of suburbia. The job of finding an appropriate vet fell upon my wife.

Since we had never owned an animal together, we didn't have a steady vet to depend on for cat service, so my wife decided to find a local vet for our and the cat's convenience. She thumbed through the yellow pages and found the closest one which was listed in Woodstock, not the infamous concert town, but the one just above Kennesaw. She dialed the number and, amid dogs barking and various other kind of animal noises where the phone was answered, a woman on the other end said, "Hello." My wife thought, "Uh oh, this group doesn't sound very professional," but after returning the hello, she went ahead and asked, "Could you tell me how much it costs to get a cat spayed?" The lady on the other end hesitated a minute and said, "I'm not sure but hold on, I'll ask someone else." My wife waited and was beginning to feel impatient, thinking perhaps the convenience of a close-by vet wouldn't make up for a lack of professionalism. The lady came back to the phone and said, "We don't know but we think it's about $50." At this point my wife asked, "Is this the veterinary office?" The woman replied, "No, you must have dialed the wrong number." This is a true story.

To get to my mental illness story, Smut, as we call her for short, was a runt. She was the smallest of the litter and last to find a home. She was a real mess when we got her, mentally and physically. My wife recollects that when she first laid eyes on her, Smut was being carried around in the mouth of a large dog within a household of many large dogs. Because of her traumatic childhood Smut has not been the friendliest and trusting of animals. Today, sixteen years later, Smut has yet to give me a friendly lick. She does have her merits, among them being a gentle individual, very clean, occasionally obedient (the only cat I know that answers to a whistle) and shorthaired. Smut is a collage of colors that amounts to a tortoise shell type pattern of mostly black with orange/brown, tan and a few in-between splotches. The cat is fat. When viewed from the front or rear, it is obvious that she lists to port, as that is where she carries most of the residue of multiple meals per day. Her cat balance goes from time to time these days, and when she bounds up on things with narrow edges like the sofa, she has to catch herself with claws to prevent losing her cat cool. Up until recently her weight had not hindered her agility, but lately I've noticed it takes a while to pull up on the sofa. She crawls up the end of the arm of the sofa, when one grab by the front claws used to do it. Now the first grab is to get a foothold so she can grab higher and eventually pull the extra bulk on up to the level part of the arm.

Smut is what is known in the trade as a yo-yo cat. She tries to see how many times she can get us to let her out, then let her in. Usually this can be successfully accomplished about 50 times a day before someone decides she can cool her heels outside awhile. You don't pick Smut up and hold her. If you put her in your lap, she is gone by the time you let go. On the other hand if she decides on her own to get in your lap you are trapped for an indefinite lap time. We call this "being cat-bound" and it happens frequently in the winter.

I remember one time we had a visitor cat. Actually the little cat was a very pretty kitten that sort of appeared one night. It sounded like the cat world had ended outside our door. Our house at this time is a California-style contemporary and has a frame of what normally would be a roof over the walk that leads to the front door. On top of the frame is Smut's combination strategic observation post and security spot. The little kitty cat had treed Smut there and she was having a holy-terror fit. All the little cat wanted was a mamma; it was lost, hungry and scared, and it was standing at the foot of the post meowing. My wife rescued Smut and fed the little cat.

That was the beginning of the little cat's time with us. It had personality and would lick you. It behaved like a dog, dragging anything around that it could get its mouth on. His worst habit was eating out of whatever bowl Smut chose to eat from. They each had a set of food and water bowls, but when he started eating out of Smut's, she would leave and go to the other. So would the little cat. We put them in the garage during inclement weather – wrong move. The little cat made a fatal faux 'paw' while in the garage. It developed a case of diarrhea on the hood of my 300 ZX. As a result he was offered up to the gods of the Humane Society ads in the newspaper. We had several candidates apply and finally we settled on a lady from up north, yes a Yankee, living alone in seriously ritzy East Cobb. We called a time or two after that to check on the kitten, and found he shared her bed at night and seemed quite content to live in the luxurious area of the county.

Thus ends my tale of mental illness in cats. Even when a cat is not under mental stress, there's never a dull moment except when they are sleep, which fortunately happens frequently.

SOME THINGS MY CAT AND I
THOUGHT UP ON THE BACK PORCH

For starters, it really isn't a back porch, it's a back deck. Deck in the sense that it's a concrete pad that adjoins our pool and affords me an opportunity to think when the mood strikes. It just so happens my cat E.J. Smut and I are spending more and more time out there doing some serious thinking. It helps when I carry my Longstreet hat and replica Confederate 1860 model Army Colt revolver.

The pistol, even though it doesn't work, looks real enough to prevent Sammy from coming into the yard. He's the "TOM" that's in love with Smut. He is also the same cat that hisses at me when I'm forced to ask him to leave. You know, of all the boy friends my daughter has had that I chased away, not a single one of them ever hissed at me. Some said a few things under their breath I'm probably just as well off not hearing, but I probably wouldn't have "heard" even if they'd yelled.

This cat courting business isn't all it's cracked up to be either.

They don't get along at all and it seems to me like he would get the message. My wife refuses to let me shoot him in the hind quarters with my BB rifle as she says she can't believe I would consider such a thing. Like on the Christmas Story, my mother used to tell me I'd put my own eye out if I owned a BB gun. I never figured out how I could do that exactly if I was the one shooting the gun. Women are smart like that, you know. But then that subject is a little deeper than I want to go today.

Anyway, Smut and I have had a few sessions together and decided if we prevailed upon my wife to stop feeding Sammy cat treats and going out and rubbing his back whenever he comes over, that he will eventually get the message. Well, my wife consented to try this for a while and guess what? It didn't work. He thinks he lives with us now. Just the other day I tried again to use a little friendly persuasion to get Sammy to leave peaceably and again I got hissed at. I wanted to get my BB gun really bad, knowing my wife was in the bathtub and wouldn't see what happened; but I remembered her words "What kind of man have I married? If I had known you would shoot helpless animals with a BB gun, I would have thought twice." That cat isn't helpless because he's got teeth and claws, and let her get hissed at a time or two and she'll change her tune. Besides he's as pushy as any Yankee I've ever known. I'm not sure he would even move if I did shoot him with my BB gun.

There he was again this morning, crouched on our deck next to the sliding glass door watching me eat breakfast. And I know he'll be there tonight when we turn the lights out in the kitchen. He's even taken to hiding in the garage before we can close the door at night. He knows Smut sleeps there, so why not surprise her right after she settles down. Of course Smut isn't always exactly a willing participant, and when she lets loose with a catly rebel yell, I know I need to rush the cavalry to her assistance. I pull her in the house, then open the garage door and let out my own rebel yell. It usually herds him out rather quickly and I return Smut to her protected domain.

I guess maybe Smut will eventually become an all-the-time house cat whether she likes it or not. This weekend we are going to the mountains for a little R&R and we're leaving Smut in the house for the time. Hopefully in that serene atmosphere, I can do a little more thinking about how to rid our lives of the tabby tom named Sammy. Of course, it'll be hard since my wife doesn't want me to take my Longstreet hat and replica Colt, not to mention my BB gun, on vacation.

PART THREE:

HOME AND TECHNOLOGY IMPROVEMENTS

If any of you out there remember Mr. V.R. Stephens, I need say no more. If you don't remember him and you remember the Tim Allen show, then I need say no more. Whether or not you are familiar with these two gentlemen, it will behoove you to read on and learn why I asked these questions in the first place. Life in the city isn't always city oriented. Sometimes it means one has to do his own building, fixing or replacing of stuff, programming and reprogramming of demented machines, and sometimes reprogramming himself. There are those times when it would be very useful to have Mr. Stephens around again. But please promise not to laugh out loud, because I don't need any more people knowing about this than necessary.

When compared to electronic skills, my home improvement ones begin to look as though they could equal Bob Villa's. Computers and I not getting along go way back, at work and home, and it saddens me to have to admit that fact. My skills and understanding of computers and other electronic devices weren't too bad at first, but then the machines got a lot smarter and more complex and eventually lost me.

SPRING CLEANING

All right, so I'm bone lazy. My daddy told me I was the

laziest boy he'd ever seen in his life. What I didn't know then is I have an under active thyroid. Okay, so that doesn't wash completely with my wife but she gives it some credence. Unfortunately for me, she tends to agree with my daddy's assessment in spite of my medical condition. I'm lazy and God made me that way for a reason. You'd think my wife would just accept that as the reason why I'm reluctant to do anything requiring manual or mental labor, especially around the house. She doesn't and says maybe I'm put here to learn to overcome my laziness, not accept it.

Here's what I'm up against this coming spring. What, spring is already here? I'm dangerous with mechanical equipment. My shop teacher Mr. Stephens could have told you I don't know a left handed hammer from a right handed one. He never let me cut stuff on the radial arm saw in shop class, not because he was afraid I'd cut my arm off, but because he was afraid I'd cut his off. I warned my wife whatever I fixed might come back to haunt her in the future. How can spreading pine straw do that? Well I don't know just yet. Nevertheless, the front yard is freshly bedded. Oh, and the twelve bales in the back yard are still there un-spread. I used to save work for my daddy because I knew he would want me to. My wife thanked me for saving the pine straw for her to spread but didn't accept the offer. Truth is I've been spared spreading it by an act of God, thunderstorms. See, I told you he meant me to be lazy.

I thought about hiring someone to finish the pine straw spreading, like I did to rebuild the pool house and install the mirrored closet doors in the spare bedroom. Can you imagine the hospital bill if I had not gotten someone to install the mirrors? Oh, and the gutters, they need cleaning, next weekend. I know because I couldn't see out any windows this week for the rain streaming over pine-straw-packed gutters. Anyway, someone already cuts the grass but he doesn't trim bushes. This winter I was unmercifully sent out into the cold to cut down or trim bushes while she did the cooking for the day. They now qualify as trees due to the fact I haven't touched them since we moved in fifteen years ago. There are certain muscle groups in your body that should never be used after you turn fifty. I know that to be a fact after this winter.

At least we don't have to take mattresses out and beat them to death, like mother used to do. Although I did sometimes enjoy beating those mattresses as it got rid of a lot of built up frustration. I certainly can't do that to the windows I have to clean this spring, even if I want to; they never go back together once I've taken them apart. I'm the only person I know that has leftover parts every time I clean a window, or for that matter anything. And don't talk to me about pressure cleaning the pool deck, just refer to the paragraph above regarding Mr. Stephens. Oh, and planting flowers. I knew there was a reason I was never a flower child, it's too much work. I don't like planting anything that requires digging holes.

But don't worry too much about my work ethic being compromised. I'll make up for it this summer. The Longstreet hat will get plenty of wear while I conjure up more articles. You see, my best thinking comes when I lie under that wide brimmed hat for a little siesta around the pool, say every weekend.

LIVING THE LIFE OF RILEY

"What a revolt'n development this is!" to quote Chester A. Riley. I doubt most of you know about the fifties TV sitcom named "The Life of Riley." Well, the character aptly played by William Bendix, the superb fifties character actor, was a good natured but bumbling idiot. Somehow after the garage door repairman left today I got the distinct feeling that maybe my wife thought about good old Riley. Of course Peg, Riley's wife, never found fault with him even the time he rewired the house and caused a flood; and outside of a daunting look neither did my wife. Don't ask me how Riley flooded his house but if you give me a month or two, I'll duplicate it for you.

Getting back to the garage door fiasco, it was about a week ago when I pushed the button to raise the door and it opened fine. Then when I went to close it, the thing got about a third of the way down and went back up. I'm not stupid, well then I didn't think I was stupid, so I tried it again to be sure. It did the same thing every time. I checked the tracks and they were clear. Then I looked at the little laser boxes at the bottom of the door that automatically return it to the up position when anything blocks its beam, like our cat Smut did with frequency, but the light was working. Just to be on the safe side, I cleared away the spider webs around it and tried again. You guessed it, nothing. So I unhooked the door from the opener and manually opened it, so I could get the car out and close it again.

When we returned from our shopping trip it was raining, so I just hopped out and manually raised the door while getting drenched. Once the car was inside I thought to myself the opener should be over its tantrum by now and work. Nope! It did the same thing one more time. Knowing my propensity from years of working for the Army where the Vision Statement includes stuff like breaking things, killing people and destroying things that do not immediately work, I decided instead to call a professional for help. That should be cheaper than calling someone to install a new garage door opener, to repair other damage to the garage and to pay a divorce lawyer, shouldn't it? I thought so. So I went inside, looked up a repair shop and gave them a call. The guy told me to go out and hold down the button until the garage door closed all the way then release it. I did and it closed all the way. Then he said don't touch it again and we'll be out next week.

Today the repairman arrived on time as advertised. He stood outside while I pushed the button and opened the door. Then I told him to observe as I pushed the button for the door to get one third down and automatically retract. It reached one third, then one half, then two thirds, and finally it closed all the way. ARGH! It's done it to me again! Yes, there is a conspiracy by all the mechanical devices in this house and others I've lived in, too, to make me appear just like Chester A. Riley. I won't tell you how much the service call cost because you'll just snicker and point at me. Of course, the technician could find nothing wrong anywhere because there never was anything wrong in the first place. After bidding him goodbye, I sneaked the checkbook back to its place in the drawer and came up here to write this all down before I forget it. Oh, my wife just came up and asked why the front door was standing wide open in thirty degree weather. That one is Gillis' fault. No, don't ask who Gillis is.

THE PERILS OF HOME IMPROVEMENT

Don't ever open your mouth to your wife about how things need to change around the house. In fact, don't open your mouth period. This sage advice comes from one who has sinned by bringing to her attention our kitchen and bathrooms which had not seen change since KC and the Sunshine Band had a number one hit.

It only took one comment before the plans were laid, and things started to appear on the kitchen table like rolls of wallpaper for accent touches. You can ask my Shop teacher Mr. Stephens if you want, but I've never pretended to be a handyman. Of course, since my wife proofs a lot of what I write, she knows I'm the only guy in shop class that actually fell for the old "left handed hammer" routine. We decided the smart thing to do was get a recommendation from someone whom we trust. There was no one better than good-old-boy Gene of Gene's Tree Service to ask. You see, Gene built the fence around our backyard to make sure we could go swimming in our pool without the entire neighborhood seeing us and also joining us with their kids. Only problem is, Gene put the horizontal planking, that holds the fence slats in place, on the wrong side, but we all can make mistakes. He did a great job taking down our trees, though, and one of them was actually a tree I selected to come down. When we asked for a recommendation for someone to do interior decoration he said, "That ain't no problem at all. There's this old boy, Dave; I know his daddy. He'll do you a good job." Well, that was good enough for us. Now we had an inside track to someone we could depend on to do it right.

We gave Dave a call the next day and he said he'd be right over. That was fast, and now I know why. He showed up with his wife and two kids. I don't remember asking him to bring the family. Anyway he was ready to go right then, but we decided an estimate was the best way to start. He measured everything in the kitchen including Smut the cat, who just happened to be having lunch. She's exactly 16 1/2 inches long if you don't count her tail. After he finished, he told us he'd go and get the new countertops ordered as well as the new ceiling light covers and paints. It sounded good. Of course my wife made sure to clear up a few little details with him, like he should make sure he sanded the cabinets before painting because we decided not to replace them. He was Johnny-on-the-spot saying, "Yes ma'am we aim to please. Me and my daddy we been in business for years and ain't never had no complaints. You can ask Gene. Why, I been knowing Gene since I was about six years old and he can tell you exactly what I can do." It was an interesting story but we had to interrupt. We were afraid if we let him finish, it would be bedtime for his kids before he could leave.

The first day Dave was there exactly as he said he would be, and he worked hard for all of three hours banging stuff, moving things and splashing paint all over the new ceiling light tiles and our fairly new carpet. If the coral paint matched those things I guess it wouldn't have been so bad. His wife made a feeble attempt at cleaning the carpet with a broom. Okay, so he isn't perfect. He actually sanded one cabinet. I saw him do it. When he took the doors to the cabinet home with him to paint I was skeptical, but when he returned them they looked pretty good except for a couple of places he missed. But that was two days later. One of his kids got sick and, whatever it was, Dave got it too, and then it was an emergency job for someone else. We patiently waited for two more days and heard nothing.

It was getting pretty close to our scheduled vacation, and Dave had promised to get finished before we left. We pointed this out when we finally reached him by phone. So he farmed the kids out and he and his wife spent the weekend with us. Finally he finished the kitchen even though my wife found a lot of touch up requirements, so we left on our trip.

When we returned, we found a leftover piece of the venetian blinds that Dave had reinstalled, sitting out on the counter. Now, I know I've taken things apart and put them back together with fewer parts than they originally had, but Dave does this kind of thing for a living. I managed to find out where the piece went after taking the blinds down and the brackets apart. Dave hadn't done that because the white paint under the brackets proved it. The trim work around the windows and the baseboards also indicated maybe Dave either didn't see them or he ran out of paint. Anyway, he owed us a bathroom counter and painting. So we called him, not knowing if he had left town or would just say, "Who are you again?" But he did come back. This time he brought his wife and only one of his kids. He told us he meant to stay until it was done. I signaled my wife to get some fresh linen out and we'd make the bed in the spare bedroom. You see Dave didn't do anything fast.

He finished in one day. I think I know how he did it now. There was still a shadow on the wall where a picture hung in the bathroom in an area that was supposed to be painted. Do you know that if you paint over those dark places, you usually cover them up? Dave dances back into the living room and reveals to us his ability to get Home Depot to mix paint so good that you can't even tell the difference between the paint on the bathroom walls and the new stuff he just bought. He managed to paint the walls in record time and still recreate the shadow from the old paint. Isn't it amazing? At this point we just wanted him to go, so we paid him and he left. Do you want to know why he came over so fast to begin with? I don't believe Dave has too many repeat customers. Now, if someone would be kind enough send me Mr. Stephens' telephone number, I need to talk to him about how to redo my kitchen and bathrooms.

JIM, THE TOOL MAN, DALE

Yesterday, I decided to work on a model ship I had started over five years ago for a housewarming gift. So what if it's a little late, it's the thought that counts. If I last long enough, I'll get it finished. But since the house it was meant for needed stuff then, and it might not now, there is no telling where this ship will end up. I just hope it isn't in something circular under the kitchen sink.

You may remember, over the course of my writing, hearing about my skills or lack thereof at assembling things. And I'm sure you'll remember me telling you about Mr. Stephens, my high school shop teacher, putting a level to the bottom of a bookcase I built in class. Of course he had my best interest at heart because he knew my parents would wonder just what kind of teacher he was, to send home a bookcase that truly "rocked". My parents didn't mind since they knew me.

Not much has changed since high school, even though I've amassed much experience assembling a number of things. My daughter never got a gift from Santa that didn't need "some assembly." I remember the night, all of it in fact, I put together a kitchen set for her. Not a single piece fell off of it until I decided to demonstrate my accomplishment. Her mother made the repairs after I lost patience and nearly ripped a nail off my finger. Recently I told you about putting together some bookcases in this very room where I sit and they're still standing. Speaking of putting things together, the ship is coming along nicely but I did discover my painting skills are still a little rusty. I'm awfully glad I remembered to buy paint thinner because it removed some of the recent smudges from the paint job of five years ago. But my major "piece de triumph" is sitting directly behind me.

The wooden filing cabinet I assembled this weekend equals anything my talented friend Cliff built in shop, and that includes his professional nine-foot-tall gun cabinet with glass in the doors. The filing cabinet has been sitting in the garage for three weeks, I know, just like the ship I'll get around to eventually. With a little "encouragement" from my wife, I did open the box to find a lot of nails, countersink locking screws, dowels, and glue in amongst the pieces of wood. This looked daunting and I figured I'd either have a serious temper tantrum and run up my blood pressure, lose a limb, or quite possibly sever an artery while constructing this thing. It likely wouldn't be level and I'd probably have pieces left over I couldn't identify.

Mulling over all this, I recalled earlier in the week taking the car in to get a headlight replaced. The guys installed the bulbs and told me to turn on the lights to test them, so I turned on the windshield wipers. Laughing under his breath, he showed me the correct switch, and that's when I realized I was the real life version of "Tim, The Tool Man, Taylor." But on this project I did something I've never done before and that is I actually read and studied the instructions; the filing cabinet went together perfectly. No tantrum, no bleeding, no hits, no runs and no errors. I wish my shop teacher had been here to see it as he'd have been pleased and may not even have turned red. Oh yes, it sits perfectly level and it's been a month and nothing has fallen off, yet.

Jim Dale

MAKING ANGELS

Just yesterday, I was pulling down the driveway to head over to the grocery store to pick up a few things so my wife could make some vegetable soup, and I noticed the yard was once again covered with leaves from our overactive elm. It isn't like I hadn't recently spent time getting rid of its latest droppings.

I can remember when it was actually fun to see leaves covering the street. That was when I lived on Marshal Avenue and my mother and Mrs. Pike would spend days at a time raking leaves and talking about everything. Life was magical then and I guess it was because I hadn't had time to grow up and learn all the realities of what it takes to manage those leaves. One thing I notice now when I rake leaves, after more than a quarter century since Marshal Avenue, is the smell of nature which never changes. I wish I could smell the aroma of the smoke from the burning leaves on Marshal Avenue, but if I burned my leaves today I'd be arrested as an environmental outlaw.

There is one thing about raking leaves and that is you don't realize how many there are until it is too late to stop. My yard isn't that big, so I decided to just pop out last Saturday afternoon and rake for an hour or so. After an undetermined period, I went to straighten up to see exactly where I was and I didn't straighten up! I pull the Tim Conway "little old man" act with my wife occasionally when I get up from my recliner. She hates it and promptly tells me to walk straight, but seriously, this time I couldn't straighten up. I thought about calling for help, but decided my wife wouldn't take this seriously. Just as I decided it was worth a try to call for help, I saw the guy walking down the street who looks for all the world like a descendent of the fellow who played the bald zombie in fifties horror flicks. He was ambling on toward me on his daily walk. Since he doesn't acknowledge anyone on these forays, I was hoping my macabre condition wouldn't get his attention. I grabbed my rake and tried to look as natural as a permanently curved spine would allow, but he glanced at me like I was auditioning for his grandpa's part.

It didn't hit me until I was finally able to get fairly straightened up that I had another problem, the leaf bags. Have you ever noticed these bags are made of plastic thinner than the epidermal layer of your skin? Ever try to open one in a hurry? Don't. After getting my blood pressure up past safe levels, I finally spit on my fingers and wriggled them on both sides of the bag and presto it was open. I've never forgotten that little trick and it works great on household trash bags too. Once I discovered how to open leaf bags, I had to master the task of getting things inside them. My street isn't a through street so you have to wonder where all the cars are coming from. I don't recall my neighbors having a half dozen cars apiece? But then we all know leaf raking is a natural vehicle attracting activity. Ever try to get leaves in an onion skin thin bag while a procession of cars cruise by at a speed only acceptable at Road Atlanta? It causes leaves to scatter to the four winds and go everywhere except inside the bag. George Patton said he didn't like to pay for the same real estate twice and I don't like to rake it twice either.

After seeing what fast moving cars do to piles of leaves and realizing I could end up in jail if I tried to burn them, I did the natural thing I always did when I would see a big pile of leaves on Marshall Avenue, I jumped into them. It worked then and it still feels pretty darn good today. I didn't know I could still make angels. Of course, I almost got stepped on by the zombie guy making his circuit back home. So next week when I do this all over again, I'll think about all the fun my mother and Mrs. Pike had raking their leaves in Hogansville. Come to think of it I never saw them making angels. They never knew what they were missing.

YARD MODE

I was lying on the flat of my back. That was the last thing I remembered shortly before I decided I needed to die. My wife and daughter were shooing away all the bees that had used my body for target practice, while I lay helplessly on the ground trying to get my breath. Soon afterwards the x-rays confirmed that my fifty percent compressed L4 vertebra was still only fifty percent compressed. I had decided to clean the gutters when my ungloved hand discovered we had guests we knew nothing about. The bees didn't particularly care for the idea of me raking their home onto the ground so they did something about it. I jumped from the ladder and you know the rest.

Since then that excuse has worked well, almost too well. My wife doesn't want me to clean gutters now unless she holds the ladder and I climb on top of the house so that I can see what I am grabbing. Only problem there is, she gets tired of waiting on me and gets distracted with other things. I never bring a parachute with me on the roof so it never fails, I always spent a few extra minutes up there until my Yvonne sweetest one remembers to come out and hold the ladder for me to climb down. And that isn't the only problem either, because I sometimes walk on the roof. She goes bonkers then because the last guy who roofed the house told her somebody heavy probably caused it to leak by walking around on it. By the way, she classifies me as heavy. But how are you going to get all that pine straw off around the now defunct solar heating system that's permanently attached to the roof? It never worked that well anyway. Logic says you need to heat the pool when the sun isn't out, right? So if the sun isn't out to shine on the solar tubes, this means the pool water doesn't get warm. Come to think of it, the water never got very warm even when the sun was out, because the solar heater leaked all the pool water out on the roof.

As you can tell, we are in "Yard Mode." My wife told me yesterday there were weeds in the new pine straw I just put down all over the yard, and they had to be pulled up. I guess when she eventually decided telling me it needed to be done didn't necessarily mean it would get done, she went out and did it herself. I just thought she was informing me out of courtesy while she was going to do a little weeding in her flower bed. Anyway I decided while she was pulling weeds, that I'd swim a bit. The "gas" pool heater warmed the water to a comfortable 120 degrees. I do exaggerate sometimes, maybe 90 degrees. I didn't want to boil so I got in the pool chair for awhile. After pulling as many weeds as she could stand, my wife came out and joined me in the pool. About three hours later, even without assistance from the boiling pool water, my skin was a very bright red; not to worry if you are a lobster.

  Was sunburn my pay back for not pulling weeds? Yep, and I still hadn't cleaned the gutters, and they needed it again. Fortunately, there were no bees and I found a place to put my ladder so no one had to come retrieve me when I finished. But I made the mistake of trying to get some excess pine straw off the solar tubing. I got the standard complaint about walking around on the roof and a stern warning that our bedroom was going to leak after I got finished. She said with all the rain we are getting, I'd be sleeping in a wet bed the rest of the summer. It sounded good to me especially with a humdinger of a sunburn.

  I agreed with my wife, as we sat in the glider underneath the shade of the wild cherry tree taking a break from our projects, that we do have our own little paradise even if it is in the middle of the suburbs. Strange, either my hearing aids were on the blink or there really wasn't any traffic to mention on the two interstate highways that parallel either side of our area. I actually heard some birds or it could have been the whistling sound when one of my hearing aid batteries is going dead. Anyway, the birds reminded us we need to load the bird, I mean squirrel, feeder. It's finally summer, and we can enjoy our little paradise if the monsoons stop, if we get all the overdue "Yard Mode" stuff done; if we can stop taking the cars in for repairs; if we finish giving Internet lessons to my eighty-year-old would-be computer hacker uncle; if we aren't needing to visit sick folks and newly born ones; if we get the house cleaned up; and so on.

ON BEING ELECTRONICALLY CHALLENGED

I don't like computers. What's more they don't like me. It seems computers are only one of the modern day contraptions I've recently had trouble with in my life. It doesn't take a complicated piece of equipment to get me confused or frustrated, ask my wife. I've never been accused of being patient either.

We have a VCR in the bedroom that defies programming. I can make it record a program I'm watching, but it refuses to film something using the timer. The remote control for the thing could easily double for a surf board. I've seen modern fighter cockpits simpler than that remote. Come to think of it, I believe the instructions said something about needing an engineering degree, or maybe it was just about the guy who wrote them. I had to use the dictionary while deciphering the guide, but that's not unusual as I need a dictionary to read the paper now-a-days. You'd think working for the government I'd be used to senseless acronyms and have a head start on those instructions. Well, I've found the government has nothing on private industry when it comes to making no sense. Anyway, you have to play the TV to program the VCR, as it prints out stuff on the screen you will need to follow. It asked more questions than my wife did when I traded cars. Some of the questions require you to make a decision, something I try to avoid at all costs. So after going against my nature, I selected a choice and promptly got an 'ERROR' message. That convinced me I was right about never making decisions.

Last week I ran out of excuses as to why I didn't have time to install the coffee maker, a Christmas present from one of the kids a few years back. It had to fit under the kitchen cabinet as a space saver for the counter. You still wouldn't have room to put anything under it? I got out my trusty electric drill and eighteen holes later decided that using glue might just do as well. My wife stepped in about then while there was still time to save the cabinets. She drilled four holes and hung the thing up. Why didn't she do that an hour earlier?

Regardless of my prowess or lack thereof with complicated electronic devices, I did manage to successfully change the light bulb in our bedroom. Best of all I did it without help. I also replaced a hose on the washing machine by myself. So far it's holding. Basking in those successes, I decided to load some software on our computer. I wasn't looking forward to it but was determined to do it myself. That is until the ice storm came and my wife decided if she didn't get away from me and The Travel Channel, that she couldn't be responsible for her actions. She found the stack of disks and promptly began to install the software. So what? I could have done it, but why not let her have fun. It may have saved my sanity and had she not done it, I probably wouldn't have learned how to save money on a vacation to Switzerland which I'll never take.

By the way, I managed to bring our computer off-line temporarily while trying to test the new software. So if you want to comment on this article or get in touch to just thank me for giving you sage advice, you are going to have to beep me. I forgot I don't have a beeper, so just call. I also don't have a cell phone, yet. So you'll just have to phone me at home. Then you had better do it when I'm here since I don't have an answering machine either. Not that I can't install or operate any of this stuff, it's just . . . .

THE REINCARNATION OF CHRISTINE

Did you ever wonder what happened to that crushed '58 Plymouth Belvedere whose radio suddenly came on, just as Stephen King's horror movie "Christine" ended? Well, some Eastern religions believe when a person dies he or she comes back later on as another person. Interesting thought, but I suspect even though she was pretty crushed up there at the end, Christine has returned in the person of the Dale family's personal computer.

It's hard for me not to believe all computers do not have a little Christine heritage in their backgrounds. You see, I've never been able to get too close to any of them nor have they cared much for allowing me to get close. Upon my first introduction to computers in the Army, I realized I'd need more than one course of college algebra to become friends with one of these contraptions. Fortunately, I had a boss who had a math degree and he saved me several times from either a heart attack or from being fired for willfully destroying government property.

When my section was transferred to the U.S. Army Reserve Command, I sometimes wondered if the division I worked for didn't have its own computer support branch just so I could keep up with everybody else. Dennis, the branch manager, was a great guy and certainly had the right disposition for a computer geek. Nothing bothered him much; well, that is except about every other day when I'd come into his office with some kind of computer glitch. Usually he and I got to work before anyone else so he expected to see me at his door with my cup of coffee in hand, asking if he had a minute to explain why my computer either just sat there and looked back at me with a blank screen or popped up a bunch of hieroglyphics that never came close to making a complete sentence. He was never disappointed in his expectation of seeing me and my computer problems. He'd laugh and then ask to see it. Usually I'd take him to the thing and he'd push one or two keys, but sometimes if the problem was hard, he'd have to go to another screen and it would graciously acquiesce to his calm demeanor. I never got around to telling Dennis I'd contemplated kicking the juice out of the thing a couple of times before coming down to get him.

Well, that was Army computers. Now to what I believe is Christine reincarnate. Our beast is a foreboding solid black plastic and just looks plain evil. The little, red, beady eyes staring at me with full defiance and the little, green lights flickering on and off daring a touch of any key without the wrath of God being struck down on me. If I so much as try to unravel its demonic chips, it quickly diverts my attention to the perverted printer that goes into convulsions. Working methodically, my wife saves the day by applying the programmatic equivalent of running it through a car crusher. This usually gets the thing back on line so I can happily return to my work; but like Christine whom we all thought was dead at the end of the movie, the evil, red lights flash on again and the green ones flicker and get stronger, then the screen freezes up. Well isn't this where you came in?

DR. STRANGELOVE, OR:
HOW I LEARNED TO LOVE THE COMPUTER

I had occasion this past week to watch "Dr. Strangelove, or: How I Learned to Stop Worrying and Love the Bomb." For those of you under fifty this is the icon of farce movies, about the accidental launching of nuclear war between the U.S. and the U.S.S.R. It's supposed to be a comedy about a computer/human glitch and a bunch of bunglers who try to reverse the error. But it's too close to reality for comfort.

I don't know if the movie just happened to air when it did or if it was an ominous harbinger of things to come. Shortly after I finished watching the movie, I sat down at the computer to answer a few e-mails and compose my column for the *Beacon*. Then, like Dr. Strangelove's demented mechanical arm that tried to choke him at the most inopportune times, the computer went north. Before my very eyes, the thing self-destructed. It took with it the address book, my favorite websites, every program on its hard disk and a few that weren't there for extra measure.

Looking and behaving somewhat like George C. Scott and

Sterling Hayden, the two maniacal U.S. Generals in Dr. Strangelove, I lost touch with reality which isn't too unusual for me when I'm normal. But I didn't shoot any coke machines to get quarters to call for help. My wife did. Well actually she didn't shoot anything, but I think she did give it serious thought when I went into my hysterics. I was banished to the basement to continue my never-ending pursuit of sorting through my stuff for something I can throw away. After getting rid of one major menace, me, she called the server help number and got someone who almost had a handle on the English language, and they began the process of reviving the machine from the dead.

After a couple of hours of no success with finding anything that deserved a trash can, I went back upstairs to check my wife's progress. I found her lower half stretched out on the floor and the rest under the computer table in a life or death struggle with wire tentacles and pronged claws, and the telephone on her ear. To gain her good graces again, I handed her a flashlight, the one tool that enabled her to successfully extract herself from the dilemma. I won't call it a draw because my wife did have the upper hand when the day ended, but the thing was still defying her efforts to bring it back to a sane state. The next day she went in with a terrible resolve and finally won the battle and that is why you see my article in print today.

If you must know, I was born too late. I should have lived earlier in the twentieth century before the advent of the computer scourge. I have been harassed, threatened and even bitten once or twice by computer, trying to end my career early. I never thought the things would follow me home after retirement. It's good the Army doesn't take to change very quickly or I'd been replaced by a computer before I retired. I'm convinced after seeing Dr. Strangelove and the movie "I Robot" that these things can be dangerous to your health and can't be trained like a dog to obey commands. I may write the Feds and ask them to start putting labels on the monsters like they do cigarettes. I think anything that contributes to high blood pressure, a stroke, heart attack, or risk of your wife murdering you to keep from being driven crazy, is dangerous to your health. I'm just glad I've got my wife working on our computer instead of Dr. Strangelove or we might all have been be singing, "We'll meet again some sunny day" while the world blew up.

PART FOUR:

HEALTH AND HAPPINESS?

What is the old saying? "If I had known I'd live this long I'd taken better care of myself." No one told me when I was younger I would have to learn to take care of my health in order to keep breathing. Well, now someone has, and it's a good thing because I might not be here to tell you a story if my wife had not put me on the road to controlling weight and watching my diet. You don't have to give up all of the wonderful food you eat, you just don't have to eat as much of it. Oh yes, when you see all the diet foods and supplements advertised on TV, showing sleek and slender models who probably have never overeaten in their entire lives, you must remember you can't look this way unless, and here comes more bad news, you exercise along with the diet. No one said it is easy but it sure feels good once you've done it, and you don't look too bad either.

WEIGHING THE YEARS

Through the years I have been troubled with weight, either too much of it or too little. I went from a plump seventh grader to a lean, skinny senior in high school. I got accused of looking like Darren on "Bewitched." If you don't remember him, you must have been "lost in space" during the 60s. Okay, I'll try and describe him. He was tall and skinny, and had short hair which he kept slicked back. He wasn't a nerd, but I was. I could never understand how he got Samantha. Then I didn't understand how Larry Hagerman got Jeanne either. In fact, I didn't care that much because for me the big question in life then was why Dan Gurney's car quit on the last lap at Sebring back in 1966.

It didn't take long before the "fat period" returned when I was a sophomore in college. I had just had the best picture ever of my life taken. My wife says it doesn't look like me. I wanted to get it made into an 8X10 glossy and sent immediately to MGM and Paramount or, better yet, distributed among the female population at West Georgia College. But before the developing fluid dried I noticed the resemblance between me and the picture had disappeared. Some of my classmates asked where my picture was in the yearbook. When I pointed it out they looked inquisitively at me and said, "Nah, they put the wrong guy's picture next to your name." I didn't say anything, as usually they were bigger than me (muscle not fat) and I didn't need bruises to compliment my additional bulk.

Fortunately the expansion ceased during my junior year when I did physical labor on the school's grounds maintenance crew, and it began to recede. That resulted in me meeting and marrying someone before my weight started to climb again. That didn't take long, as her recipe book contained such things as fried chicken and steak smothered in onions and gravy. The steady meals along with a reduced work schedule soon began to show results. When I graduated from college, I weighed a hefty two-hundred pounds and pictures of me and my wife looked like John Candy and Twiggy.

Needless to say, the military reduced me to one-hundred-fifty trim pounds in six short weeks of Hell. I bought thirty-four inch waist pants for the first time since I was a freshman in college. They lasted six months until I resumed the fried chicken and steak diet again, with no exercise. This rocked on for thirteen more years. My remarriage to someone who rarely fried anything resulted in stabilization but no loss of weight. Loss is what I needed, so I resorted to the dreaded weight loss companies. If I mention the one I went to they will probably sue me, but just as in the Air Force I lost thirty pounds in a short period. Actually, I lost ten more than the weight loss folks wanted me to. Yes, as a true Methodist I backslid and regained much of the weight resulting in another visit to the weight loss plan and a more serious effort to really change my habits.

I've maintained, as my daughter likes to say, my Karen Carpenter figure for almost twenty years now but recently I've noticed I've grown fond of fattening food again in my old age. The cheese will have to stop with the glass of wine in the evening. I also will have to cease buying Texas Toast and the "fat free" ice cream bars my wife and I have taken to splitting with our nighttime vitamin supplements. Oh yes, my present wife has maintained her Karen Carpenter figure all her life, so with that example at hand I should have no problem. Should I?

A JACK AUBREY DINNER

"A glass of wine with you Mrs. Dale," as Captain Jack Aubrey of Patrick O'Brian fame would have said if my wife had been at the dinner table of HMS Surprise's gun room during the Napoleonic Wars. No one ate better than a Post Captain of one of His Majesty the King's ships, and no one I know of makes a better meal than my wife.

Tonight we decided to grill out, in spite of the heat that suffocated the back deck of our own HMS Surprise. We had just gotten back from looking at the deal of the century and turning it down. One of our sister-in-law's friends has a leather sofa and love seat that cost a lot more than we'd have cared to pay when I was gainfully employed. The seller and her husband are moving to a new house and starting over by buying all new furniture. The sofa and love seat weren't that old, but then they wouldn't do in our house according its Master and Commander. We bought a steak to celebrate our decision one way or the other. So after returning from our outing, I fired up the grill and went to assist in the preparation of an artichoke. My wife made garlic mashed potatoes and oversaw the entire meal making process.

I don't do that well cooking on the grill or the stove; however, I do have my specialties such as Gumbo and Traylor hamburgers. Usually when I'm left in charge of the grill we have company, so I get carried away talking and sometimes forget what's cooking. We've had some pretty well-done stuff and some burnt stuff, too, as a result of my watch or lack there of. Tonight there were no distractions, well maybe one, a thunderstorm. After I put the half inch sirloin on the hot grill and watched the flames lick its bottom, I went back in to check on the artichoke. I didn't stay long before I heard a rumble. When I checked again the steak had browned pretty well on one side so I turned it over and raised it up from the fire a bit. Then there was another rumble. The wind picked up and then I felt a few drops of rain. My wife hurried out and decided we could finish the steak in the microwave. By the time I made myself a Caesar salad neither of us had thought to put the meat in the microwave.

We sat down to a rare steak, a level of rareness neither of us had wanted to experience. As a kid, and even as an adult, I sent steaks back that weren't cooked through and through. I can also remember having to saw my way through a few of those steaks. Over the years I figured out if you don't cook meat too done, it seems to be a bit more tender. This time though it was red throughout and in my humble opinion almost ready to moo. But after a couple of bites along with a few artichoke leaves, salad and those wonderful potatoes, I decided this meal would have pleased Captain Aubrey prodigiously. No one enjoyed a meal more than this man and tonight he would have been right at home.

Oh by the way, the storm didn't totally materialize after the prelude chased me from the grill. How in the heck did we mess up that many dishes? Well the crew, which is composed of my wife and me, cleaned up the mess in short order. Now I'm sitting here in my great cabin thoroughly contented and wondering if we are going to be in for a serious blow tonight before the last dog watch.

PIZZA TO GO-OOOO

My wife is not a fan of eating out. Don't read it again, I wrote it right the first time. I've done the unforgivable by making her go out to dinner so much it isn't special anymore. You've heard about doing something so much that it loses its mystery? Well, would you call going out to dinner four nights a week too much? She does, and I do now.

How did we come to go out to dinner so much? Before you get any wrong ideas, it's not her cooking. She thought that too. But honestly my wife is a good cook and I will defend her gourmet delicacies with my life. Well, maybe not with my life but certainly with my fork and knife on the ready, which by the way is what she says is the first thing she sees every evening when she gets home from work. Okay, so I love food. Sometimes I can't wait to get it cooked so I insist on going to a local restaurant to unwind from the day. We can have a meal and not worry about who will wash, dry and put away the dishes. Recently we replaced our automatic dishwasher with a new one because the old one died from lack of use. You see, my wife doesn't believe in running it unless we have occasion to feed a combat division at Ft. Mac which doesn't happen with any frequency. She hates loading and unloading it worse than washing the dishes, so we manually do the dishes most nights.

Anyway, doing the dishes isn't the only reason for my wanting to eat out. We save time from cooking and cleaning too. Lately I've stopped pushing my wife to go out and eat, and I just pick something up on my way home. This sort of remedies the "I hate going out so much" syndrome, except when she decides to start one of her self-imposed diets to lose a pound or two from the one twelve she normally carries. The bumper-to-bumper rush hour traffic just up our street has also put a damper on eating out. So to break the monotony of bringing in fast food, I occasionally order something to be delivered. Last Friday night my wife came home in the mood for pizza. I picked up the phone and called our usual take out place to learn they were renovating and not doing delivery for a while. I searched the phone book for an alternate and found one two miles away, meaning we'd be lucky to see our pizza in an hour, with rush hour traffic you know.

After ordering the pizza I went back to the "computer room" to peruse the Internet. This room has a view of the driveway so I could see the guy as he arrived. When the delivery guy made his way to the door, I dashed for the checkbook. But the expected knock and doorbell didn't come; instead I heard a slam and a yelp akin to a rebel yell. As I looked through the narrow window running parallel with our front door, I saw a rampaging gray car with a guy chasing it down our steep curved driveway. I didn't think he could catch it and I wondered what he would do if he did. I remember remarking to myself that he wasn't as quick as most dogs I'd seen doing that. The car veered off between my mail box and driveway running lights and went across the street to hit the only tree that would prevent it from plowing into our across-the-street neighbor's house. In spite of all the noise and chaos, the episode gave me a chance to see my neighbor again, meet some new neighbors who stopped to offer assistance, and learn there's a guy on the other street who owns a tow truck company. He just happens to keep one of his trucks in his driveway. The gathering got really festive after a while.

As for the pizza guy, well, he picked up a few potential customers and found his car wasn't any worse for the wear. When he drove away, the neighbors wandered on back home and I found my pizza intact exactly on the door step where it was abandoned for the chase. You can't get that kind of service, entertainment, and food at a restaurant without spending big bucks, so I think I'll order out more often. Besides, my wife is happier, I developed a closer relationship with my neighbors, and who knows I might just need that tow truck myself someday.

BUTTERMILK CHICKEN

I can remember it well, not how long my wife has been on this diet, but the last time we had Buttermilk Chicken for dinner. If I tell you exactly how it is prepared then I'll have to have some, and it wouldn't do on this diet. You see, my wife decided she was fat. This woman who weighs a hundred and fourteen pounds soaking wet with her clothes on noticed she could almost feel a little something around her waist. With me I see and not just feel something around my waist, and it's not little.

I'm not officially required to be on this diet but you know when the one who is dieting also possesses all the institutional knowledge on cooking skills (a diplomatic way of saying she knows how to cook and I don't) then I'm subject to semi-starvation too. Well, no one really starves because you get squash and onions steamed in a microwave, green beans and onions (she like onions), and carrots (and I bet you thought I was going to say onions again) without any seasoning except salt and pepper and no butter. Maybe I might prefer starvation after all. It doesn't taste as bad as it sounds, though. That doesn't keep me from making an excuse to go to the kitchen so I can rip open the fat-free potato chips that taste like gourmet cardboard and wash them down with a caffeine-free Diet Coke. If I'm still starving after that, I open the refrigerator and devour the leftover salad (lettuce, tomatoes, and you guessed it, onions). If I wanted to splurge I could eat a fat-free sugar-free frozen juice stick (fondly called a popsicle by my wife). Who says she doesn't have an imagination?

She did go out to a restaurant with me, although she reminded me she never coerced me into such a temptation when I was dieting. When I was trying to lose weight I wasn't dieting, I was being slowly murdered by Jenny Craig. At the restaurant I ordered Sicilian Zita with a ton of cheeses, pasta and eggplant. Incidentally, it was accompanied by an endless salad covered with all kinds of oil and rolls swimming in butter and garlic. She ordered a plain salad and dressing on the side (which she almost never uses). While I stuffed my face, she sat there and tried to figure out how I could get all that in my mouth at one time without doing irreversible harm to my jaw bones. Eventually even I felt guilty. Between bites of butter-dripping rolls and pasta, I pictured her as being a political prisoner of the Viet Cong slowly being starved and threatened with water torture. Oh, that reminds me she drank water with the salad, too. I really couldn't enjoy making myself sick on Italian food knowing she was watching and possibly starving. So for the time being, I've given up the idea of eating out while she diets. Back to the kitchen for snacks I guess.

My wife has been on this diet now for about a week I think. Just yesterday she announced it won't be much longer. I was hoping she was talking about the diet and not her imminent starvation. I've been meaning to have a look at our scales. I'll bet they are broken. If I do just a little fine tuning on them I'll bet I could get them to work just fine. Once she realizes her true weight is really three pounds less than she thought, this diet thing could end quicker.

One good thing about all this is we have saved money at the grocery store. Now-a-days we buy more stuff than food when we go there. I even bought an umbrella last week just to make the trip worthwhile. You need to go to the grocery store whether you buy any food or not; you don't want to forget how to get there just in case you decide to start eating again. It also provides me with an opportunity to try and steer this woman toward some tempting item that might snap her out of this non-eating comma. She especially likes ice cream. But wouldn't you know it, when I got her near the freezer section she found these low fat ice cream sandwiches. I think the chocolate sides are made of some space age carbon fiber material. They sorta taste like chocolate, but then I haven't tasted real chocolate in so long I'm not sure.

Okay, so I'm exaggerating some of this. You probably guessed. You can't be so sure though how much is exaggeration until your wife decides she needs to get ready for the pool. She won't admit it but my wife is a little self-conscious of what she believes the swim suit will reveal. That I couldn't see the little bit of what she claims is there, doesn't mean that for her the form fitting swim suit won't make it as obvious as a wart on the nose. So, I'll tolerate the diet. Who knows, maybe I can "get into" my swim suit this year because of the indirect benefit on me or maybe if I get that Buttermilk Chicken again I won't care.

BACK IN THE SALAD AGAIN

The old Gene Autry song "Back in the Saddle Again" comes to mind when I think of what's happening to me lately. It's been a few years since I made up my mind I wasn't going to be fat and lost weight. Once I make up my mind to do something, according to my wife, I can usually do it. So why am I not rich? Anyway, getting back into the saddle might mean giving up my old eating habits and it definitely hurts to do that at my age.

Lately, I've noticed my belt is a bit tighter and my sword belt too. The sword belt is a story for later. I'm diligently sticking to my exercise; well, occasionally between car repairs and visiting my new twin granddaughters. On these visits my daughter has taken to calling me Karen Carpenter. Of course, she's judging by my past eating behavior and I can certainly understand why she would say that, since eating for me hasn't always been a controlled sport. I can't get away with it now since I'm not twenty nine anymore like my daughter.

There are many temptations out there to help climb back into the saddle and the worst offender isn't my sweet daughter, it's Matilda. You've no doubt heard of office wives? Well, I can't identify her here so I'll just refer to her as the Divine Mrs. M, our office mother. She brings donuts, cookies, candy, ice cream, vegetables cooked at the local greasy spoon in tons of lard and grease (only the proprietor know how many fryings it'd been through), and yes, Cuban Sandwiches. Mrs. M specializes in birthday celebrations, retirements and special occasion luncheons, as well as impromptu eating frenzies at work. I'm beginning to believe we have people in my office who have birthdays more than once a year. She has a knack for knowing not only American holidays to celebrate but every country on earth's national holidays. I don't think I've ever celebrated the invention of the rubber band but I guess it was worth a visit to the local Mexican establishment. Although Mrs. M prefers the all-you-can-eat Chinese buffet, she'll occasionally break down and arrange for the office to go to Ryan's or Golden Corral's food bars on occasion.

It's hard to resist Mrs. M's sweet motherly siren song to eat just one, or if you fail to resist temptation just one more. She should be selling used cars. If you say you'll eat it, then the Divine Mrs. M will even buy it and bring it to you. If she comes in at lunch with a full course meal from Gene and Addy's Country Cookin', she'll offer you some. By the way, don't say yes even if you are just being nice, because she'll tear the top off that styrofoam container and fill it with better than half of what's she's just brought in before you can say Jack Robinson. Then she'll make sure you scrape that sucker clean. So far I've only fallen for the Cuban sandwich she brings, but then anything with hot peppers on it is a weakness for me and my ulcer. Hey, that's it! I'm eating too many Cubans. Nah, jalapenos have reverse calories, don't they? Guess until I discover for sure what's putting the weight back on, I'll just get back in the salad and not the saddle, again.

PART FIVE:

A RELUCTANT RETURN

    Reluctance to attend one's high school reunion is typical of a late bloomer. I was not only a late bloomer but a wallflower to boot. It wasn't until I began writing a column for the *Hogansville Herald* and was drafted by the editor to write an introductory article for a special section on the last reunion of our Alma Mater, before it closed it doors forever, that I was coerced into attending a reunion. It was a tragic mistake not going to earlier reunions but I've long since made up by attending others. If you haven't attended one of your high school reunions, don't put it off, as you might not get another opportunity. Don't worry that your classmates will not remember you as you think they should. They won't. And you'll be surprised to find they are happy to see you just the way you are.

WORKING WHERE I DO

    Working where I do, I meet many people. Being the unreconstructed Rebel that I am, most of them appear to be Yankees that came south to finish Sherman's work from an economic standpoint. Don't get me wrong, a lot of them are good folks, but slightly misguided about the South. I am a Senior Management Analyst with the U.S. Army Reserve. My work requires me to coordinate with other staffs within the Headquarters prior to releasing decisions I've made. While performing this task, I've had occasions to see an individual that possessed a rather unusual name on his desk plate. I drew no connection until I returned to see a Yankee Colonel who had non-concurred with one of my actions. While waiting to see the Colonel, I stood in front of the cubical with the unusual name. The man sitting there was staring at me because I was staring at his nameplate. I then spoke and asked him if he was from around here. He replied that he definitely was a Georgian. I then told him I had grown up with two guys named Eason in a little town a hundred miles south named Hogansville. His response was, "I also grew up in a little town a hundred miles south of here named Hogansville". I was ready to either smack the guy with a right hook or walk away as I believed he was a real smart-alec Yankee pulling my leg.

I decided that I would string this guy along and eventually put him on the spot. I asked his whole name. When he said "Al Eason," I looked at him closer, trying to remove the beard and see the face I obviously didn't discover the previous visit, or on this one either. As I looked closer, there was no mistaking either Allen's or Mike Eason's faces. There was something about the way they held their mouth that set them apart from everyone else, heredity I guess. The mouth set was there, and I knew he really was one of the Hogansville Easons. We renewed our thirty year hiatus for close to half an hour. The Colonel, who finally agreed to concur with my action, had been an acquaintance of Al's when they flew helicopters together in Vietnam. He was an Alabama boy and not the Yankee I had assumed, because he lost his southern drawl over thirty years in the Army. In nineteen seventy Al had become disabled due to a car wreck, cutting short a promising Army career in flying. He was like me now, a government employee with a less than adventuresome life.

Al and I have talked several times about our classmates and caught up on their current statuses. He attended my thirty-year high school reunion that I didn't, even though he was a year ahead of me graduating. From what he said, I wish now I had made the time to go and see his brother Mike and a few others who showed up. I expect to not let the next reunion be missed and I'll make a point to stay in touch with Al. It's good to be able to go home to Hogansville in my mind and even better to see those folks that I knew when it was home.

WAXING NOSTALGIC

It was about eight o'clock the other evening when the phone rang. Well, sorta/kinda as we have had phone problems for a long time. The portable phone hasn't been the same since it was inadvertently caught in a quick shower during the summer of 1992. My wife had grabbed up the wet beach towels from the pool, but not the portable phone. After that you couldn't call out because it didn't recognize numbers, and sometimes you couldn't hear what the other party was saying. Well, maybe that was just me and my normal hearing? Anyway it did ring, and that was something our kitchen phone suddenly decided not to do. I finally replaced the kitchen phone since we had to keep the portable's hand set with us to know when someone was calling. The new kitchen phone didn't ring, either. When I went back to return it, I asked the salesman to make sure the next one worked before I left the store. It rang beautifully and loud in the store but not at home. It was then that I decided that the jack and not the phone was the problem. I called the phone company.

Oh yes, the phone call. Well, we were perched up in bed watching one of my wife's favorite Sci-Fi series when her keen hearing detected the new phone in the kitchen ringing. Once she could hear conversations in the next town but that was before my daughter Emily, while I was tickling her, screamed in her left ear. Now she can only hear cars on the interstate five miles away and, of course, the phone ringing in the kitchen. It was tough for a guy in his forties to leap over a full grown woman and a bunch of cover, and arrive at the kitchen at the same time that the answering machine was delivering its message. But I did it. When the voice on the other end asked if Jimmy was home, I was convinced my mother was in critical condition as no one except family in LaGrange still refers to me as Jimmy. It wasn't until I was able to get the answering machine to quit and let me talk to the party on the other end that I found out it was a positive, not a negative, call. And it wasn't from LaGrange, either.

I didn't recognize the lady's voice when she asked again if I was Jimmy Dale, the same one whose articles were appearing in the *Hogansville Herald*. My blood pressure had returned to normal by this time and my thinking was clear enough to say that I was one and the same. She identified herself as Linda Plant, former schoolmate and friend from the sixties. It was like no other call I had ever experienced. Here were two friends who had not seen each other since we walked off the stage at Hogansville High School with that rolled up piece of paper saying we were officially literate. We talked for close to an hour reliving our high school days and talking about those we had known and what happened to them over the years. Linda said the articles had brought back many happy memories and helped her through a difficult period of recuperation from a recent surgery. I'm glad my writing has touched someone in a positive way.

After Linda and I hung up, I was wide awake. I grabbed up the 1964 "Hohian" (Hogansville High School Annual) and began to page through the memories. Over the years our class had lost quite a few of our members. But out of that sixty, there are still a lot of us around, for now anyway. I noticed Eddie J.'s picture was included with the majorettes. I wondered if that was a mistake or possibly someone's attempt at being funny. I saw Mr. HHS, Cookie C. I learned he is now a successful pharmacist in Dalton, Georgia. Franklin T. is an attorney in LaGrange, and Clifford T. works as an accountant at Southwire in Carrollton. I wondered what had happened to the others.

My wife made the comment that people don't change very much. She clarified it by saying that anyone could look at almost any year book before and after 1964 and see the same people, just a little differently dressed, but essentially the same people. In the case of the 1964 yearbook, it seems we in 1995 have gravitated back to the same dress and even hairstyles.

I read the half page I marked reserved for my then girlfriend, Angela. It was late when I put the annual down. I began to feel I had accomplished about all the reminiscing I could handle for one evening. It was easy going to sleep knowing I had regained a piece of my youth without ever leaving the house. I slept well and woke up a much rejuvenated middle aged man.

CHAPTER V

ONE SOUTHERN VIEW OF VALUES AND IDEALS

Before launching into a controversial area I should tell you I am, and have always been, politically conservative. No, I don't try to force my beliefs on others, well, not anymore. On some occasions I have managed to be open-minded to others' opinions, as I am hopeful they were of mine.

Have fun with these musing and don't make yourself angry and mark all over everything in red ink and start poking yourself on the forehead with your fore and middle fingers until your whole faces turns red, saying "Jimmy, Jimmy, Jimmy." Lord knows, I've had enough teachers do that to me already.

PART ONE:

CHANGING TIMES

You don't know sometimes what you have until it's gone. We cannot call back a few score years to re-live the kind of life you see described so lovingly within these pages. We have to accept changes that have occurred over the years and face new problems created by current times. There is a line from a movie where a warship's captain says to a young officer, "It's unfortunate business . . ." It is indeed unfortunate business we have allowed so many of our small towns to die. The most important factor in rebuilding a community isn't money, but the spirit of the people. So one wish is left with Hogansville, the hope that it never loses its spirit.

ALIEN BEHAVIOR

It was my friend Homer Brown who said, "He doesn't even know you exist," right after I brought it to his attention someone had just walked in front of me and slammed the door in my face. In spite of all my haranguing and carrying on, Homer knew he was correct. The guy never even knew I was there, and for that matter anyone else. Homer was raised in St. Louis and Chicago, so he is used to people just plain ignoring you as they pass.

It's a little difficult for me to comprehend being ignored. I didn't see much of that when I was growing up in Hogansville. It seemed like when people were in a hurry, that somehow they managed to take time to speak or throw up their hand as they passed. I can remember my mother rushing around in the Colonel Store trying to beat Lucille, Ellabee or Mrs. Rainwater to all the specials. Even then she had time for a few friendly words with her competitors, before piling on to get the half price streak-o-lean Tommy had just put out on the meat counter. And when folks weren't able to stop and talk because they had their mouths engaged already with someone else, they managed a friendly smile or nod.

I guess after growing up in that kind of atmosphere, I expect folks to return my greetings, even if they are bent on slamming a door in my face. But I've noticed lately, more often than not, some people will go out of their way to avoid speaking. I'm prepared not to get spoken to when I meet someone with their head down, but it's the ones who look you right in the eye and just ignore you, as if you aren't there, that I don't understand. My natural southerness makes it hard for me to keep my mouth shut, so when I pass someone I have to speak, and if I can't speak for some reason, like having my mouth full of food, then I find other ways of acknowledging their presence. We southerners consider acknowledging others as a sign of respect. That may not be the case everywhere though. Perhaps being afforded your space and privacy in overcrowded cities is a sign of respect there.

I've noticed on trips that people in cars generally don't acknowledge each other. Often I get treated as if I'm not even there, or my car either, and I almost get run over. I contemplated all this in the grocery store parking lot the other day while cranking my window up and locking the car door, practices we never needed in Hogansville. Yes, I have crank windows in my Chevy because we decided we didn't need something else to go wrong in a car. Anyway, lost in thought, I was unaware I had left my middle finger inside the window railing until the obvious happened, pain. I let out a rebel yell that would have towered over any raging battle. Realizing what I had done caused me to cringe in embarrassment, but as I looked around red faced and cowering I found no one had noticed. Just as Homer said, they didn't even know I existed. I guess we have all become a little immune to car alarms and maybe they thought my scream was just another version.

When I finally arrived inside the grocery store, I saw lots of people but I don't think they saw me. Not forgetting my Hogansville manners, I spoke and smiled, getting no reactions. Okay, it's entirely possible aliens have taken over their bodies and made zombies of them just like in the movie "Body Snatchers." I could be the first one to notice? But these aliens must be the stupid ones. You'd think in the South they would make themselves friendly to avoid detection. Next time you mash your finger in the car window at the grocery store, take notice of who doesn't acknowledge your cry of pain. They may be the aliens.

SAVING STAMPS

This morning as I was booting up my computer, one of my co-workers came up to ask if she could borrow an envelope. She was looking for a "civilian" and not a military envelope. I dug around in my desk, and finally found such an animal I had brought to work, for some reason which I don't recall anymore. So I gave it to her and she explained she needed it for the only bill she couldn't pay in person. Did I hear her right? She drives to the offices of those whom she owes to pay them in person, and they let her do it? In 1998 I decided to pursue this; it was just too good to pass up.

Well, it turns out she lives in a small town not yet overtaken by developers, where the big companies maintain small satellite offices that will indeed let you pay bills in person. That is, except the one place she had to send the envelope. I sat enthralled while she described how on Thursday afternoons she made her payments, and how overall she saved about two or three dollars a month on stamps since these places were one her way home anyway. How fortunate, I thought, this lady can still live in a community where life is a little bit more simple, and personal too. Not many of us can appreciate how much fun it can be to pay your bills to real people.

It took me back to a time when I sat in our car at the Old Mill, waiting for my daddy to come out and take me home. There were those days when he would decide to go by town to pay some bills before we went home. Our route took us by the Post Office first, in case a new bill happened to be there. Then we would park in front of Whit Barrett's Western Auto Store and go in to find Kaiser sitting behind the counter. He'd take daddy's cash and open the old metal ledger containing individual clips for all the store's customer's accounts; then he'd stamp "paid" on all daddy's bills for that month. Afterwards, they'd talk a while and I'd look at all the Western Flyer bikes and footballs in the store. Finally, daddy would leave when I got to the bins with all the small hardware stuff. After that, we would go up to Ray Cheatham's Economy Auto Store to pay the light and phone bills. Ray had models there, so I'd check out all the good airplanes and car kits he had that week. He also had lots of small hardware stuff I couldn't stay out of, too. Since we traded mostly with Whit, it was a thrill to go in Economy Auto because I never went there that much.

After my friend at work got the envelope, she moved on. All this is really fun to think about, knowing it's still possible to pay bills in person in some places, and it gives me some hope that community spirit isn't totally lost today. While my daddy paid bills, he also took part in our community. He saw and talked to people, got to breathe fresh air, and above all was an active participant in the life of a small town.

This stopped happening here in Kennesaw the late 70's. Before Kennesaw became just a zone for my zip code, I knew the Mayor, the Police Chief – who drove one of the two cruisers, and the Postmaster. I occasionally went downtown to pay a bill or two in person and spoke to people who seemed to be glad to see me. Now-a-days there are scores of city policemen who are interested in you only if you violate a law; and you have to stand in line at the post office to be served by people you don't know, who only speak to tell you how much your transaction costs. I don't even know if Kennesaw has a mayor anymore. All my bill payments go to some other state or downtown Atlanta. But I feel comforted knowing there are places where you can still pay bills in person.

HOGANSVILLE DOWN THE ROAD

Stealing a theme from my cousin's column in the *Franklin County Citizen* newspaper located in beautiful downtown Lavonia, Georgia, I want to talk about the future for small towns. His recent column entitled "A View From the Lake" lays out what Lavonia can expect. Although our writing styles differ, his being of a serious socioeconomic/political nature, we occasionally find common ground. In this case we agree change or progress, whatever you want to call it, cannot be prevented. Therefore, small town folks need to get ready to deal with major culture and lifestyle shifts.

Don't say I didn't warn you, because I did many columns ago, when I wrote for the late *Hogansville Herald*. Even then I hoped I was wrong and maybe overreacting, but it seems I was very nearly right on the money, just a little early. I recall a fellow a while back buying up huge tracts of real estate around Hogansville and even threatening to buy downtown. I suppose he had a vision of renovating stores and establishing a shopper's paradise in a small town setting, retaining the small town atmosphere. I've since noticed that some of the buildings of original restaurant and hotel ventures that originally brought the town to the attention of developers no longer exist. I, for one, am glad developers haven't totally caught up with Hogansville yet.

As I said in the first paragraph, things are going to change. When I was down last year for the Hummingbird Festival and annual Class of '64 mini-reunion, new housing developments were already starting to pop up; and of course to support this growth, infrastructure will surely follow. Government officials love developers because they mean more money and more government, and show me a government that doesn't want to grow in wealth and power! So don't depend on government to save the day, because it'll be fixated on adding more revenues, collecting more taxes, and increasing regulations.

By the way, don't expect to keep the small town atmosphere you've had. I know because I saw it swept away in Kennesaw, my second hometown. It wasn't much different than Hogansville until developers turned it into a bedroom community and Atlanta engulfed it into the metro area with businesses, wall to wall shopping centers, restaurants and traffic snarls. Now it's just a name for an area of NW Atlanta and the small community flavor has ceased to exist. It's home to people from all over the country, as well as the world, and it seems few speak to each other; I'm suspecting in part because of a language barrier. The same symptoms are just beginning to show in Canton, a few miles down the road from where I currently live. The North Georgia mountains that were once home to bears, bobcats and other wildlife is already on the developer's radar; and as soon as they can figure cheaper ways to level those mountains and strip off the trees for massive subdivisions and businesses, they'll be there.

PART TWO:

LET'S GET SERIOUS

TWENTY-EIGHT YEARS LATER

It became clear to me yesterday, while I was deeply engrossed watching a film of Dan Gurney pushing his GT-40 across the finish line at Sebring in 1966, that I haven't really been listening or paying attention to anything since that race. In some ways it's good, because somewhere down the line I missed becoming a drug addict, flower child or a victim of Vietnam War Syndrome; although I came pretty close to that last one. I missed a lot too, things like finding a high paying job, getting advanced degrees and maybe even running for political office.

I do recall the day my mother told me I needed to decide what to do with my life. This was around my sophomore year in college, just after I had returned from Spring Break at Daytona Beach. I was fortunate she apparently didn't notice a massive hangover and a headache from too much fun and frolic. I was reluctant to listen, much less understand, what she was trying to get across to me. Had I been able to comprehend all this deep and serious stuff, I might have majored in finance instead of history. Instead of "Thomas Crown," it would have been Thomas Dale, Thomas being my middle name. I'd have had a high rise glass-walled private office, a Rolls Royce coupe and a multi-million dollar home in the most fashionable neighborhood. But would I have been happy with all this opulence? Outwardly the answer is yes, but like Mr. Crown I'd still want something else. In spite of how the movies portray them, people who have this kind of lifestyle usually pay for it with long hours of work and no time for their families. Their lives are anything but fun.

It's better to come home and ask my wife, "What's in the

refrigerator, or what do you want me to help make for dinner tonight?" Come weekends, there's usually time to spend a cozy Saturday afternoon. It's this kind of life that gives me a feeling of involvement and not sitting in a stuffy boardroom lording over subordinates.

I have never understood two things that seem to dominate current thinking, politics and the economy. They weren't tops on a twenty year olds list of things to care about in 1966. I just figured then, if we ever got to the point where we could just put the government on auto-pilot, maybe there would be time for worthwhile endeavors. But then reality sets in, and I see the only way I can disengage from the effects of politics is to be deceased. Not favoring that remedy, I decided to participate and learn, but as little as possible. I succeeded beyond my wildest dreams.

IN NINETY-NINE YEARS

It was my wife's great-grandmother who said, "In ninety-nine years, no one will know the difference." If that's true why do we work hard to make an impact on life in our world? The Christian Work Ethic tells us worth is vested in hard work. If we give everything to our work, then we usually achieve a high rate of success in our jobs. Is that what's made America great? Maybe so. I can't disagree with hard work, but like anything else work can be over done.

Today's society demands more than it returns. But that's nothing new. I remember my parents working weekends and double shifts. I missed my mother not being home in the evening to help with homework and soothe an occasional hurt feeling over disagreements us kids had. But there was no choice. She had to work the second shift. My daddy did a good job doing double duty as both mother and father during those times, but it just wasn't the same. Don't get me wrong, I fully understand why both my parents had to work. We could not have survived on just one salary, even in a time when one salary was supposed to do the job. And of those rare occasions when mother could be home for the evening, I have some pretty wonderful memories.

My parent's lives were consumed with making and saving money. They wanted me to have the opportunities in life they missed. I appreciate that. The Great Depression earlier in their generation caused them to fear for their jobs more than any generation before or after. It sometimes created a misdirected priority between family and work that prevails to this day. The ballad "Johnny I Hardly Knew Ya" sums up my feelings about how much I wanted desperately to know my parents and spend quality time with them before it was too late. After I grew up, there was a granddaughter who'd need money for college so they felt obligated to help with that by continuing to work past their retirement age. It wasn't until ill health forced them into retirement, I finally got to spend the "quality" time with them I wanted. It was almost too late.

I'm grateful that just before I lost my daddy, the two of us were able to spend some uninterrupted time talking. He came along on trips with me to Savannah and the coastal islands for seminars I had to attend there. We spent time walking on the beach and learning things we meant to tell each other years earlier when there was no time. I now know what shaped his outlook on life, things that happened in war he never told mother about because he loved her too much and didn't want her to know how cruel the world can be. In these conversations, I also discovered things about myself I never knew. I was determined not to wait that long before taking this kind of opportunity with my daughter. We're spending that quality time together, what of it our world will allow today, talking about what life means to us. She knows the ideals that drive me and hopefully will use them to form her own.

Yes, my career has suffered because family has always come

first with me. This direction has cost me promotions and hasn't made me the most popular guy at work with management. But I was the most popular guy where it counted, at home. Do I regret not pursuing a professional career more aggressively? Will it make any difference in ninety-nine years if I had? My answer to both those questions will always be a resounding no!

KNOWING YOUR HISTORY

History isn't a subject most folks relate to, but it is important to remember the past, if for no other reason so we don't make the same mistakes twice. If you couldn't remember when you busted your knuckle using a certain wrench, the likelihood is you'd do it again the next time you had a project involving that wrench. It's isn't that simple, but that's a pretty straight forward example of why it doesn't hurt to have a little recollection of what happened before. It also doesn't hurt that some fairly interesting things happened back there and are worth reading for enjoyment, if you are a history nut like me.

Unfortunately history has become a weapon in the war to win hearts and minds. Politicians, and others who seek to have us follow them, don't mind revising a few things in our school texts to suit their purposes or political attitudes. I found out quite by accident that my daughter, who is thirty years old, was never taught about the Alamo. She just thought it was some old building in Texas. I asked her if it was omitted in her history class or did she sleep through it. This is a girl that not only went to high school, but she also graduated from college. And she said, "No, I was awake." So I told her the story.

I had to wonder why no one put it in a history book and why a professor who obviously knew of the oversight didn't fill in with personal knowledge. Then it occurred to me, maybe the professor needs to keep his job and perhaps the attitude of higher-ups calls for a little censorship to keep everyone happy. Offensive or not, history happens, and kids today no matter what their heritage have a right to know what actually happened. Hispanics need to know some of their own ancestors might have died defending the Alamo from a tyrannical regime. I'm one who believes truth in history and today's attitudes can coexist. We have to give those, whom we believe we are protecting from their own history, the opportunity to face facts that may not be pleasant and vice versa. You can't grow until you know what you need to change to, to get where you want to be. That goes for all of us.

Changing history to suit current attitudes isn't a new idea. I was never taught in school about Kasserine Pass, Savo Island or Anzio because they were American defeats in WWII. Pearl Harbor was the only defeat I studied and that was because it started the war for the U.S. Then in the late sixties and early seventies things changed, and all we heard about was American defeats. The media glossed over victories and it wasn't until recently in a wave of patriotism as a result of 9/11 we got a glimpse of the truth of the courage of the American soldier in Vietnam. The movie "Once We Were Soldiers" told the story of a resounding American Victory. We were led to believe Kah San was an American tragedy, but in actuality it broke the back of the North Vietnamese Army and it practically ceased to exist after that battle.

So if my daughter doesn't know about the Alamo, I wonder how much today's student knows about real history. After reading some recent text books, I find students are being taught the most tragic of America's wars was fought for only one reason, slavery. I was taught states rights and to repel an invasion were also reasons. If our society doesn't stop trying to protect everyone with less than the truth, we are surely going to bust our knuckles using the same wrench our forefathers picked up.

LEVELING THE BATTLEFIELD OF LIFE

Yesterday, I attended a luncheon for a female of Hispanic origin who has just been promoted to Sergeant Major in the Army. "Well," you say, "What's new? Minorities hold a priority in government and business today." I say this is not your common story of promoting minorities to level the playing field. I worked with this soldier several years and can say without a doubt she'd earned every stripe and star sewn on her uniform. The Army isn't just about combat arms; it's largely a force that supports combat arms. Just a small percentage of soldiers actually fight the battles, and a large percent provide the necessary tools to help them win. In every case that support is the edge needed for victory. This top sergeant's devotion to provide soldiers the support they need on the battlefield should command the respect and admiration of us all. You might say she helps soldiers master the un-level battlefield, for in truth no battlefield is level.

National civil rights advocates call for leveling life's playing field to bring things equal by legislation, even if it interferes with the rights of non-minorities; this may not be on the right track for achieving equality. This kind of support might work for a while, but as a permanent fix-it breeds contempt and wins no victories, even though it's done with the best of intentions.

Coming home from the luncheon, I tuned in a news radio station just as a prominent talk show commentator came on. Now, I don't know how you feel about radio commentators but I like to listen to them over some of the so called music on radio these days. We all need to keep an open mind and viewpoint, even though some talking hosts gag me. Most popular music makes me tense and soft rock can easily put me to sleep at the wheel, so I tuned into talk radio. This fellow was talking about the argument of leveling playing fields to achieve minority equality. He said he'd never had the opportunity to play on a level field himself, had to come up by his own means, and never got a break he didn't have to make for himself. He also said people do unfair and unscrupulous things to other people's careers, and that's just human nature no law or society can govern. This is about the time things started sounding familiar. One of the people at the luncheon yesterday could easily fit that scenario where my career is considered, but I can say without doubt I did all right in spite of this person's efforts to un-level the playing field for me.

This brings us full circle. Respect and equality aren't gained by leveling the playing field, but only by one's efforts to earn them. My Hispanic friend never gave any thought to playing on a level field; she applied herself and did the work, overcame obstacles placed in her path by others, and gave no favors nor solicited any to achieve rank. And that's the point; one has to be willing to run the gauntlet of an un-level field to achieve success, respect and equality. We've had a mindset for over fifty years in this country that sends the wrong message, that a level field is all that's necessary to gain these things. If society and government would understand that respect, equality and success are not things to be legislated, bought or forced by soliciting guilt for past indiscretions, but have to be earned through hard work and perseverance. Only when that is understood will we overcome the un-level field. The playing field of life, like the battlefield, is never level for anyone regardless of race or origin. Those who apply themselves don't need someone to level the field; they simply succeed regardless of the odds. There is a sergeant major out there who will tell you this first hand.

IT'S NEVER TOO LATE TO FOLLOW YOUR DREAMS

I just got an e-mail from a Master Sergeant who retired from the Army a couple of weeks before me. She's in Hawaii going to a church supported school. Yes, having fun too, but learning how to help others. She's a dedicated Christian and is making it her life's work, even if she had to wait a few years to be able to do it. I've known several people who have always known what they wanted to do and never strayed from that path no matter how long it took them to achieve their dream. It has to do with being focused and willing to do whatever it takes and never admitting "it's not over till it's over."

One friend always comes to mind when I think about being focused and determined. He and I started to West Georgia College together, and his first declared major was Art. Back in high school he was the art editor for the HOHIAN, our school annual. This guy spent his time after school and on weekends working for the late Jim Lassiter, delivering prescriptions and manning the cash register. He never had a particular talent for science or chemistry, but his artistic talents are God given. So I fully expected to see him develop into a fine commercial artist. He didn't. He's now a pharmacist, and very happy, thank you.

There aren't many who can stay as focused as the two people I've mentioned. So what does one do when he's finished a career where he really didn't pursue his dream? I guess another good example of this is another friend I've known since my Air Force years in the 70s. This guy is now a senior guard at the Utah State Prison in Salt Lake City. He is also a historian; and like me, he collects plastic models, so many he'll never get around to building all of them. He wanted to teach history so badly he formed his own classes for prisoners and taught them two nights a week. He was so good they kept him teaching several years. Now that he's contemplating retirement, he told me in a recent e-mail he may just go back to school and finish that degree in history. He's already put two kids through college, so why not himself? I think he's serious because for the first time in the thirty plus years I've known him he's thinking about selling off a good many of his model kits to help finance his venture, and also to make sure he doesn't get deterred from his objective.

The trick is to not let age or situation work against you. There are too many examples of people who didn't reach their goals until they were past the age when most of us think it's useless to do anymore. I happen to think it's never too late. Money is the reason we did what we did when we were young, and its lack is sometimes still a deterrent for today's young people. But it's not a trap you have to remain in. My daughter is contemplating going back to work when her twins are a year or two older and in school. She didn't enjoy her previous job and isn't looking forward to entering the work force again. On our visit with her the other day she told us about a paper she wrote in college that was so good the professor kept it. It was on law. Dare she go to law school with twins and a husband to take care of? Well, if she wants it bad enough and if she is willing to do it in steps, it can be done. I told her if she didn't try she'd never know. I'm telling you the same thing.

PART THREE:

PATRIOTISM AND DUTY

"DO YOUR DUTY IN ALL THINGS. . ."

It was me, the twelve year old kid who wore the black leather motorcycle jacket with two silver stars on each epaulet and the collar turned up. That was in the late fifties when I was trying to imitate James Dean, a movie star who I'd heard of but didn't know anything about except he was supposed to be cool. Then in the early sixties, when fad told me to wear a madras shirt with jeans, white socks and loafers, I succumbed. Later on as a freshman in college I blindly followed the stream of look-alikes, wearing buttoned down oxford cloth shirts with neatly pressed khaki slacks and penny loafers without socks. I don't recommend wearing leather shoes without socks unless you want the shoes to develop a permanent odor even after you've exhausted Dr. Shoals' entire product line.

Still enthralled with the pop-culture, I noticed halfway into my college sophomore year things were changing a little too much for me. I can't deny I was a child of the sixties and pretty self-centered, although for whatever reason, I couldn't break with tradition and be drawn into the hippie movement with their anti-establishment lifestyles, violent protests, and disrespectful treatment of our soldiers and society in general. It could have been self-discipline on my part, but then my mother would have respectfully disagreed that I ever had any. So whatever it was, it steered me on course with the country I felt pretty comfortable living in. Its laws, a few I sometimes had to scratch my head over, were I felt, for the most part, fair and I had no reason to lose trust in or disobey them.

My rejection of the anti-war movement, plus growing up hearing my mother tell family stories filled with anecdotes about those ancestors who had gone off to fight for their country, left me wondering perhaps if one day I would also have to make such a commitment. It gave me lots to think about over the four years I spent in college. I had serious thoughts as to how it would feel getting shot at by people who might really want to kill me. Friends and classmates returned from the war talking of how frightened they were each time they faced combat, and it wasn't a reassuring piece of news to a kid who'd never been much further from home than Atlanta.

There were kids from my generation claiming to be conscientious objectors, some of whom I'm sure were sincere. I didn't then, and still don't, feel any animosity toward them. I wasn't totally sold on the Vietnam War either, as I didn't necessarily agree with the way it was being run by the politicians. Their strategy apparently was getting a lot of people killed and maimed for no good reason. Though I objected to that part of what was going on, I could never have gone to Canada or signed a piece of paper as a conscientious objector. I knew I would be deceiving myself to think that I didn't need to serve the country which gave me freedom to form my own opinions.

Upon graduation and with the war still in progress, I had to make the decision I'd dreaded for so long. I spent many soul searching days and weeks agonizing over what I should do, as there was always a chance I could go on to graduate school after I had my degree. Finally I came to the conclusion I had a duty to my family and country to repay what they had done for me. Fate was good to me though, and my service never required I be in the direct line of fire. It might have been easier to decide had I known about the quote by General Robert E. Lee who said so eloquently in a letter to his son, "Do your duty in all things. You cannot do more; you should never wish to do less."

PLAYING ARMY

You'd think a guy who just retired from thirty years of service with the Army wouldn't concern himself with anything do to with the Army. Well, that's not true. I just spent the weekend doing what I used to do as a kid. Well, not exactly. I did wear a uniform, carried a sword and pistol, and ran up and down a lot of fields with some other guys charging stationary targets while yelling and screaming. I also did some marching, some flag carrying and just joking around. No, I haven't reverted to my childhood entirely, because I have never really grown up. My wife will attest to that fact. I don't know why but I couldn't interest her in going with me on this adventure.

From the earliest time I can remember, I've always played army. When I was about five or six, I used to go across the street to the parsonage and play army with the preacher's two sons Curtis and Carlton. The preacher's house had a huge field behind it, covered with weeds that stood taller than us boys. We pretended to be in Burma looking for Japanese. I never found any, but had plenty of fun pretending we did. When my family moved up on North Highway, the huge yard behind my house was similar to the preacher's, but my daddy had it bush-hogged regularly. That didn't stop me from charging down the uneven furrows and falling, pretending to be "hit" and firing my

M1 (BB rifle) at Germans pill boxes. Were there Germans in our yard? Actually, my vivid imagination conceived about two battalions of the finest they could rally.

  When I was growing up, I envisioned myself in the Army carrying a sword and marching in a parade with my pristine uniform. Of course, none of that ever happened but I did become a civilian equivalent of a Lieutenant Colonel and was called a Senior Management Analyst. My boyhood dreams weren't realized until I began to assist the historian in our Command on outings the Army calls Staff Rides, teaching young officers and non-commissioned officers (NCOs) about leadership. This part of my job I didn't retire from, and I still assist the historian as a fulltime member of the teaching team. I dress as a soldier from the Civil War and deliver lectures on real battlefields where soldiers fought and died. Of course, just like when I was a kid, I don't get killed or wounded, and I can see some of the lessons we teach go a long way toward helping these future leaders learn how to deal with situations on the spot and learn to resolve them.

  Sitting here in my cozy house listening to the thunderstorm outside, I realize that fantasy and imagination are wonderful gifts we humans share with no other of God's creatures, although I sometimes wonder about squirrels, cats and some dogs. If you haven't "seen the elephant", as Civil Wars soldiers called being in actual combat, then we cannot conceive of the horror it presents. Fortunately I haven't had to endure that experience, but I've studied enough to put aside my ideas that war is glorious and to focus my efforts on helping teach these young leaders of tomorrow how chaotic and terrible actual combat can be. If you thought this was going to be a lighthearted and funny tale, well you are probably disappointed. Sometimes I just say what's on my mind. Right now I'm hoping you don't take for granted our soldiers in Iraq and Afghanistan, as some in my generation did our soldiers in Vietnam. Young people are our nation's leaders of tomorrow, so don't discourage your kids from playing Army just because someone says we shouldn't encourage our children to violence. It just might some day save their lives and maybe your own.

PART FOUR:

RESPONSIBILITY AND MORALS

SCHOOL TEACHINGS, NOW AND THEN

Going to school was not among my favorite endeavors while growing up. I went because there was a penalty to pay if I didn't go, and it was worse than sitting through English in Mrs. Allison's sixth grade classroom in late May with no air conditioning. That's right, we didn't have any A/C except for that large bank of windows that ran lengthwise on one side of our classroom. That's the same bank of windows that drove one of my friends and classmate from sheer boredom and heat to leap out of, during class one day. I don't believe the paddling he got bored him too much but he didn't think it worth repeating either.

When my classmates and I went to school, we were taught the basic curriculum of English, math and the other academic disciplines. Our rights were only good when we behaved and listened. The teacher's hands were not tied when it came to discipline, and their lesson plans didn't include teaching us to favor a particular political attitude. Their job, as they saw it, was to make sure we were educated, used proper grammar, solved arithmetic problems and knew who the President was when asked.

Earlier this year I was involved in a living history program at a local college, making presentations to several middle school classes from the surrounding area. My colleague and I were representing Civil War soldiers from both sides of the conflict. After our presentation, my colleague asked each class who the

President and Vice President are. A handful knew the President's name, but none except for one kid knew the Vice President's name. You can guess who most of them named, movie or rock stars and sports personalities.

Last week while watching the news, I saw a story that made me wonder exactly what our kids are learning today. It centered on a parent who was arrested and taken from his local Board of Education meeting in handcuffs. Seems all the man was doing was politely disagreeing with teaching political ideology in the classroom.

I've always believed political leanings should be personal, something we develop as individuals from information we gather by our own ways and means. In my civics classes, I was taught what the government branches are and how they operate, period. It would never have occurred to my teachers to sway our easily-influenced minds, but it's happening often today, with little or no opposition. Could it be parents in our complex society just don't have the time to spend finding out what is going on in their children's classrooms? Or, I hate to say this, they just don't care.

I am fortunate to have had teachers who spent their time teaching the three R's. These teachers would have considered it un-American and intolerable for their professional organizations to endorse teaching of a single political viewpoint. I didn't have a hard time at all figuring out what my political position was, without help from opinions taught in the classroom. And guess what? I can name all of the presidents from the very beginning of this nation.

CAJUN KITCHEN

For several years now I have worked in one capacity or another for the U. S. Army. One of my favorite jobs was that of a Staffing Standards Analyst. Staffing Standards is short for a statistical application of correlation and regression models to manpower. If that isn't confusing enough, we went to various military reservations and confused them too.

The visit to Fort Polk, Louisiana, still stands out in my memory as stellar. Several things happened on that three-week temporary duty. I think they purposely put Fort Polk where it's located so that you have to become physically fit to survive working there. You must not be afraid of alligators or horse flies, horse flies being the most dangerous. Heat is a given, and if anything you have is dry it won't be after a couple of days at Fort Polk. To let me know just how wonderful the place is, the Chief of the Contracting Office for whom we were doing the study gave me a T-shirt that said, "Happiness is Fort Polk in your rear view mirror." It didn't last me until I left Louisiana. It was so popular I guess someone made off with it before I could get it safely back to Georgia.

Being in bayou country, there aren't that many places to eat. We had the only motel with refrigerated air conditioning, and when we walked outside, the temperature change affected our minds and so the choices of restaurants. This being a good excuse, we selected for our second visit a combination Mexican, Hungarian and Italian restaurant in a nearby hamlet that didn't serve fried chicken. The waitress looked vaguely familiar and I realized she was also at a Popeye's Fried Chicken we ate at the day before in another hamlet. The restaurant business in the area was short of waitresses and since she was also taking a correspondence course to be an airline stewardess, she thought it to be good experience. Besides, my boss liked her and it was worth it to him to eat something different occasionally, to enjoy the same female scenery. I expressed some doubt about that logic because there is a limit to what I can take and goulash and enchiladas don't like each other inside me.

There were four of us on this trip. Homer was a large, black guy who was experienced and knowledgeable in his trade and was always willing to go an extra mile for you. He did for me many times and we always worked together on projects. But never underestimate his sense of humor. His favorite line to me was, "You're the most aggravating white man I've ever known," but he was only kidding, I think. Usually Homer preferred stopping at the local 7/11 and stocking up on "pop" and munchies for a wild and woolly evening with the local TV stations and a good book. Not including the munchies I had a similar routine, so we got along great. I always enjoyed doing a study with Homer.

Then there was Nick, a good old boy from North Carolina, who usually did studies with our boss. This time we were all on a rare trip together. Nick was a big knife/gun lover but a very religious fellow too. He didn't let those things get in the way of a practical joke or a good-natured ribbing. He was well educated and sharp as a tack, but used his light North Carolina down east brogue at any given moment to advantage, since he was straight out of coastal North Carolina. One night Homer and I concocted a scheme pretending to be the Miami Vice guys and stationed ourselves on either side of Nick's motel room door prepared to jump at him with our pretend guns when he answered our knock. We got into position and called out to Nick to go to dinner. We were going to give him a real surprise when he opened that door, but the only trouble was Nick came out wielding his Bowie knife. Homer and I almost tripped over each other trying to get out of the way. So who played the practical joke?

Carl, our boss, was a New Orleans gambler type of guy. He was familiar with Louisiana and felt right at home, mainly because it was his home when he was being raised. Of course, if there was a female around Carl really felt right at home. But he was also a task master who concentrated on doing a through and professional job, and gave himself as much work as he did us. Later in the second week we were joined at our hotel by another team from our office who was there on a separate project.

It was Stan's team. I always believed Stan was really Gabe Kaplan but wouldn't admit it because Roshak might find him. His trusty right-hand man was Tom. Tom is no longer with us but he was a low key joker who used intelligence to keep you from knowing you were had, fifteen minutes before you realized it. There were a couple of others who were also along with Stan. It was a muggy evening and after Nick jumped into the motel pool and ducked two of the females on Stan's team, we all decided to get some food. Tired of seeing our standard waitress, we decided to go out of town to a more upscale restaurant. Someone at Fort Polk recommended the "Cajun Kitchen." It sounded like it was right up our alley, except it was about ten miles into the bayou. Expecting to see expanses of glass and modern steel with rock fireplaces, we found a quaint, slightly dirty, naturally ventilated but accommodating little restaurant, with a mailbox at the entrance and a dirt driveway about a mile long. Well, we were there, so why sweat the small things. The real heat didn't last long before we were blessed by the night and a cool breeze from the swamp blowing through the natural air conditioning. Our waitress was a different girl and that was refreshing.

Olin, our analyst emeritus, since he was retired but back as a consultant, was struck by the natural decor and quickly asked if they had corn flakes on the menu. The rest of us spent a little more time perusing the offerings. I asked the waitress if the boiled shrimp was cold or hot. She said they were hot and spicy so I thought that might be good, but the frog legs were also tempting since I had never had any. She was very gracious and offered to bring a frog leg with my shrimp. I took her up on it and asked if I might also have some drawn butter to which she replied, "I don't think we have any of that but we do have Land of Lakes, will that do?" I said, "Sure just melt it before you bring it out."

I would not have wanted to see the frog that leg belonged to when it was attached. It was a meal in itself. After dinner we sat around and finally she brought the bills. Everyone had spent about twelve bucks except me, and mine was twenty-five. After a little serious addition and menu checks, I determined I had been charged for two dinners. When I handed the bill to the male cashier, I mentioned the problem and he asked, "Was your waitress Judy?" I answered, "Yes, I believe it was her name." He just laughed and said, "She did it again." Apparently, Judy had succeeded with this little trick in the past but this time she was caught red-handed. He reprimanded her and said, "You gotta stop doing that because people don't like it."

The next day Homer and I related the story to the Contracting Officer at Fork Polk, the Colonel who gave me the t-shirt and for whose office we were doing the study. He seemed amused and asked a few more questions about our cashier. The next day, he told Homer and me he was President of a court-martial for the cashier at the restaurant, and we had just saved his military career. We were puzzled and he explained the cashier who helped us at the Cajun Kitchen was a platoon sergeant who had moonlighted there because it belonged to his girlfriend. This had kept him from properly managing his troops and, in turn, got him charged with not following regulations. He had been wounded on two different tours in Viet Nam and was in his nineteenth year, having never been in trouble with the Army previously. He only had one more year to go before retirement. The Colonel said our story gave him a better perspective of the man's character and provided a way to let the sergeant retire honorably instead of being dishonorably discharged, as the court martial board had been considering. The morale to this story is, don't let Judy get away with it and you may save more than your customer's money.

TYING ENDS

It's fourth and two on the ten yard line and there's twenty seconds left in the game, with the home team four points behind. A field goal won't do, they need that touchdown. Sort of sounds like one of the old Greenwave games, doesn't it. Well it could be that, or it could be the first string Tying End Team about to push through and get the job done for the Reid Mill. From the thirties to the seventies my mother was on the first string, if I can use that pun, of the Championship Tying End Team. Her teammates were Elmira, Corrine and Lena Pearl. This combination made the Dallas Cowboys, and even Lombardi's legendary Packers, look anemic.

Before I go much further, I guess I'd better tell you what tying ends is all about. When the looms weave the string into cloth it is a pretty rough process and a lot of individual bobbins of string break. It was mother's and her teammate's job to make sure those broken ends were all tied back together so the loom would keep going and not have to stop. That loom represented everyone's pay check so it was necessary to keep it running. Very few ever stopped on my mother's team's watch. Their commitment to the job of tying ends is something hard to comprehend in the work world of today. Simply put, that commitment is pride in one's self to be the best. It worked for Lombardi's team too.

I see people around where I work get angry with management for placing us in intolerable situations, and they not do their best because of it. I, too, get frustrated. However, while I agree some management today is a long way from being "enlightened," I don't see my effort as something I'm doing for them. I see it as something I'm doing for me. When the work is sloppy you know who will get the blame, but more than that, I don't want to be perceived as sloppy. In short, my work is a reflection of me and not management. There are times when it would be easier to just call in sick and not face the tribulations of uncaring bosses and customers who think if you don't please them with what they think is right, then all you do is wrong.

Mother's Tying End Team generation called staying home from work "laying out." The very term conjures up visions of no account and lazy behavior. Now-a-days as I get older and nearer retirement, using sick leave seems more appealing than when I knew my career depended upon me being there. Nevertheless on some occasions when I'm sick and have a good reason to "lay out," I force myself to go in and take care of things that shouldn't be left "hanging fire". Now don't mistake this for being an overzealous workaholic because I'm not one to spend any more time at work than I can help, but I'm also not one to leave a job half done when it needs to be completed.

I never experienced the Great Depression and World War II like my parents. I'm sure their generation's work ethic was heavily influenced by those events. But then I also believe they already had a heavy dose of the Christian Work Ethic passed on from previous generations influencing their behavior. Those former generations were expected to go to work and support their families. They didn't have nursing homes, child care centers and government programs to take care of older family members who could no longer work. The older kids in the family did this duty until they too had to begin work. And many began working at an age before our kids today start high school.

The Great Depression made such deep scars on our parent's generation that I think it caused them to overkill a bit, guarding us against having to suffer similar hardships. They saw to it we weren't deprived of our childhood as they had been. But did my generation lose the work ethic as a result? I don't see as many Saras, Elmiras, Corrines and Lena Pearls being produced for the workforce of today; but there are still a few out there. Yes, our folks made our lives easier; but they didn't spare the rod too much and they led by example. The Tying End Team's example of self pride and seeing things through to a successful conclusion is not lost on my generation. That's our legacy and we must pass it on to our kids, if we want the kind of world tomorrow that we are used to today.

PART FIVE:

A LITTLE COMIC RELIEF

HOSTAGE OF HALLMARK

Yesterday while sitting on the deck at "Dux" in fashionable Buckhead, I was thinking how much my wife was enjoying Mother's Day. Her son and daughter treated us to this genuine Cajun lunch as recognition for all the hard work she had done to get them here. I thought it a well-deserved afternoon together with folks she sponsored into the world. There were the presents, one of which was the lunch, and yes, the cards. The cards were mandatory. Not by any of us, by the card companies.

How much time did my wife spend with her cards? Not much even though she appreciated them. She read the verse written by a guy who was actually paid to make up personal messages to people he didn't know, and smiled lovingly as she put them down. But they will become part of the already mounting stockpile of stuff that's crowding us out of house and home. Oh, before you say it's the thought that counts (where've I heard that before?), think of this. Her kids spent around two dollars to have her read something they had already said better themselves. They spent time they didn't have, looking for the thing. The card companies are very big on this aspect in their guilt-trip advertising.

It seems I'm buying cards on a daily basis for my wife, mother, daughter or anyone else I decide to recognize on one of the hundreds of obscure occasions set aside as days for cards.

By the way, who started Valentine's Day? Secretary's Day is one of those days that I think the industry created for card sending. That goes along with Boss's Day. While they are at it, the card companies ought to create Assistant's Day for people who aren't secretaries or bosses. My wife is one of those and that would be another card I'd need to buy, adding to the twenty other cards I'm urged to get her each year for various holidays or dedicated to something else she is. I've unintentionally given her the same anniversary card for three years in a row. I didn't even know I was doing it until she opened the envelope one anniversary and said, "It's the same one I got last year." We checked, because as I've said, she keeps them all and clutters up her dwindling supply of closet space in the bedroom, and sure enough, she had two more just like it. Big seller I guess.

When I get recognized by my family on "Viet Nam Veterans Who Didn't Get Wounded or Develop the War Syndrome Day," I have to open the card as necessary protocol before tearing into the presents. Now I have no problems with presents for recognition on holidays. Let's see, if I could get presents for all the "official" holidays plus those the card companies invent, that means I could probably fill my Civil War library in less than a year and still have some presents left over to get all those Penske and Honda racing caps I have on my want list. Opening the card only delays the excitement of ripping off ribbons and paper, also sold by the card companies. You just can't win. I'm very touched all of half-a-second by the verse, while my wife and daughter are sitting there wishing I'd finish reading the thing and put it down. I'd rather hear all that affection from their lips, no matter if it isn't as poetic and original as the guy who got paid to tell me this stuff. Wonder if he'd be as poetic if he had to say it to my face?

DOCTOR BILLS

We all get them, starting at mid-month and running until the end. They come in many sizes and shapes and usually catch us totally off guard, even though we know they are coming. Yes, they are bills, and in my case doctor bills. Recently, my mother managed to sling shot herself out of the bed while turning out a light. She didn't suffer any broken bones but the fall stirred up her arthritis and got it excessively active again. She had to have all sorts of medical tests, x-rays and a cat scan. You might think it would have been cheaper to let our cat scan her, but then E.J. Smut isn't that inexpensive either. A good scan from her could cost us about $8.00 in cat treats and take about five hours if we are lucky. By the way, mother is fine now, but I'm not. I got the initial bill from the hospital with a warning the insurance wasn't about to pay for it all.

I anticipated the flood of bills from the hospital and primary care physician, even though I couldn't understand any of their modern hieroglyphics except the bottom line charges. But now I'm beginning to get bills from doctors I've never heard of, and from places I never heard of either. So I called my mother's doctor and asked about these bills. "You know, Mr. Dale, I had to consult with so-and-so in order to make the best diagnosis." I thought, this guy went to medical school on and off for twenty-five years plus took all those specialist courses, and he still can't make a diagnosis on his own? Anyway, he explained he had just needed reassurance in case anything went wrong. I could read between the lines, and it said in case he got sued he wouldn't have to pay all of it himself.

Well, I can see it now: The doctor runs into an associate in the hospital corridor and says, "Charles, I'm treating Mrs. Dale for a fall and arthritis, what kind of test you think I should order next?" "Well, Fred, have you thought about doing a . . .?" Then out of the blue I get a bill from Charles for a professional consultation. Over a drink after work Charles tells Harry, another specialist, and he suggests something neither Fred nor Charles has thought about. Next thing you know I get a bill from Harry. Harry happens to mention his conversation to Neil, an anesthesiologist who also sent me a bill. An anesthesiologist sent me a bill? For what? Mother wasn't put to sleep during any of these procedures. That does it! Something has got to be done. I'll be getting bills forever if these guys have their way. I'll know something is just a little suspicious when I start to get bills from these fellows' wives and children.

I may have to get the Post Office to start returning the bills marked "Moved and left no forwarding address" or "Died of cardiac arrest after receiving a bill from the doctor's dog." So my suggestion to you is that if you are going to get sick and go into the hospital, find a doctor who is anti-social or has an ego the size of Philadelphia and thinks he knows more than anyone else. He might not be the easiest one to deal with, but you can bet he will rarely ask another doctor for an opinion. Whatever you do, don't find a friendly doctor who likes to talk and schedules you for unnecessary additional visits. That's a clue right there to avoid them like the plague. Did I say plague? MORE BILLS!

"CAN'T COME TO THE PHONE..."

I recently had occasion to call our local community college and request a catalog for my daughter. Instead of a helpful admissions person, I got this recording that did a thirty second advertisement for the company that developed it. This was shortly before it launched into an eighty option menu, all in fluent Yankee. The thing was too fast for me to translate into Southern before it told me I had ten seconds to make a choice or it would hang up. I decided it was a good thing I already had a college degree because it wasn't going to give me enough time to find out how to get one there. I also considered myself lucky I had only called a community college and not a major university.

Every morning when I get to work, I have to check my voice mail; and every evening when I get home, I check my message machine. It seems like today you can't talk to humans anymore because they're too busy, disinterested or just plain practicing avoidance. I guess before I get into a tizzy over all this, I should explain that coming from Hogansville I'm used to picking up the phone and getting someone who is really there. They may not always have the right information, but just in case they do, you don't have to leave a message to get it later.

When I tried to get a real person on that community college answering system, it hung up on me, twice, even though I pushed the right buttons to stop it. When I finally did get someone she insisted on rerouting me back to the recording. Unfortunately, for her, I was persistent enough that she finally took my request, even though I'm sure I detected hostility in her voice. By the way, I never got the catalog.

It wasn't too long after that I called an electrician to come and repair the light and exhaust fan in our bathroom my wife had blown out, without even going in there. The first call was taken by, you guessed it, a machine. After my call wasn't returned in a reasonable time, two days, I placed another call. The second time was no different than the first; I got the machine again and no one showed up at my house. Yep, not learning anything from the first two tries, I called a third time. This time, lo-and-behold I got a real living breathing person or a real good imitation by a machine. The voice could care less whether my electrical problem got repaired. She told me she would beep the electrician and he would call me right back. If he did, then he didn't get my machine or me either, for that matter. The light and fan are still in need of repair.

In the past I've talked to you about traffic snarls here in the city, developers that kindly provide florescent and neon lighting to help the few remaining trees grow, and my fighting other never-ending problems from overpopulation. Now you can add to the list recordings that never let you talk to real people. Do you get the impression I miss my hometown lifestyle a whole lot? I am certain some of this has extended to small towns in

America, and possibly Hogansville too. But I'll bet in spite of the answering machines, traffic and developers, you can still go to town and find people that talk to you in a friendly manner slow and pleasant enough to understand. Not always so friendly here in the big city, even when you are fortunate enough to be able to talk with a real person. This may make you wonder why I choose to knock the friendly and courteous recorded voice on the machine, when I end up with humans who make me pay in spades for causing them to have to answer the phone. I wonder that too. So, if you'll excuse me, I'm going to go back to 1966 now. Should you need me just leave a message on my machine, and "I'll get back to you as soon as I can".

PART SIX:

YANKEES AND REBELS

UNRECONSTRUCTED YANKEE

Old Ed is having a birthday today. He really isn't old, at least not by my standards. He's only nine months older than me. What's so special about this birthday you ask, or did you? Well, you see, Ed's a Yankee. Not just your average Yankee but a Yankee that knows how his side won and respects my side as a worthy foe. He also knows everything in between the beginning and end of the War for Southern Independence. Of course, you can't get Ed to use that title. What's important is, we are friends and he is my mentor for something I hope to do in retirement, staff rides.

Ed works in the U.S. Army Reserve Command Historian's Office and part of his duty is to conduct Army Staff Rides. In short, this is a tour of battlefields with the intent to teach tactics, use of terrain, leadership, and instill Esprit de Corps in junior officers and NCOs. Coming from a background of teaching at the U.S. Military Academy and the Army's Command and General Staff School, and retiring as an Army Lieutenant

Colonel Ed is imminently qualified to lead staff rides. But just like undertaking any military operation, you must do a reconnaissance before initiating the real thing. Ed's trusty recon staff consists of me and our mutual friend Mike.

It was a chilly spring morning when Mike was supposed to pick Ed up at his home in Douglasville and then me at I-75 and Highway 92. We were going to head up to Chickamauga for a recon of the battlefield. I arrived at my pre-designated spot at 0730 hours and posted myself in clear view of the intersection. I watched traffic and anticipated the day's activities. After an hour or so of anticipation, I walked a couple hundred yards to Shoney's to call Ed at home. I got his wife Jill and found he had walked up to the corner and waited for Mike for an hour and then returned to call Mike. Mike hadn't answered so Ed had gone back on guard for some more anticipation. By the time I made my third call to Ed's wife, she was quickly tiring of Ed's returning home every fifteen minutes to call Mike, and me calling every twenty minutes.

It was nine o'clock when I saw the government van finally pull up at the intersection. The two of them were laughing, and as I got in, they accelerated throwing me even further back than the rear seat position I occupied in that monster. The story was Mike had gotten lost, which I still don't believe. The man takes nothing serious and his Tennessee brogue gives up nothing to convince you otherwise. Arriving at the battlefield, Ed was in his element walking down one of the many trails to check its condition, dragging me along. Mike took the van to meet us at the other end of our walk.

When we arrived at the open field at the end of the trail, Ed was engrossed in describing a magnificent turning action. Suddenly, realizing the van wasn't there, Ed dropped everything and broke into an uncontrollable and not so magnificent charge across the field. Running for the road at full speed repeating expletives I won't share with you, Ed was totally incensed. He couldn't understand how Mike could get lost again, especially in an area he knew like the back of his hand. We soon learned what had caused the delay, when the jovial Tennessean drove up laughing uncontrollably. He said, "Bet ya'll thought I got lost again, didn't ya? Nah, had to stop at the visitor's center and jaw with a few friends." Fortunately for our late arriving friend, Ed is a Yankee and I'm a Rebel who doesn't shoot first and ask questions later.

I just got a message on my e-mail this morning from Ed responding to comments I made about a meeting on the command history. He acknowledged my suggestions and signed off saying he would accept them even if they were from the unreconstructed rebel. I like Ed, even if he is an unreconstructed Yankee.

Captain James Dale, Company B, Third Regiment, Confederate Engineers leads an Army staff ride at 'The Battle above the Clouds', Lookout Mountain, Tennessee. The unit identified is my re-enactment unit from which I am now retired.

A RHODE ISLAND YANKEE
ON MAIN STREET HOGANSVILLE

So, what is it that endears Hogansville to a New England Yankee? Never in a hundred years when I was growing up would I ever think a New Englander would discover Hogansville, much less like it. Then again as I've said often, what do I know? It turns out this guy works right here in the same building with me. Now, you have probably surmised it wouldn't be too difficult for him not to know about Hogansville, working only a floor away from yours truly. Well, you'd be wrong; he discovered it all by himself. It doesn't hurt that Hogansville advertises itself as an antique haven. He likes antiques; maybe that's why he and I get along so well? I won't go into names here, although I don't believe he would object. I know my New England friend will soon be down again and I want to respect his privacy. Then again, how can someone speaking with a New England accent in Hogansville remain anonymous for very long?

It appears my Yankee friend picked Hogansville as a second hometown, so I asked him why. Would you like to know? Thought so! Not so much that Hogansville is an antique haven; he likes the sense of tranquility he finds walking on our quiet tree-lined streets. Funny, while I was growing up it didn't seem so tranquil when Larry Joe and Ted drag raced down Main Street, and when Joe L. tried to outrun Otis, our octogenarian police officer, in order to avoid getting his '55 Chevy impounded for no mufflers. My Yankee friend might not think the Rock Hole so tranquil if he could see us kids diving from the cliffs. Finally, as he walks our quiet tree-lined streets today, he probably won't be hit with a water balloon on Halloween, or witness the mayhem on Friday nights in the fall when the Greenwave played at home.

It seems, in addition to enjoying the nostalgia of current Hogansville along with antiques and pretty good food to eat, my

New England friend met some interesting people too. Things get a bit sticky here. You see, some of these folks remember me from my unreformed days, growing up in this adopted hometown of my friend's. No, I didn't spend time in reform school, but I did spend a little time making my neighbors wonder if I didn't need to be there.

I'm happy my New England friend finds something of home in Hogansville. It proves our little family altercation of a little over a hundred years ago between the North and South didn't separate us completely. We still share a common heritage and a common love of things that remind us of home. I didn't notice much difference between the rural communities of New England and Georgia when I vacationed at Cape Cod a few years ago. When people and their values are the same which I'm certain they are all over this country, with the possible exception of California and New York, we Americans can find a touch of home everywhere we go. Even if we can't go home again, especially me after this article, it's nice to know it's possible to find a substitute hometown.

SAME CHURCH, DIFFERENT PEW

Lives of Southerners seem to relate, no matter what part of the South they are from. I have written several articles about my youth, the love I have had for cowboys and Indians, and the fifties which were a part of my generation's era. Later in the sixties it was sports, sports cars and girls, not necessarily in that order. So the other day when I had occasion to stop and talk with an Army friend from Arkansas, I gave him a copy of my latest offering, "Cowboy Hats and Pistols I Have Known and Loved." He read it and later we discussed childhood memories the article brought back. We agreed ours were similar, even though we grew up in different parts of the South, hence his statement, "Same church, different pew."

I've found from talking to my Northern friends they don't view change in the same way we Southerners do. In the North many children are exposed to change early in their lives by parents who travel frequently, who move to where the jobs pay better, or perhaps even move for adventure or to escape the cold. Whatever the Northerners' reasons for accepting change, one thing is clear, most Southerners don't like it much. I'm guilty, and I'll be the first to admit I had rather be pulled inside out than to change something I feel comfortable with or be forced to accept something new. It's a wonder I ever trade cars. But I guess things like that don't count? It's the big things, like trading houses, my mother and daddy didn't like and neither do I. Nevertheless it was done a couple of times and we lived through it; believe it or not, we did manage to get over it. Would I do it again? Probably, but with much hesitation and not without the terrible guilt about leaving a house I've come to accept as part of the family. It feels almost like you would feel giving one of your kids away.

It warms my heart to occasionally run into someone like my Arkansas friend. We're still in the same church even if we sit on different pews.

A FEW WORDS ON BEING SOUTHERN

How often is it said we Southerners are different than the rest of the country? Well, I know we say it about ourselves, but when someone else is saying it, we naturally take the defensive.

I remember when it first came to my attention that maybe the rest of the country didn't exactly believe we were fully integrated into the main stream. I had just arrived at my Air Force duty station in Tucson, Arizona, and getting ready to set up my desk. I was approached by one of the guys in the office who began a conversation that seemed to be going nowhere. After working there for a while, I noticed he was doing this a lot. Then one day he came up and engaged me in conversation again. Suddenly, I stopped in mid-sentence and asked why he was so interested in me. He said he wasn't particularly, he just liked to hear me talk. The fellow wasn't being rude, merely honest. He meant no harm and I took no offense, but I did realize that being Southern meant I was different even if it was only in the way I talked.

Boy, did I find out just a little bit later how much different some people think we Southerners are. My wife and I were lucky in that we found a refrigerated air conditioned apartment in Tucson. Most of them were cooled by what is referred to as Swamp Coolers, which are large units sitting atop an apartment building or house pumping cooled water through a kind of radiator unit inside. It creates an atmosphere something akin to Georgia humidity in August. You stay wet all the time, but cool. Our apartment looked across a swimming pool that lay not more than five feet from our door, and it faced a similar apartment on the other side of the square courtyard. In the other apartment lived two people who proved beyond a shadow of a doubt that Southerners are the most misunderstood of all regional people in our country.

They were an Air Force couple too. He was a navigator trainee from New York and she was a housewife trainee from California. They were both Jewish and had never been South. One Saturday she came over wringing her hands and in a major tizzy. I knew he was flying that day so I immediately assumed there had been a flying accident and he was the centerpiece of it. When we got her calmed, she told us he was all right. Whew! Anyway, she had just opened a letter to find a set of orders sending them to McDill Air Force Base which is located in Tampa, Florida. It sounded pretty good to me.

As we sat down, she said she had some very blunt questions for me. Without batting an eye she began, "We are Jewish (I already knew that) and of course you know how they feel about us in the South." I said, "Well, no I don't." I got a cold stare so I decided to have a little fun. Then I said, "Too bad, you may be in worse trouble than if you were assigned to Saigon." She said, "We've never gone South and I'm afraid we will get a cross burned in our yard or worse yet be killed by the Klan." I did know some folks from Hogansville with Scottish backgrounds but they didn't belong to any clan I knew about. Then she said, "The KLAN, you know." I said, "OH!" Then I reassured her that I would have my uncle plead her case to the Imperial Wizard, and he could virtually assure her safe passage through Georgia and most of the rest of the South. She was thrilled. Then she asked me to describe what they might encounter as they traveled through the South. I said she would have to overlook all immense poverty of the small towns, and sacked plantations Sherman burned that we haven't had the time or money to rebuild just yet. I also told her she should buy a washing machine and dryer before she left, that many of our stores didn't have much merchandise since the "WAR." Then I told her to befriend some local farmers or she would never have fresh food. And by all means avoid speaking Yiddish.

This was the most grateful woman when she left our apartment. And as she left she stuck her head back inside to remind me not to forget to call my uncle with the Klan. Alas, we Southerners may be slow, but we have a sense of humor. I wished I could have been there to see her face when they rolled into Tampa.

IT'S A GOOD TIME TO INVADE THE NORTH BOYS, THE YANKEES AIN'T AT HOME

Lately, I've again gotten interested in the one passion that consumed me throughout my high school years and toward the end of my college years. The passion is the War Between the States. Notice I didn't call it the Civil War, and that's because to us Southerners it wasn't a civil type of war, in fact there was nothing civil about it. It was, and still is, to some of the more hardened Jubal Early types the "War for Southern Independence." So now I'm interested in finding my Southern roots and investigating all the famous Georgian heroes like Longstreet, Gordon, Benning, Toombs, Wheeler, Hardee, and Alexander.

While I was, so to speak, serving time at West Georgia College, a fellow history major made a terrific find at West Point, Georgia. Digging in a private yard, he found a box of muskets; they were still packed in grease and most of their metal parts were still salvageable. They were, of course, U.S. weapons. Even before then, when I was a kid going to visit my grandmother in West Point, I wondered about the Confederate cemetery there. It sits at a major intersection (for West Point anyway) of Hwy 29 and the highway going across the Chattahoochee into downtown West Point. Well, recently I read an article about the "Battle of West Point." Did you know it was fought a week after General Lee surrendered? And also, did you know the Yankee commander's name was LaGrange? Neither did I, and was I surprised to find out that there was a fort at West Point too. It was named Ft. Tyler, after a Confederate Brigadier General (Tyler) who died defending the city. He's in the cemetery too.

After renewing my interest and finding out so much I hadn't known about my past, I began to look at my future. To my regret I find that so much of our Confederate past is under attack and threatened with extinction, due to the current belief all we fought for was bad. It also occurred to me maybe there is no one in the South to defend the Southern cause much less care. That's because my neighbors are from Michigan, Illinois and Ohio. These are my neighbors at home and at the office. Why is this? Why did it take them a hundred and forty years to figure out it was warm down here? They've always said they won the war because they were smarter than us, but I don't know about that. The more I read the more I find that their losses were much greater than ours, number-wise, and you'd think they might figure out why they kept getting so many of their people killed. But there were enough of them to get through, and apparently that was all that mattered.

They talk fast, but do they say anything that makes sense? Well, you don't know if you are Southern, because we are accustomed to listening to slow talk, and can't keep up with what they are saying. Just because you talk slow enough to be understood, some Yankees think we are slow thinkers and therefore dumb. Can you imagine a fast talking Yankee Forest Gump? Most Yankees say they don't really like the South, but that doesn't stop them from coming down in droves and wearing shorts in fifty degree weather. Then they look at me weird when I have on a winter jacket and jeans. I've had a couple of them ask me about what I consider cold. Anything above freezing up north calls for a beach party or nothing short of a cook out. But anything under seventy degrees is cold to me and calls for a long sleeve flannel shirt and jeans.

I also don't try to drive in Georgia snow, either. When I worked in downtown Atlanta I was the lone native Georgian in my section. I tried to tell my boss, who was from Illinois, that a half inch of Georgia snow could be treacherous, but he said he was used to driving in five to ten foot drifts and this was nothing. He didn't let me finish to tell him there was an inch of ice under the half inch of snow. He asked me later, after he had spent the better part of the next day doing wheelies in his Crown Victoria in front of his house, why I didn't warn him about the ice. I reminded him that I tried, but he had said he didn't have half a day to listen to me make a sentence. I didn't realize it took that long? I enjoyed the infrequent snow day at home watching the local news showing Yankees playing car ice hockey bumping into each other, and sliding down hills that they just climbed. It reminded me of the battle for Marye's Heights at Fredericksburg, They scaled the slope, only to come sliding back down as a result of Longstreet and Jackson's entrenched troops behind the stone wall.

In more recent years apparently the Yankees either got too

cold, or ran out of stuff up north. Their companies were spending lots of money on labor and operating costs. It seems there were no unions here, labor was a lot cheaper and costs were lower. They wouldn't need to have those huge heating bills to maintain their factories. But just like they did in reconstruction, Yankees brought all the high paying jobs with them, already filled. That's why I have neighbors who don't speak the "King's English." I don't know if they are talking about a card or a cod, or if they own a "kaa" or a "car." You get used to it after awhile, but you could probably learn Spanish or French almost as easily.

I find we Southerners can hold our own with the Yankees when behind the wheel. I guess it come from our prowess with horses in the century before. You know Jeb Stuart, Nathan Bedford Forest, Wade Hampton, Cobb's Legion, Fightin Joe Wheeler and our cavalries literally rode circles around Yankee armies. Only trouble is, the Yankee armies were still moving south while we were doing it. Today modern day carpetbaggers roam our streets in search of wealth, and our willingness to accept them make us to a small degree "scalawags". There's nothing wrong with being nice to visitors provided they understand they are visitors. Why did they go back north in the first place? That brings us around full circle. Well, I must admit it is a little easier on them down here now that we Rebs have stopped shooting at them.

I figure that by the end of the century, most every Yankee that is still up there will be down here. That gives me an idea. Since they don't pay us "no mind" anyway we can put together another army without them knowing it. We wouldn't have much trouble getting it up north, 'cause they came down here so fast they probably didn't remember to lock the door when they left. Just think we could easily take Chicago, Detroit, New York or Boston. Can you see the pages of Southern newspapers, "SOUTHERN ARMY OCCUPIES YANKEE CITIES WITHOUT A SHOT." Who can shoot at us if there's no one there? Only question is, would that make us Yankees if we occupied the north? I just thought of a second question, too, "Would that make the Yankees Southerners since they are down here?" And I just thought of a question that might make all this stuff null and void, why would we want to go up there in the first place? They came down here to get away from up there didn't they? We'll never know until we do it, so I say, "It's a good time to invade the North boys, the Yankees ain't at home, they're all down here."

CHAPTER VI

A SOUTHERNER COMES FULL CIRCLE

As my friend Homer "The Great" Brown says "Life is good," and it definitely is when you are doing something you want to do regardless of whether you are retired or not. Retirement doesn't necessarily mean the end of life. It can mean the beginning of life, depending on how you look at it, and what you do with it. We usually have the freedom and time to do whatever we want once we retire. I know today money is definitely a deterrent to doing everything we might consider fun, but what I'm talking about isn't driven by what we can and cannot afford. We have the opportunity to be useful in volunteer work and making sure those grandchildren are a part of our lives. It costs little or nothing to take a walk with your wife, spend time fishing on the lake, or just sit with a glass of wine or a cup of coffee on your back porch. Some people simply leave one occupation for another and there's nothing wrong with that, if it's something you do because you love the work or you really need the money. If it isn't, then you need to take a good hard look at yourself. I'll leave you with one thought. Whatever you do when you do retire, do it with every bit of energy and enthusiasm as you did that job that got you there.

PART ONE:

RETIREMENT, TIME TO GO TO THE BEACH

IT'S GETTING CLOSE

Just this past week after seeing a friend retire, I had a rather traumatic realization. I'm getting close to retirement too. I've been talking about it for years and doing a lot of smiling. I'm not smiling now, and I'm thirty-six days from the big event. It's not that I'm not happy, I am, but it's scary. Actually, I'm entering the final phase of life where I've earned a rest. I'd like to do a few things before really resting, such as traveling, just sitting around and watching a few old movies on TV like my just retired brother-in-law, working on my various collections, and finally the most important thing, spending some quality time with my family. Of course, the kids we have in common are all grown and out of the house doing stuff like working, racing bikes on weekend, tending to twins, and traveling. My wife is free from a paying job too, so I suspect we'll have a lot of quality time together. That's worth smiling about.

So why am I scared? Well, I can't think of a time when I didn't have to work. Maybe in high school, but since then I've had some kind of job for my livelihood. Yes, I could get a part-time job or maybe even another fulltime one, but if I want to continue working why not just keep the one I have and not retire? Makes sense to me. No, I don't want to keep working; I just want to know I am useful after I've stopped. I suppose that is what really is taking my smile away. I've never been one to do handyman chores or gardening. I figure if something is broken around the house, it's better to let people who know what they are doing fix it. The price for handyman duties may have to be evaluated a little closer after my income decreases. I may actually be forced to do handyman work myself. It won't hurt to learn a few things, I guess, but I may end up destroying the house while I'm learning. The results of that could require more than just a handyman.

Yes, I've gardened some and found I get much better tomatoes at the fruit stand. I've also cut grass, reluctantly. That reluctant part is what inspired my wife and me to have our new house built with a "natural" yard. That means there is no grass. But there are occasional weeds that need to be pulled and leaves to be raked. I was cleaning a drain last week and picked up a bunch of leaves in which was napping a small (and fortunately for me non-poisonous) snake. I don't need a heart attack just before I retire. So maybe next time I'll wear a glove and use a rake before I move suspicious leaves; or maybe a kid down the street might be interested in a part-time job.

So with my thirty-six remaining days of work, I'll try to figure out just what kind of uses I might have as a retired person. There must be something to make me feel useful in retirement and not end up costing me more money than I'll receive in my pension. Maybe I'll ask my wife; she retired a few years ago. She'll know something I can do. Just had a thought, if I ask I might end up learning to vacuum the house, cook, wash clothes, scrub bathrooms and pay bills. Come to think of it, with an imagination like mine surely I can find something worthwhile on my own to do after retirement. Maybe like writing? I think I'm getting that smile back again.

"NEVER APOLOGIZE: SIGN OF WEAKNESS"

Who do you think would say that? No, it's not a quote from a rap group and it's not attributable to George Patton or Vince Lombardi either. It's certainly not a quote you'd hear from one of today's flawed heroes. Give up? Well, it's from John Wayne. Not John Wayne the man, but a character he played in the movies. The character is Captain Nathan Brittles in "She Wore a Yellow Ribbon." My wife still can't believe how much trivial stuff I can remember.

At age ten I'd passed my Roy Rogers, Gene Autry and Tex Ritter stage so I enlisted myself in the cavalry. It would be fairly accurate to say John Wayne at that stage of a boy's life is a hero. I admired all his characters and when I grew up, I admired the man himself. But the purpose for writing this piece is to remember where I've been and to draw some parallels with Captain Brittles. You see when the movie begins, the Captain is a week away from retiring from a thirty something year career in the Army and he is finding it hard to deal with leaving. He "Xs" off each day on his calendar with a bit of remorse and goes about the job as if nothing is happening, right up to the last minute. I've found myself doing exactly the same thing and with only two more weeks left in my thirty year career as a civil servant, most of which was spent with the Army, I'm a bit sad about leaving it too.

When I was growing up in Hogansville, I dreamed of being in the Army and wearing dress blues complete with a saber and sash. Over my Army career, I've found soldiers handle more paper and computers than rifles and swords. So I've had to supplement my army visions with a lot of make believe through my volunteer associations, and I've managed to fulfill my childhood dreams. I've led soldiers on a charge over a real battlefield (of the past) and taught them about tactics and strategy during staff rides. I've also participated in ceremonies and living histories at the Army in Atlanta Museum at Ft. McPherson, standing at attention in uniform with sword drawn, and giving the command to "Present Arms" while general officers passed and returned my salute.

So as I leave the Army, I can say I've achieved not only my professional objective but a childhood dream. I've gotten to play army and be in the Army all at the same time. I've served in a fighting organization my daddy spilled blood for in World War Two, have two great, great grandfathers who wore gray that fought against it in a previous century, and another ancestor who fought for independence in 1776. When I think back over my career and the very small contribution I've made to our country, I have no reason to apologize, besides, it's a sign of weakness. Wait up Captain Brittles!

BEING JIMMY BUFFETT

Don't laugh. We have more in common than you know. We were born in the same year a month apart (I'm older); we're both male; we both grew up in the South; we both play guitar (I play at it); we both married and have a daughter; we are both dreamers; and we both write. Of course, that's where the similarities end. He's rich and I'm not. He's had an extremely successful career, and well, I've managed a career that's allowed me to retire so far. I have no talent for singing and no real adventuresome spirit that drives me on to take risks the way Mr. Buffett has done in pursuing his talents.

I've often wondered what I could have done had I been adventuresome. I may never find out in this life, at least by conventional methods, so I'll have to portray myself as a risk taker in books I just might begin to write. What started all this Buffett and writer thinking? Well, it's due to e-mails earlier this week from a friend at my former workplace whom I've shared Buffett concerts with in the past. She alerted me that tickets for the event go on sale around Atlanta this weekend.

Last year I fatefully arrived in front of my Publix three hours in advance of the ticket sales, to be first in line. But being first in line doesn't always mean you will be first to get tickets, because now-a-days a lottery is held and you could easily go to the back of the line regardless of when you arrive. It was raining last year when I went to get tickets. My night blindness kicked in, just as I turned on the eighteen lane parkway going to my Publix where the tickets were being sold. That parkway doesn't have any businesses along the sides. Matter of fact it doesn't have anything on it much at all. Maybe somebody is planning ahead, way ahead. Anyway there were enough white lines to confuse anyone, but I managed to steer my Prelude completely across the road and into a turn lane for the Post Office.

I finally figured out where I was going and salvaged the day, but I have to admit I thought the guy behind me was also after tickets and it was painful to see him blow right past me. Fortunately, he didn't turn into the Publix parking lot. In fact almost no one does at that time of the morning. After arriving, I spent those lonely three hours dodging rain and wind and sipping cold coffee, until a few other diehards began to arrive.

When the lottery started, I selected the lowest number and everything worked out perfectly, with me officially first in line to buy the coveted tickets. Turns out my daughter also was first in line at her Publix and neither of us had a way to communicate, forgetting to swap cell phone numbers, so we ended up with three extra tickets. I wonder sometimes why luck can't be spread out instead of happening all at once.

This year, rain or not, I won't be going to the concert and I'm having serious withdrawals pains because I won't be getting up in the middle of the night and once again forging through rain to vie for Buffett tickets; but life must go on. Oh, the reason I'm missing the concert is my wife and I just this week rented a condo on the Gulf coast for the month Buffett will be in town. Yvonne, my wife, always knows what to say to make me feel better on these kinds of occasions and this one is no exception. Her words went something like this, "Instead of seeing Jimmy Buffett this year you can be him. We'll have Margaritas every day and you can take your guitar." Oh, and I mustn't forget the sponge cake and the flip flops.

HANGING OUT SENIOR STYLE

It was a typical Friday night with nothing much going on in Hogansville. We drove by the Legion Home to see if we recognized any of the cars and then cruised by a girlfriend's house to see if she'd gotten home yet. No luck, so we made a pass through downtown hoping to see if some of the luckier guys were back from their dates. We parked my daddy's shiny sleek Chevy hardtop with the big engine and tried to look cool sitting on the trunk, but only attracted the local cops who asked why we weren't home at that hour. Such was life in my hometown in the mid-sixties.

It was another Friday night in Hogansville, but not a typical one. We made a similar circuit checking a classmate's house instead of a girlfriend's, but we didn't stop downtown because it was already occupied by what looked to be a gang and not one we'd normally expect to see. There were a few other differences this time around, too, the main ones being we weren't eighteen anymore and my wife was along for the ride with us. My buddies' wives didn't make it to this reunion. We had two-thirds of the evening left and nothing to do except cruise around in a four-door Saturn nowhere near as cool as that fast Chevy. My wife, trooper she is, asked to be dropped off at the motel where we were all staying and turned me loose to hang out with my three friends.

Well, what do a bunch of fifty plus guys do having been set free by their wives for an entire evening? One thing is not ride around in a small car all night, especially one that our stiff legs don't lend to climbing in and out of well. So we went to the International Café to listen to live music and talk about the sixties. Did I say listen to music? Actually, my hearing aids went ballistic with the noise and I'm certain Tommy thinks I heard at least half the conversation we were carrying on. I did hear enough to find out why we lost the regional football championship our senior year. I also heard an interesting expose on a former girlfriend I once spent a whole night crying over while at work in the mill, getting cotton lint stuck to my face. Tommy assures me I was most fortunate to be dumped by her. We stayed to close the place down and I was shocked any of us were still awake at that hour. What was more shocking is when we got back to the motel there were other classmates sitting outside talking. Of course, we had to stay a while just to be polite but the real draw was one of these folks happened to be a popular girl back in school who tended to still draw attention. I didn't get around that much back then and didn't know her well; besides a guy my age starts winding down after midnight, so I took my leave. Naturally the slide key card didn't work so my wife had to get up and let me in.

After settling down in bed, I had time to think about all the male bonding and just plain fun I'd had with my former school buddies. I also realized how lucky I was to get dumped by that girl from LaGrange because I might never have met the woman who's been sleeping next to me for these last many years. Knowing she was there waiting when the fantasy evening ended, made it all the more perfect. I wonder if maybe we shouldn't make this cruising thing a permanent part of our class reunion fare? Nah, not a chance, wives will only tolerate so much.

THE SHELL THAT GOT AWAY

"Murderer!" she cried after stepping into the room where I had placed the spiral shell only a few minutes before. We are on vacation at a condo on the South Carolina coast where there is an abundance of beautiful large spiral shells, huge horseshoe crab shells that look like German World War II helmets, starfish, and sand dollars washing up on the shore each day. My wife is very conscious of life of all forms especially if it cannot talk or tell me I'm killing it. Of course, once I told her the shell was no longer inhabited, things almost got better.

The main point to our seashore vacation was to walk on the beach a couple of times a day, enjoy the beauty of nature, revel in the warm ocean breeze, relax and eat too much. We seemed to manage to get to the beach at low tide every day when the shells mired up in the sand and finding them was easier than looking for Easter eggs. The problem is whenever we found something that looked like we wanted to keep, it was occupied. When this happened I knew the answer was to throw the thing back into the ocean and hope it would not be foolish enough to get washed up on shore a second time. I should understand this concept fully, since I have a tendency sometimes to need saving more than once a day from some of my own foolish deeds.

Anyway, about the first day or so we were at the beach I found the most strikingly beautiful shell I'd ever seen. It was a relatively small spiral and had vertical strips of delicately soft shades of brown with perfectly delineated lines all the way from light beige to soft chocolate. I determined this one would stay with me, that is until I heard scratching and looked into the opening to see a very brave aggressive hermit crab with the deed clutched firmly in his claw. My wife wasn't near but it didn't matter because her morality about all things living had long since ingrained itself into my brain, and without another thought I tossed the beautiful shell back into the ocean, knowing full well with the strong waves it would be back on shore before the next day. I didn't see that one the next day but I found another spiral shell not even comparable and it didn't seem to have an occupant, at least one that was still breathing water or air. To make certain I prodded it gently with a stick to assure myself it was vacant, not believing the sign on the front saying "for rent or lease." So I brought the shell up on the porch of the condo to save for my granddaughters' collection back home.

By the way, this is where you came in. I'm not a murderer but I'm also nowhere near being a Green Peace type, which is just slightly left of Ralph Nader. I don't need a shell bad enough to evict its occupant, especially if the occupant needs the shell to stay alive. So without too much argument I ambled back down to the beach, braving the alligators in the marsh over which I had to traverse by boardwalk, to get and toss the shell back into the surf. By the way, I never saw any of those alligators in the marsh but I did see a bunch of really friendly microscopic frogs hopping all over the sidewalk and boardwalk, and a couple of pretty cute bunny rabbits munching grass in the side yard. Oh yes, and there were a couple of very nice black snakes in our shrubbery. I decided not to try to make idle conversation with the snakes since they seemed to be in a great rush to get somewhere. Overall it was a pretty restful vacation of reading and eating too much and throwing back shells.

LIVING IN THE PAST

You don't need to know much about me after reading this

column to know I'm a history buff. This past week I had a wonderful opportunity to demonstrate to a bunch of school children how life was lived a couple of centuries back. Reinhardt College is a beautiful little school about five miles from my house. Every October it holds its annual Georgia Timeline for local elementary schools, and I was invited to take part as a presenter. Actually, earlier in the year I stumbled into this great opportunity by showing up on the doorstep of the Funk Heritage Center on campus dressed as a Confederate soldier on the wrong day; I was supposed to help a re-enactment unit. I was greeted in the parking lot by the Assistant Director, who is a charming girl near my daughter's age. She looked at me a little funny but gave me the correct date for the reenactment and said she was thrilled to have me participate in the scheduled Living History.

I'm no stranger to living history, having broken in my act at Fort McPherson's museum and on Army staff rides with my old command, whose historian insisted we leaders wear Civil War uniforms. Reinhardt sets up "stations" in a field behind their museum where each era of Georgia history is presented from the earliest Native Americans through the Civil War. They have an impressive array of professional and volunteer living history folks. I was impressed by the camps of professionals portraying James Oglethorpe, early American Indians, and by the volunteers who do pioneer life at a period cabin with a blacksmith shop. They do a great job and our Civil War camp was good too. We had a lady who talked about civilians during the Civil War while wearing a widow's black hoop skirt, a Union soldier portrayed by a real descendant of General James B. McPherson, and me being a Confederate staff officer. Our camp had pup tents, a flagpole, a Dutch oven, and we fried bacon and hardtack over an open fire. If Civil War soldiers ate this stuff, then no wonder we had more deaths due to causes other than bullets. The grease was an inch thick in the half canteen we used as a frying pan. We introduced the kids to lye soap, raw sugar, and of course hardtack. Then I demonstrated how a sword and black powder pistol were used in combat, and the Union re-enactor fired a dummy round from his rifle. The kids ate this stuff up.

  This is the kind of history children do not get from a book or classroom. They saw how people dressed and lived during each era of Georgia's history, and got to ask questions that would never have come to mind elsewhere. It wasn't our job to explain the sociopolitical aspects of the Civil War, as our station emphasized soldier life. They were a little young to understand the politics of war anyway. We got some surprising answers to our questions and lots of questions from these third through fifth graders that surprised us. Before telling them who fought in the Civil War, I asked if they knew. I had answers ranging from Indians to British with one finally saying the United States; most were quite knowledgeable even knowing what the Confederate States were. I got a few thumbs up when they learned I was a Confederate soldier. One little boy asked if my sword was real. I resisted a smart-alecky answer because when you think about it, that's a legitimate question. I told him it was real but didn't come from the Civil War time which I'm sure is what he meant by "real;" he still wanted to hold it in his hand. Touching history is something else you don't often get in class. Who knows, maybe I've awakened another history buff who one day will step into my boots. Come to think of it, I wish he'd hurry. Now I know why those soldiers' feet hurt after a day's march.

DID I SEE THAT?

  Now there may be such things as other dimensions and other worlds, but I've yet to see them for myself. My wife says there is a reason why my middle name is Thomas and it becomes clear when I try to deal with abstractions. Just recently a professional counterpart told me I should avoid at all cost the abstract until I can learn to connect the dots. What was he talking about?

Considering the possibilities of things you're not sure are there, is abstract to me. I dealt with this theory back in college psychology and I could only manage a "C" in that course. But then again a "C" is passing, so having successfully completed Psychology 101 I'll attempt to tell you a story about the abstract that happened early this spring.

I like history so I spend a lot of my free time pursuing that interest. Recently, I assisted in an exercise to train three history detachments at Kennesaw Mountain, where my job was to be a Confederate Officer POW getting interrogated by modern day Yankee soldiers. This meant I had to wear the uniform and report to Cheatham Hill Battlefield in Marietta, Georgia, to await the arrival of each detachment to practice on me.

Fortunately the park was devoid of civilization, so in the early morning no one was around when I strolled down the trail admiring the beautiful mist and heavy green canopy of tall hardwoods surrounding me. It's puzzling how such a beautiful place could have been an awful killing ground at one time. Even with this past history I never gave much thought to ghosts being around there, but the lady I saw walking towards me may have. This early in the morning, it never occurred to me as to what she might think she was seeing. But then I am used to eliciting such looks from my wife when she tries to get the cowlick I've developed over the years to stay down before I go off to work. She says my hair looks like Strom Thurman's. If he were still alive, I might not take that to mean anything too bad.

Well, back to the story. As the lady continued toward me she swayed off the path a little until I realized why she was acting so peculiar. Here she was alone in a misty and possibly eerie quiet setting, meeting a Confederate soldier on a Civil War battlefield over a hundred years after the war. In spite of my problems dealing with the abstract, I realized I needed to say something before she had a heart attack. The appropriate words escaped me even though I was still trying to figure out what to say, as we began to close the distance between us. Then it hit me and I said, "No ma'am, I'm not a ghost." She took a deep breath and said, "I wasn't so sure." We both managed a smile. I felt the better part of valor was not to try and explain my dress and presence so as we passed I dipped my kepi, and hoped I wouldn't disappear.

PART TWO:

I NEVER THOUGHT I COULD LOVE AS MUCH

I have been fortunate to have been blessed with a great set of parents, a wonderful wife for the last thirty years and an intelligent and beautiful daughter. I never thought there would be anyone I could love more than these people, until. . . . well, truth is I love my granddaughters, all three of them equally with those others I've just named. But my granddaughters are special people I know I probably won't get to see through to their adult lives, so I have to love them a little more right now to make up for that time I won't get to spend with them later on. I mentioned three granddaughters but you will only read about two of them here because the third one, Deliliah, decided to wait until I stopped writing before making an appearance. I think she was smart to do that, don't you?

LEARNING THE HARD WAY

I don't think I'm that old, but to a twenty-two year old daughter I'm pretty old. We have talked about things and I've tried to tell her how to live, hopefully saving her much unneeded effort by learning from my experiences.

Did I listen to wisdom and experience? Well, one of my daddy's favorite sayings was, "One of these days boy, you'll have to learn the hard way." Pain seems to stick out in my mind when I remember the "hard way" experiences I endured.

For instance, there was the time my daddy was trying to teach me to catch fly balls. I didn't want to support my gloved hand with my bare hand to stop the forward momentum of a hard baseball traveling at somewhere near the speed of sound. My nose didn't grasp the theory that gloved hands can do as much damage as a baseball by itself. So when the baseball landed in the glove and they both whacked my nose it responded by bleeding. Had I listened to my daddy's instruction, I wouldn't have had to miss the second game of that double header.

Anyway, he explained the little tidbits of knowledge he expounded came from his learning the hard way. So why did he expect me to follow his advice when it seemed pretty clear he didn't follow his own daddy's advice? I guess for the same reason I expect my daughter to sit there and soak up all my fatherly information on how to avoid the pitfalls of life. I get this really good feeling when she occasionally laughs and intently listens to me, as if hanging on to every word. I just know she's filing this stuff away for the right time. Trouble is, she's probably thinking about that concert next week and hoping I'll finish before she goes into a deep coma.

Apparently the hard way isn't too bad a way to learn. It definitely allows you to appreciate the real life experience of making a mistake. If it hurts enough you eventually learn not to do it too often. That can't be relayed any other way. I know I won't forget to support my glove on the next occasion I have to catch a fly ball. But then again, have I really learned from my father's advice? Just this morning while rushing to the bathroom in the dark, it happened. I knew the very instance I struck the door jam with my left little toe that it was broken. Not the door jamb, the little toe. You would think I wouldn't forget how much it hurt two months ago when I broke it the first time doing just what I was doing this morning. I was running around in the dark and not paying too much attention to where my feet were going. And you know it hurt just as bad the second time.

So much for learning the hard way, since my accident happened right after the alarm went off, I tried to subdue the scream of agony, so as not to further awaken my wife. It seemed to work, or she figured I had broken my toe again and there wasn't much she could do about it anyway. So I took my shower and slowly pulled a sock over my left foot. I noticed it sorta looked the same as my right. My big toes on both sides were in the same place, meaning I had two right feet. However what I was looking at was my little toe on the left foot slowly becoming the same size as the big toe on the right. Maybe, I thought, I ought to wear two right shoes to work today.

So how can I keep a straight face when telling my daughter bits of wisdom I've learned the hard way when I'm still learning them? And can I tell her I didn't get this old by being stupid?

JIMPA'S STICK

There was a stressful period in my life when I took up smoking. After a couple of years of that, I finally quit back in 1984 and it wasn't too tough for me. For some reason I stopped cold turkey. You see, when I quit smoking I began to chew toothpicks. I don't think it's a replacement for cigarettes. I think it's because I have gaps in my back teeth. I have to use a toothpick after every meal in spite of the usual floss, depending on what I've eaten. So there! But toothpicks are fun to chew, there's no doubt. I've found myself chewing them at work, home and when we have gone places. I had a boss at work who also chewed toothpicks. Now, don't try to tell me it looks hokey like a hick on the farm with a piece of hay between his teeth and a straw hat and overalls. My boss looked like a Harvard Business School Professor. He was trim, wore the best suits, thin wire-framed glasses and was a clean-cut guy and he was three positions above me in the hierarchy.

I've drawn a few comments from coworkers and family about my toothpick chewing, and I guess I forget they are there sometimes. I chew them when I drive too and get some really strange looks because neither my cars nor I look like James Dean. It was during the fifth grade in school, the last time I turned a collar up on a shirt or jacket. Oh, and that black leather jacket with the silver stars on the epaulets I had in seventh grade doesn't fit anymore, so don't even think about it. Just today I noticed my spare tire is returning. I'm not paying as close attention to my diet now that I'm retired and I don't exercise as frequently. So I asked my wife if she knew which one of her husbands was gaining weight, and because she was busy and didn't want to answer silly questions, she said, "No, but I know which one is my husband because he has a piece of wood in his mouth." Then she sent me down the street in drizzling rain to the mail box to mail some bill she'd just paid.

It wasn't until my granddaughter Madelyn, one of the twins, told her mother who was chewing a toothpick one day, that she had JimPa's stick. That's when I realized maybe I was chewing toothpicks a little too much. With that and my wife's comment, it's clear I need to stop chewing toothpicks. Good thing I know all the bad stuff about cigarettes now, and the fact you can't smoke just about anywhere in the USA, otherwise I might be tempted to go back to them to replace my toothpick chewing habit.

"I JUST DON'T UNDERSTAND WHERE THE LEAVES GO."

We were almost at the end of the day's long session of baby sitting our three year old granddaughters. Madelyn had collapsed on the sofa for a nap and Audrey took "Vonnie" up to her play room and in no uncertain terms told JimPa he wasn't invited. While she styled Vonnie's hair, Audrey made a few scientific observations like, "I just don't understand why the leaves fall off the trees. I just don't understand why the wind blows." The girls are not only at that age where they are curious about everything, they are also at the age where they are into everything. Their mommy had had them on a successful potty training program but they still needed a little help while getting their clothing back in order.

They may not have taken totally to getting re-dressed, but one thing the girls have mastered is confusing their grandparents and keeping them off balance. After downing her fruit juice, Madelyn announced she had to make a trip to the bathroom. Dummy that I am, I let her get ahead of the game and she locked the bathroom door behind herself before old JimPa could stop her. It took some serious discussion to get her to open it again. Then Audrey, before I could get Madelyn fixed back like a normally clothed kid, went into the bathroom and locked the door. Audrey is the scientific one, so it took a great deal of negotiating and a lot of time to get the door open. Of course, when she did come out, I was so relieved I didn't think much about it when she pulled the door shut behind her. After we got Audrey put back together, I went to open the door to see what kind of damage the bathroom had incurred while the girls had held it captive. So when I twisted the door it was locked. Who went in this time? I took stock and on the outside were two twins and two adults. We were all accounted for. Then who's locked in there now? No one! Their mommy didn't have one of those little push tool that builders put above the door sill to jimmy the lock in case someone accidentally locks themselves out. So we had to look for a substitute.

My daughter is the descendant of a pack rat. I know, because it's me. We eventually decided she had everything but a tool that would unlock the door. I found a set of small screwdrivers but we had no luck and finally decided they wouldn't do the job. Time was of the essence, since I needed to get the door unlocked before my daughter got home and decided I was too incompetent to keep her children. The only recourse left was to take the door knob off. I managed to locate a Phillips head that just fit. Pack ratting can be a good thing, just glad I didn't need a left handed hammer for this task. Ten minutes later with a blister developing on my palm and lots of sweating, I got the door knob off and released the lock. Success, the door was open. But now I had to put the door knob back together. I'm here to tell you it's easier to take one off. I got one screw back in and soon discovered just because one was in successfully the other hole wasn't necessarily lined up for the other screw. My wife then took over and put the thing back on. She has a smaller hand you know, to maneuver into tight spaces.

Well, this is where the tale started. Madelyn got bored and took a nap and Audrey decided she could best get her scientific questions answered by someone who can put a door knob back on successfully. Me? I did some reading. And mommy was never the wiser, until now.

PIRATES IN THE FAMILY

It had to happen sooner or later, there are real pirates in my family. Well, real in the sense that they say they are pirates, and they sure sound like pirates. I'm sitting here at my desk looking at a picture of my daughter and myself at a Jimmy Buffett concert about four years ago. It was the last one we were able to attend together, as after her twins came along there's never been much chance to get to another. Over the years I've managed to convert my daughter from a heavy metal maiden into a bona fide "Parrothead" – Buffett speak for fan. If you haven't been to a live Buffett experience, you haven't lived. It's difficult to explain the atmosphere but it's akin to a massive beach party where everyone knows one another. It's also filled with a lot of piratical behavior and wild dress, and his best songs are about the ocean and imagining life as a Caribbean pirate.

Well, if that isn't enough to whet your appetite as to who the real pirates are in our family, then I might as well go ahead and tell you about them. It was a couple of weeks ago when my wife and I were taking the twins from their house to the playground up the street. You'd think since they are three and a half they'd want to walk, but they insisted on riding in their wagon and having JimPa pull them the couple of blocks. As we passed the car, I opened the car door to get my ball cap and Madelyn said, "Pirate, I wanna wear it." Sure enough the light blue cap had stenciled across it a white skull and crossbones, along with the latitude and longitude of Wolf's Bay Marina near Gulf Shores, Alabama. After they climbed into the wagon I placed the cap on Madelyn's head, bill to the front. I was surprised she wore it the whole way to the playground since the last time either of them had caps placed on their heads, they gave a yelp and slung them to the wind.

This past week we took the girls a few seashells we had gathered on our South Carolina vacation. Right after that both Madelyn and Audrey began speaking fluent Long John Silver. My wife and I, along with their mom Emily, took them to the playground with JimPa pulling the wagon once again. When we arrived, the girls climbed up onto a wooden platform housing the top of a slide. The platform had hand rails, similar to a ship's so young pirates don't fall off, and a steering wheel, ah, I mean ship's wheel. This time it was Audrey who pointed a long straight stick at me while steering her ship and said, "Harrrr matey! Come aboard." The stick I soon learned was her imaginary cutlass. Of course, Madelyn was not without words either and she was speaking to herself about hoisting the Jolly Roger. To their mother's amazement the pirate talk continued throughout the afternoon.

Well, you'd think now that between their mother and their granddad, these two little pirates got a good dose of Mr. Buffett's world but you'd be wrong. They picked up their pirate ways from their dad, who's never cared for Buffett's music and prefers rock groups I've never heard of. I thought I knew him pretty well, but maybe I need to spend more time with him. It's entirely a possibility a Parrothead isn't buried too deeply within. So in honor of the two budding Parrothead pirates of Lullwater Main, I ordered a door sign from the Margaretville store for their room. It has lots of parrots, pirates, and palms on it and bears the Buffett song title, "We Are the People Our Parents Warned Us About." HARRR!

TWIN TORNADOES, OR WAS IT HURRICANES?

If you think I'm talking about Florida this last season I could be, but then I'm not. I'm talking about our house this weekend. The devastation wasn't much different than from a Florida storm though. The weather change started about 1030 hours Friday morning when a tan van pulled up in our yard. Just like all those tourists who ignorantly and happily stand on the beach awaiting the first waves to kick up in a hurricane, I was there on the front porch happy as a clam. Well, after all it was my twin three year old granddaughters Audrey and Madelyn and their mother in that van. Once Audrey was released from the belts and buckles of her car seat, she was bounding around the van in a motion not unlike some destructive winds that come out of Kansas. Then Madelyn was released and she, too, joined the fury.

Two circling tornadoes were about to land at our house. At least they were dispelling some of their energy before coming inside. Our house is not too child proofed since we mostly visit the girls at home where their toys are abundant. We keep a few things such as coloring books and crayons their mother used to play with, when she wasn't much older than they are. So in order to entertain the girls, we had to let them create their own toys. This isn't advisable, and you shouldn't try it at your house. They went for the dominos, a very nice older set, which had belonged to my wife's grandmother. Then I introduced poker chips from a game we haven't played in a score. They also got out a couple of decks of playing cards for good measures. Then the winds began to pick up and the storm started in earnest. Their mother provided a coloring book and I some computer paper. I still can't figure out how they got the paper coverings off the crayons without tearing them. I couldn't put them back on, and I can't figure out where they put half the dominos and a small model cannon I had on the wall unit. No one swallowed any thing, I don't think. Most of all I can't figure out how they got into our office? I only left it for a minute to check on my wife and daughter who were surfing the Internet.

The girls proceeded to color everything in sight and transport their art and other paraphernalia into the office which also houses my model collections. Want to talk about panic? Well when they spotted a wall full of brightly colored models, I saw lightning flash as their eyes opened wider. I took a couple down and let them look closer and touch. They liked the big bird on the hood of one of the cars and wanted to know what the silver things were they thought should be pulled off all the cars. Then, as if drawn by the light reflecting off the blade of my Civil War sword, they changed directions. I spent most of last week cleaning and polishing it and still wasn't quite finished, so I had left it out on the office floor. They immediately wanted to confiscate the blade which convinced them JimPa is a pirate. For whatever reason, as I mentioned, they're very pirate conscious these days. I did manage to talk them out of making me walk the plank.

After sweeping through the house and eating all their blueberries, most of my yogurt, and drinking all the orange juice, they stormed back into their car seats for home and we set about cleaning things up. I still can't account for all the dominoes and chips but next morning I found a wooden duck in the powder room. Maybe it would be a good idea to invest in a few toys for future visits? Oh yes, my wife convinced me the sword should be stowed away for next time. Now, how do I lock that office door?

YVONNE (LILLIAN'S GIRL)

There was a frenzy of e-mail going on between my wife Yvonne and her cousins. They were scanning and sending pictures of the family between each other's computers with a vengeance. I had just settled down to watch the latest Formula One race and was trying to find an open space to put my Coke glass on the end table that sits between our two recliners. Seems it was covered up with all sorts of pictures she had been scanning from a period I was able to identify as pre-color. One of them in particular caught my eye; it was a smiling little girl about two or three with golden blonde locks and no shirt. She was smiling and squinting into the camera. Written on the back of the picture were two words, "Lillian's girl." When my wife came back into the room I asked if the picture was of one of her cousins. I was quite surprised when she replied, "It's me."

Something happened in the ensuing years. My wife developed brunette hair and the lily white complexion in the picture became the characteristic coloring of the south of France. In my opinion her adult characteristics are much more pleasing and now-a-days she wears a shirt, or blouse, or top, whatever they are called. You see, I never knew my mother-in-law as she died when my wife was three years old. She talks about her mother but I don't associate the name enough to put the two together. When Yvonne was born, it was her Aunt Ruth who brought her home from the hospital as her own mother was very ill. When she was only three years old her mother died, and her grandmother raised her to maturity with the help of her father, aunts and stepmother.

I've often wondered how my wife developed all her motherly abilities, as she was deprived of a full-time mother herself. She raised two responsible, supportive and loving children and was a caring part-time mother to a stepdaughter. Whenever she sees them, she kisses and hugs them like she may never get the chance again. There is a very strong bond between her and those kids. She doesn't look much older than they and it seems they don't mind treating her as an equal, as opposed to a superior, which makes them friends too. That doesn't mean she wasn't a firm parent and that included her step kid, my daughter. I see too many parents today blaming dysfunctional children on their own experiences as kids. If there was ever a set of experiences that could be used for such an excuse, my wife's childhood had to be it. She never had a firm home as a child as she got passed between relatives until she was seventeen. Don't get me wrong, she was loved and not deprived or abused, but it has to have had a profound effect on one's outlook to get raised under such circumstances.

She never had a lot of material possessions as a child so there is no one I know who appreciates the simple things of life more than she does. She puts more emphasis on relationships than things. Give her a good book, a comfortable chair, a reading lamp, a warm room with a fire, and someone near she loves and she will remain content on the cold rainy afternoon when most of us decide the mall and spending money is the only way to avoid boredom. I enjoy those kinds of days and every other day with her and the fact there is something inside her that weights our relationship and life itself with a little more thought and dedication than I could imagine. She is, as my baby boom generation puts it, deep. Again, I think it comes from the way she partly brought herself up, and I didn't make a mistake in wording this sentence.

When I look at this woman with rock solid faith in life and a glow in those sparkling blue eyes set in a classic French Mediterranean complexion, I see someone who is more than just special; she is one of a kind. Maybe it's because of the way she was raised or maybe it's something that was going to be anyway; whatever it is, she has a gift for loving to the fullest all the people around her including my granddaughters. And if anyone is the lucky benefactor, it's me for being loved by "Lillian's girl.

THIS BOOK

I'm sitting here with popcorn all over my robe wondering how I can tell you what's on my mind. I have a hard time saying things I don't want to say. I had a great time writing the columns, and most of these stories came from my life and the lives of my family and friends in Hogansville. I guess there comes a time when you have to focus on other things and that time has arrived for me. I suspect after I finally accomplish this book, I'll be back to telling more stories about a time, as Margaret Mitchell so aptly put it, will only be known in books because it is ". . .gone with the wind."

I told my family and friends for years I would attempt to write a book that would try to encompass life in the South in a time when it was okay to occasionally be fallible but truthful about things and people. The fifties and sixties were a time when no one easily took offense and when we were all considerate of each other as a matter of fact instead of a requirement of law. There was no need for "hate crime legislation" or for quotas or affirmative action. No one expected special treatment, only a fair day's wage for a fair day's work. Hate was a word for things we didn't want to do, instead of for people and cultures that did not suit our own. We spoke one language, albeit with a number of different dialects, depending on what part of the South or anywhere else we were from.

We all had a common link with the past and most had ancestors who fought a war that pitted brother against brother. Southerners were proud of their Rebel stand, and the battle flag did not have negative stigma. The flag was prominent at NASCAR races named the "Southern and Dixie Five Hundred" and the "Rebel Three Hundred" and there were car clubs named "The Confederates" that used the flag and a gray uniformed mascot as their logo. Blacks and whites in the South got along and helped each other out and no outside agitators were welcome. We knew that slavery would have come to an end without the war. Everyone was proud to be called Southern and Georgian and most of us were born and raised in little towns. If God grants me a little more time, there just might be more to tell you about later. So until then I'll say, "happy trails to you until we meet again."

ABOUT THE AUTHOR

Jim Dale is a graduate of Hogansville High School and West Georgia College, now State University of West Georgia where he also did graduate work. He served during Vietnam as an Air Force historian. Afterwards he served as Assistant Registrar at Kennesaw College, now Kennesaw State University. He pulled a stint as a technical writer for General Dynamic's Electric Boat Division in Atlanta. Finally he served thirty years in the Department of the Army as a Senior Management Analyst, retiring in 2003. During his Army time Jim lead Military Staff Rides and conducted Military History Detachment training for officers and NCOs, and updated the official history of Fort McPherson, Georgia. Jim served on the Boards of the Army in Atlanta Museum and the Kennesaw Mountain Historical Association as Vice Chairman of the latter until retirement in 2012. He was for many years a member of a Civil War reenactment unit, and performed living history for the Army and Reinhardt University. He was Second Lieutenant Commander and Newsletter Editor for the Marietta camp of the Sons of Confederate Veterans. Jim currently serves as Secretary for his chapter of the Sons of the American Revolution and is currently working on a book about the Battle of Kennesaw Mountain. He and his wife Yvonne and their Siamese cat Princess Nim live near Waleska, Georgia.

CPSIA information can be obtained at www.ICGtesting.com
Printed in the USA
LVOW130845041012

301445LV00005B/3/P